T0323518

Catching Up to America

China's rapid rise is doubtless the most significant economic and geopolitical event in the twenty-first century. What has led to its rise? What does it mean for the rest of the world? When will China overtake the US? Will the conflict between the two superpowers derail its further rise? Can China's development experience be emulated by other countries? These are some of the important questions addressed in this jargon-free, yet rigorous, book. It debunks many popular explanations of China's rapid economic growth ranging from abundance of cheap labor, export promotion, demographic dividend, and strong government, to mercantilist policies and IP theft. Taking a global comparative approach, this book demonstrates convincingly that the true differentiating factor making China grow faster than other developing countries over the past four decades is the Confucian culture of savings and education. This cultural perspective yields powerful new insights into many questions regarding China's rise.

Tian Zhu is Professor and Santander Chair in Economics at China European International Business School (CEIBS). Before joining CEIBS in 2005, he taught at the Hong Kong University of Science and Technology (HKUST) for ten years. Zhu is an expert on China's economy, having published many articles and also two books in the area. He was awarded the 2017 Bergson Prize by the Association for Comparative Economic Studies for the best article published in *Comparative Economic Studies*. Educated in China and the US, Zhu received his BSc, MA, and PhD degrees from Tsinghua University, Peking University, and Northwestern University, respectively.

Catching Up to America

Culture, Institutions, and the Rise of China

TIAN ZHU
China Europe International Business School

CAMBRIDGE
UNIVERSITY PRESS

CAMBRIDGE
UNIVERSITY PRESS

University Printing House, Cambridge CB2 8BS, United Kingdom

One Liberty Plaza, 20th Floor, New York, NY 10006, USA

477 Williamstown Road, Port Melbourne, VIC 3207, Australia

314–321, 3rd Floor, Plot 3, Splendor Forum, Jasola District Centre,
New Delhi – 110025, India

103 Penang Road, #05–06/07, Visioncrest Commercial, Singapore 238467

Cambridge University Press is part of the University of Cambridge.

It furthers the University's mission by disseminating knowledge in the pursuit of
education, learning, and research at the highest international levels of excellence.

www.cambridge.org
Information on this title: www.cambridge.org/9781316510612
DOI: 10.1017/9781009038997

First published 2021

A catalogue record for this publication is available from the British Library.

Library of Congress Cataloging-in-Publication Data
Names: Zhu, Tian, author.
Title: Catching up to America : culture, institutions, and the rise of China / Tian Zhu,
   China Europe International Business School.
Description: Cambridge, United Kingdom ; New York, NY : Cambridge University Press,
   2021. | Includes bibliographical references and index.
Identifiers: LCCN 2021020767 (print) | LCCN 2021020768 (ebook) | ISBN
   9781316510612 (hardback) | ISBN 9781009017657 (paperback) | ISBN 9781009038997
   (epub)
Subjects: LCSH: China–Economic conditions–2000- | Economic development–China–
   History–21st century. | China–Economic policy–2000- | BISAC: BUSINESS &
   ECONOMICS / Development / Economic Development | BUSINESS & ECONOMICS
   / Development / Economic Development
Classification: LCC HC427.95 .Z47228 2021 (print) | LCC HC427.95 (ebook) | DDC
   330.951–dc23
LC record available at https://lccn.loc.gov/2021020767
LC ebook record available at https://lccn.loc.gov/2021020768

ISBN 978-1-316-51061-2 Hardback
ISBN 978-1-009-01765-7 Paperback

For Xiaoling, Liefu, Liewen, and Liewei

Contents

Figures

Tables

Acknowledgments

Seven years ago, a group of executive students enrolled in the Adolfo Ibanez Business School at the University of Chile came to China Europe International Business School (CEIBS) where I teach. These students came from several Latin American countries. I gave a lecture on the Chinese economy for half a day. During recess, a student came to talk to me. He said that he was from Paraguay and had worked for the government's economic research department. He pointed out that in the early 1980s Paraguay already had a GDP per capita above US$1,500, while it was only $200 in China; three decades later, Paraguay's GDP per capita was still less than $4,000, but it was over $5,000 in China. So his question was, why had China been able to grow so fast while Paraguay had grown so slowly? What was China doing right? Or what was Paraguay doing wrong? I did not know anything about Paraguay at the time, and naturally I could not give him an answer. But the question raised by this Paraguayan student has stayed with me and has become a question that I have been studying and trying to answer for the past few years. The result of my research is this book in your hands.

Most of the ideas in this book have been published in my Chinese books and articles. My dean at CEIBS, Professor Yuan Ding, thought that I should spread these ideas to non-Chinese speakers and encouraged me to write a book in English. Together with the associate dean for research, Professor Bin Xu, they initiated a research grant scheme to support faculty to write books and I was one of the first beneficiaries. I am therefore most grateful to Yuan and Bin for their enthusiastic support, without which this book would not have been written.

During my research for this book, I received help, encouragement, and constructive criticism from many colleagues and friends. I would like to express my heartfelt gratitude to them. They include Jiahua Che, Shimin Chen, Kim-Sau Chung, X. L. Ding, Albert Hu, Yuhchang Huang, Carsten Holz, Dipak Jain, Mingjun Li, Shan Li, Neng Liang, Yimin Lin, Yingyi Qian, Rama Velamuri, Xiaozu Wang, Yi Wen, Dingbo Xu, Lixin Colin Xu, Yang Yao, Fang (Frank) Yu, Hua Zhang, Weijiong Zhang, and Dongsheng Zhou. I am especially grateful to Fang Liu and Jun Zhang with whom I collaborated on the research summarized in the Appendix. I also want to thank Danni Chen, Cheng Li, and Sophie Song for their excellent assistance in searching the literature, compiling references, proofreading, and translating Chinese materials.

The main arguments of this book have been presented many times both in and outside CEIBS. I have been constantly inspired and encouraged by discussions with many CEIBS colleagues and students and other attendants in my lectures. I thank them all. I would also like to thank four anonymous reviewers for their very helpful referee reports on the original manuscript. I am especially touched by the extraordinary professionalism of one reviewer who wrote a seven-page report giving detailed comments chapter by chapter. Thanks to the many helpful comments and constructive suggestions from the reviewers, I believe that the revised manuscript is much improved.

I am deeply indebted to Joe Ng, the acquisitions editor at Cambridge University Press, for his unfailing professionalism and support for this book project. I am also grateful to Zhifeng Hu of CEIBS Publishing for his effort and patience in facilitating publication.

Last but not least, I want to thank my family. My wife, Xiaoling, has been my most diligent reader, editor, and critic. She is a literary writer with no particular interest in economics. However, I wanted my book to be easily understood by a layperson like her, so in this sense, she is actually my perfect reader. I must also thank my two adult sons, Liefu and Liewen, who proofread the whole book. Because they also majored in economics in college, they were often my first readers and commentators. I dedicate this book with love and gratitude to my wife and children.

Abbreviations

BIS	Bank for International Settlements
BRICS	Brazil, Russia, India, South Africa, and China
CCP	Chinese Communist Party
COVID-19	coronavirus disease 2019
EU	European Union
FOF	flow of funds
GCF	gross capital formation
GDP	gross domestic product
GFCF	gross fixed capital formation
GII	global innovation index
GNI	gross national income
GNP	gross national product
HCA	highly cited articles
ICOR	incremental capital–output ratio
IMF	International Monetary Fund
IP	intellectual property
LTO	long-term orientation
M2	broad money
NATO	North Atlantic Treaty Organization
NBS	National Bureau of Statistics, China
NSF	National Science Foundation
OECD	Organization for Economic Cooperation and Development
PCT	Patent Cooperation Treaty
PISA	Program for International Student Assessment
PPP	purchasing power parity
RCEP	Regional Comprehensive Economic Partnership
RMB	Chinese renminbi
R&D	research and development
S&E	science and engineering

SEZs	special economic zones
SOEs	state-owned enterprises
TFP	total factor productivity
TIFA	total investment in fixed assets
TVEs	township-village enterprises
UCLA	University of California, Los Angeles
UK	United Kingdom
US	United States
WIPO	World Intellectual Property Organization
WTO	World Trade Organization
WVS	World Values Survey
WWII	World War II

Introduction

On November 6, 1957, thousands of delegates from sixty-four communist and workers' parties around the world gathered in the brand new Central Lenin Stadium (now Luzhniki Stadium) in Moscow to celebrate the fortieth anniversary of the October Revolution. In his long keynote speech, Soviet leader Nikita Khrushchev boasted that the Soviet Union would catch up to or even surpass the United States in fifteen years in terms of total output of major industrial products. At a follow-up meeting on November 18, Chairman Mao Zedong, inspired by Khrushchev's speech, made an impromptu speech and enthusiastically declared that China would follow the example of the Soviet Union and surpass Britain in fifteen years. What Mao had in mind was to surpass Britain mainly in terms of steel output, which he considered to be synonymous with industrialization.[1]

On New Year's Day in 1958, the *People's Daily*, the mouthpiece of the Chinese Communist Party (CCP), published an editorial officially declaring that China would overtake Britain in the output of steel and other heavy industrial products in fifteen years, and after that, China would take another twenty to thirty years to catch up to America in economic power. "Surpassing Britain and Catching Up to America" (*chaoying ganmei* in Chinese) thus became the goal and slogan of the Great Leap Forward. In the heady days of mid-1958, Mao even believed that China could overtake Britain in three years and America in ten in steel output.[2] But his dream of rapid industrialization was soon shattered by realities, and the Great Leap Forward

---

[1] See Mao (1999, pp. 325–326) and Qi and Wang (2002).   [2] See Qi and Wang (2002).

ended up being the greatest self-inflicted disaster in Chinese history.[3] When Mao died in 1976, China was one of the poorest countries in the world.

In December 1978, China's new leader, Deng Xiaoping, explained to the visiting Japanese Prime Minister Masayoshi Ōhira that the medium-term goal of China's modernization drive was to become a "moderately prosperous society" (*xiaokang shehui* in Chinese) by the end of the twentieth century. Specifically, Deng said that China aimed to quadruple (*fan liangfan*) its gross national product (GNP) per capita in the next twenty years, implying an annual growth of 7 percent in per capita income.[4] At the time, this was an ambitious goal, but it was actually realized in less than twenty years. Clearly, Deng was not only a more pragmatic leader than Mao but also more informed in economics. Mao equated steel production and heavy industry with economic development and had no idea about realistic growth rates, whereas Deng already understood the concept of GNP and the fact that a growth rate of 7 percent per year was an admirable goal requiring great effort to achieve. On April 30, 1987, during a meeting with a Spanish delegation, Deng looked beyond the twentieth century and set a development goal for China in the first half of the twenty-first century: quadrupling its per capita income again from US$1,000 in 2000 to US$4,000 to become a middle-level developed country in thirty to fifty years.[5] By setting this long-term goal, he allowed per capita income to grow at a much slower rate of 3 to 5 percent per year. In reality, China realized a world-beating 8.5 percent average annual growth rate of per capita GDP between 1978 and 2018. Deng, an ultimate realist, never mentioned anything about China ever catching up to America.

In 1978, few people, not even a visionary leader like Deng, could have predicted that China would become by far the fastest growing economy in the world over the next forty years. In 2010, China became the second largest economy, having surpassed Britain in

[3] See Li and Yang (2005).   [4] Deng (1994, p. 237).   [5] Deng (2001, p. 226).

2006, then Japan four years later. It is still growing rapidly, albeit at a slower rate of 6 percent. Now that China is quickly catching up to the United States, many questions of paramount importance in economics and world affairs have arisen. What has led to China's rapid rise? Will China overtake the United States economically and technologically, and if so, when? Is there a Chinese model of development that can be emulated by other developing countries? Why is China's economy currently slowing down? Will the rapidly declining US–China relations slow it down even further? Will the United States, the incumbent superpower, and China, the emerging superpower, be able to coexist peacefully or fall into the so-called Thucydides Trap?[6] Opinions on these questions are sharply divided. The answers largely depend on how one understands China's rapid economic growth over more than three decades after the reform and opening-up policy of 1978 and its economic slowdown in recent years. Different interpretations of these two phenomena will lead to different answers to the aforementioned questions.

In China, many pundits, economists, and, of course, policymakers are understandably proud of the country's rapid rise and are confident about its future, crediting it to China's unique institutions and good policies. Many commentators outside China have also been impressed by its rapid growth and have made bold predictions about China's rise to the top position in the global economy.[7] However, there are many others, both within and outside of China, who see more of the challenges and headwinds facing the Chinese economy, including a rapidly aging population; debt-ridden corporations and local governments; excess production capacity; insufficient consumption; export dependence; inability to innovate; rigid exam-oriented education system; delay or even reversal of market reforms; renewed statism; and distortionary industrial policy. They are less worried

---

[6] See Allison (2017).

[7] See, e.g., Jacques (2009), Fogel (2010), Subramanian (2011), Lin (2019), and Mahbubani (2020).

about the consequences of China's rise and more about whether China can sustain its economic growth and avoid a deep recession or financial crisis in the short term and escape the so-called middle-income trap in the longer term.[8] The COVID-19 pandemic and the tensely antagonistic US–China relationship have added further uncertainties to China's economic prospects.

THE CHINESE GROWTH PUZZLE

If someone told you that China's economy has grown rapidly over the past four decades or so, you would find it a trite statement. But if they told you that China's economic growth has been the fastest in the world, and not by a slight margin, but several times faster than the global average, you might be a little more surprised. In fact, if you are an average reader rather than an economic expert, this might even be the first time you hear such a statement. The truth is that China's relatively more modest growth rate of 6–7 percent in recent years is by far one of the fastest in the world.

With more time to contemplate, you might venture that China's growth is no reason to brag, as China had a very low income base to start with, so it is no surprise that its growth is faster than that of other countries. After all, China has been growing rapidly for many years, but is it not still relatively poor compared with more developed countries like the United States? Indeed, based on data from the World Bank, China's per capita income is just above 15 percent of the US level, and even on a more generous purchasing power parity (PPP) basis, which takes into account the price differences between the two countries, it is still just over 25 percent of the US level.

But do low-income countries naturally tend to grow faster? Alas, this is not generally the case! Since 1980, the growth rate of gross domestic product (GDP) per capita in low-income countries has generally been lower than that of high-income countries. China's growth rate is not only much higher than that of developed countries

---

[8] See, e.g., Pettis (2013), Shambaugh (2016), and Magnus (2018).

like the United States, Britain, and Japan but also much higher than that of other developing countries – be they middle-income countries like Brazil, Mexico, Turkey, or the Philippines, or low-income countries like Haiti, Kenya, or Bangladesh. After forty years of rapid economic growth, China has grown from one of the poorest countries in the world to one of the richest poor countries in the world. Measured by the total size of its economy (i.e., GDP), China has gone from eleventh place behind the Netherlands in 1978 to the second largest economy in the world today. Moreover, if the current trend continues, China will overtake the United States to become the largest economy in the world by 2030.

So, the puzzle here is not why China has grown so much faster than developed countries to become an economic superpower, but why it has also grown so much faster than other developing countries. I call this the Chinese growth puzzle.

Today, we all attribute this achievement to the reform and opening-up policy that began in 1978. This is of course correct. However, China's reform and opening up can only explain its faster growth after 1978, not why it has grown faster than other countries – and not just a little, but much faster.[9] Most developing countries have implemented policies of market reform and openness to varying degrees over the past three to four decades, and many of them have freer markets than China, but no country has grown faster.

Some commentators, either approvingly or begrudgingly, have attributed China's rapid rise to its state-led economic model that favors state-owned enterprises (SOEs) and pursues an active industrial policy, to its protectionist and mercantilist trade and investment policies, and to its technology transfer policy without regard for

---

[9] The small African country of Equatorial Guinea can be considered an exception. Equatorial Guinea quickly grew rich thanks to its oil discovery in the 1990s, and its average growth rate of GDP per capita between 1981 and 2018 was 9.9 percent, faster than that of China. However, its oil-based growth occurred mainly during the 1992–2008 period, while its growth rate was negative in most other years.

foreign intellectual property (IP) rights.[10] China hawks in the United States seem to subscribe to this view.[11] However, if a statist economic model can produce a growth miracle, why has no other country achieved or tried to achieve similar success by adopting this model? In fact, for many academics, statism is not China's strength but its weakness.[12]

Why, then, has China been able to sustain its rapid growth in the past four decades, when most developing countries have grown slowly during the same period? In other words, what are the distinctive strengths that have enabled China, but no other developing country, to catch up to the developed countries so quickly?

Explaining the Chinese growth puzzle will not only help to understand the reasons for the rapid growth of the Chinese economy in the past but also predict its prospects for the future. Indeed, China's economic growth has fallen sharply in recent years, causing many to worry about its future. What are China's strengths (if any) going forward? Will a deteriorating US–China relationship in a post–COVID-19 world derail or at least significantly slow down China's rise? What are the chances that the Chinese economy will collapse under the weight of the superpower conflict with the United States, a debt-ridden corporate sector, and increasing state control of the economy, as some pundits have predicted or even hoped? To answer these questions, it is necessary to first understand the driving forces behind China's rapid rise. I focus especially on the thirty-year period between 1982 and 2012 preceding the recent downturn, during which China experienced an average annual growth rate of 10 percent. I then address the issue of growth slowdown after 2012.

China is a big country, and its population size is an important factor to consider in matters such as national defense, international trade, e-commerce, and social media. However, when studying economic development and growth, it is often more meaningful to use

---

[10] See, e.g., Wen (2016) and Bremmer (2017).   [11] See, e.g., Navarro and Autry (2011).
[12] See, e.g., Naughton (2011), Huang (2011), and Lardy (2019).

per capita statistics. Therefore, in this book, I use GDP per capita to represent the level of a country's economic development and the growth rate of GDP per capita to represent the speed of economic development or simply economic growth.[13]

CONTENT AND STRUCTURE

Some may argue that the Chinese growth miracle has been exaggerated because it is based on official figures from the National Bureau of Statistics (NBS) of China. There is a widely held suspicion that China's GDP statistics are manipulated by the government. Even if this is true, the conclusion to be drawn is far from simple. An inflated GDP growth rate is not the same as an inflated GDP level, and vice versa. The key question is then: How inaccurate are these figures? I investigate this question in Chapter 1. The short answer is that China's economic growth may have been overstated in official data and that the level and growth rate of GDP in any given year may not be accurate. Nevertheless, after taking these factors into account, the facts are still very clear: China's economic growth has been the fastest in the world. In this chapter, I also place China's growth performance in a historical and global comparative perspective.

There are many popular explanations for China's rapid economic rise besides the aforementioned initial low-income level and the reform and opening-up policy, including, for example, the abundance of cheap labor, the demographic dividend, and its export orientation in the age of globalization. I evaluate these explanations in Chapter 2. For now, suffice it to say that if these explanations are correct, at least some, if not all, developing countries should have been able to achieve rapid growth similar to that of China. Compared with developed countries, all developing countries have low income and cheap labor, and most have declining fertility rates, leading to

---

[13] My view of economic development as per capita GDP growth is relatively narrow, unlike that of Nobel laureate Amartya Sen who defined development as the enhancement of various types of freedoms or the removal of various types of unfreedoms. See Sen (1999).

potential demographic dividends. They could all have also relied on exports for growth. Indeed, it is much easier for a small developing country to pursue export-led growth, as it is less likely to become the target of foreign protectionist policies than a big country like China.

Economists have distinguished between two levels of causes of economic growth.[14] The first level is called proximate causes, including investment (i.e., accumulation of physical capital); education (i.e., accumulation of human capital); and technological progress (or increased productivity). An economy grows as it accumulates physical capital through investment and human capital through education and as it makes technological progress or improves its productivity. But what are the factors that cause physical and human capital to accumulate and technology to advance faster in some countries than in others? These factors constitute the second level of causes of economic growth. They are called the fundamental or ultimate causes of growth, including institutional, geographic, and cultural factors.

Professional economists and political scientists have tended to explain the Chinese growth puzzle from an institutional perspective. I refer to them collectively as institutionalists. Among them, there are two contrasting schools of thought: the free market school and the active government school. Both schools acknowledge that the reform and opening-up policy has been a key factor in China's rapid economic growth, but the free market school believes that China's economy is still not free or open enough. This school of thought argues that if China does not further accelerate its pace of reform and opening up, its economic growth will be difficult to sustain and could even suffer a total collapse. In contrast, the active government school attributes China's rapid growth to its strong government and active economic intervention (e.g., effective industrial policies), and tend to give high marks to China's political system. These two contrasting institutionalist views are evaluated in Chapter 3. The short conclusion is that

[14] See, e.g., Acemoglu (2009).

neither view can properly explain the Chinese growth puzzle. The free market view cannot, because China's market is not much freer than that of most developing countries. The active government view cannot either, because China is not particularly well ranked in terms of government effectiveness, even among developing countries, and because it is highly unlikely that out of some 150 developing economies in the world, only China has been lucky enough to have discovered or stumbled upon the right industrial policies for economic development over the past forty years. There are, of course, many other institutionalists who hold different or more fine-grained views than the aforementioned two schools. I also evaluate some of these views in Chapter 3. I conclude that institutional and policy factors may be important contributors to China's economic growth, but they do not appear to be the differentiating factors that have made China grow faster than all other countries.

As other factors such as geography, climate, and ethnic homogeneity are unlikely to offer good explanations for China's growth, culture remains the only major factor to consider. The cultural view is not new. Confucian culture, especially its emphasis on hard work, thrift, and education, has been used by sociologists to explain the growth miracle of the East Asian economies of Japan and the four Asian Tigers (Hong Kong, South Korea, Singapore, and Taiwan) from the 1950s to the 1990s. But how exactly (i.e., through what channels) has Confucian culture promoted economic growth? How do we prove that China and other East Asian economies value thrift and education more than other developing economies? If Confucian culture is so conducive to economic development, why has China's rapid growth only occurred in the past four decades and not earlier? Is Confucian culture a substitute or complement for effective institutions and government policies? I try to answer these questions throughout Chapters 4–7. In particular, I argue for the role of a thrifty culture in China's investment-led growth in Chapter 4 and the role of Confucian culture's emphasis on education in China's high-quality schooling in Chapter 5.

One may very well agree that China's economic growth over the past four decades has indeed been remarkable, if not miraculous. However, this does not necessarily allay a prevalent concern about China's macroeconomic structure. China's growth is often described as seriously imbalanced with lackluster domestic demand, especially consumption. It has been mainly driven by investment and exports, which seems unsustainable. According to this view, as the Chinese economy continues to grow, export demand will not be enough to compensate for the shortage of domestic demand; moreover, investment-driven growth has led to overcapacity and a rapid accumulation of corporate debt, which will ultimately lead to an economic crisis. In Chapter 4 (and also later in Chapter 8), I show why these popular views are misplaced. Much of the misunderstanding is caused by the failure to distinguish between long-term growth and short-term growth. Long-term growth is determined by investment, education, and technological progress, not by consumption or exports, which only affect short-term growth.

China's economic growth over much of the past forty years has indeed been driven by investment and cheap labor, although cheap labor is not specific to China. Now that China's high investment may have run into the law of diminishing returns and its labor is no longer cheap compared with other developing countries, it seems that China needs to switch to a growth model driven by innovation. Yet is China's ability to innovate up to scratch? There are tendencies either to exaggerate China's innovative capacity and its threat to Western competitors, or to dismiss it and attribute its technological progress to imitation, or worse, to the theft of foreign technologies. I address the role of technological progress and innovation in China's rapid economic growth and evaluate the country's ability to innovate in Chapter 6.

In 2012, the Chinese economy entered a phase of declining growth. Its GDP growth rate of 6.1 percent in 2019 was the lowest in nearly thirty years. What are the causes of this severe slowdown? Is the Chinese growth miracle finally coming to an end? After all, China is already an upper middle-income country according to the World Bank classification. Historically, only a small number of middle-income economies have successfully developed into high-income economies. This fact has given rise to the popular but misleading term the "middle-income trap." Is China falling into this trap? I discuss these questions in Chapter 8.

In 2018, the Trump administration started a trade war against China, followed by technological sanctions against some of China's hi-tech companies, notably the Chinese tech giant Huawei. In 2020, the COVID-19 pandemic broke out and the global economy suffered the worst contraction since WWII. What are the growth prospects for the Chinese economy in a post–COVID-19 world? How may a prolonged trade and tech war with the United States affect China's economic growth? Can China's further rise be derailed or significantly slowed down? How will China's further rise affect the world, and how should the world reckon with it? I try to answer these questions in Chapter 9.

A GLOBAL COMPARATIVE PERSPECTIVE

Political sociologist Seymour Martin Lipset (1922–2006) once said, "A person who knows only one country knows no countries."[15] There is a similar saying in Chinese: "One who lives deep in the mountain cannot know its true appearance." What Mr. Lipset advocated was the importance of a comparative perspective. For this book, this means that China should not be observed and studied in isolation, but in perspective with other countries. Of course, everyone knows how to make simple comparisons. In China, people like to compare *guonei* ("inside the country," i.e., China) with *guowai* ("outside the country," i.e., foreign countries). In these comparisons, China, perhaps until very recently, is often painted in a negative light. Indeed, when Chinese people think of *guowai*, they almost always have developed countries like the United States or Japan in mind.

[15] Quoted in Fukuyama (2007).

People are rarely conscious of the fact that there are many more developing countries than developed countries. A similar mistake is often made by Western observers when they compare China with their own country or with the West in general. It is certainly appropriate to make comparisons between two countries, for example, China and the United States, if the objective is, say, for China to learn some best practices from the United States in certain areas. However, if the objective is to understand why some countries grow faster than others, simple comparisons will lead us astray. In statistical terms, the sample size in simple comparisons is just too small and unrepresentative. A distinctive feature of this book is that I adopt a global comparative perspective, comparing China with all the countries in the world.

A global comparative perspective on economic growth is certainly not new to economists, as there is a large body of cross-country studies of economic growth. However, all of these studies have used statistical regression methods with cross-country data to identify factors affecting economic growth. These regression analyses cannot and are not meant to answer the question of why a particular country, such as China, is growing so much faster than other countries, although they can help us find possible answers to the question. In this book, I examine the potentially important factors identified in these studies that can affect a country's growth and compare China with all countries based on these factors. I conclude that conditional on the market reform and openness policy adopted, the main differentiating factor behind China's rapid growth in recent decades is not some unique institutions or judicious policies, but traditional Confucian culture, especially its emphasis on thrift and education.

This book is intended not only for economists but also for other social scientists and general readers. The questions I address matter to a great many, if not all, people around the world, and I hope that its theme will be of interest to readers across disciplines and well beyond academia. Therefore, in writing it, I have kept economic jargon to a minimum, and whenever it is necessary, I try to make its meaning clear to any educated layperson.

I Just How Rapid Is China's Rise?
A Global Comparison

The Chinese economy has grown rapidly in most years since 1978. Between 1982 and 2012, the thirty-year period focused on in Chapters 1–4, China experienced an astounding average annual GDP growth rate of 10.2% and an annual GDP per capita growth rate of 9.12%, according to official figures.[1] In contrast, over the same period, global GDP per capita registered an average growth rate of just 1.48%, while the same figure for high–income developed OECD countries was only 1.86%.[2] Even after 2012, when the Chinese economy began to slow down, its growth remained one of the fastest in the world. Note that the headline measure of a country's economic growth is normally the growth rate of GDP. However, in this book, I use the average annual growth rate of GDP per capita (over a given period, say ten years or longer) as a preferred measure of long-term growth to capture the speed of the rise in the standard of living.

CHINESE GROWTH FROM A GLOBAL COMPARATIVE PERSPECTIVE

The fact that China has grown faster than developed countries is not remarkable. Most readers will probably attribute this to China's very low initial per capita GDP. Economists call this the "catch-up effect."

---

[1] I will comment on the accuracy of these official figures shortly. Unless otherwise noted, all growth figures in the book are real (i.e., adjusted for inflation) and not nominal.

[2] OECD refers to the Organization for Economic Cooperation and Development, headquartered in Paris, France. It is an intergovernmental economic organization founded in 1961 and composed mainly of Western countries. It was later expanded to include some non-Western developed countries, such as Japan and South Korea, and some developing countries, such as Mexico and Turkey. It currently has thirty-six member countries.

Table 1.1 *Economic growth around the world: 1982–2012*

Country or Group of Countries	Average Annual Growth Rate of GDP Per Capita (%)
China	9.12
India	4.41
United States	1.92
World	1.48
High-income OECD countries	1.86
Low-income countries	1.38
Middle-income countries	3.08
Latin America and the Caribbean (all countries)	1.21
Sub-Saharan Africa (all countries)	0.45

Note: Unless stated otherwise, all data in this book are from the data set of World Development Indicators published by the World Bank (https://datacatalog.worldbank.org/dataset/world-development-indicators). The version of the dataset used in this book for the 1982–2012 period was published on December 18, 2013. All average growth rates between 1982 and 2012 were calculated as an average of thirty annual growth rates from 1983 to 2012.

But do low-income countries always grow faster than high-income countries? Not really. In fact, it is usually the opposite. Table 1.1 shows that between 1982 and 2012, the average annual growth rate of GDP per capita in low-income countries was only 1.38 percent, which was lower than that of developed countries. The average annual growth rate of middle-income countries, including China, was 3.08 percent. Thus, in terms of economic growth, China has outperformed not only high-income developed countries but also low- and middle-income developing countries, and by a large margin. It is this last fact that constitutes the Chinese growth puzzle.

In this book, I use the World Bank classification of all countries into low-income, middle-income (including lower middle and upper middle), and high-income groups. Both low-income and middle-income countries are referred to as developing countries, while high-income countries are referred to as developed countries. The World Bank's latest classification criteria were based on countries' gross national income per capita (GNI per capita, which is roughly the same as GDP per capita). In 2012, low-income countries were those with a GNI per capita of US$1,035 or less; lower middle-income countries were those with a GNI per capita between US$1,036 and US$4,085; upper middle-income countries were those with a GNI per capita between US$4,085 and US$12,615; and high-income countries were those with a GNI per capita above US$12,615. These income criteria were adjusted slightly downward in 2018. According to this classification, all Western countries, Japan, and the four Asian Tigers are high-income developed economies, while developing countries include upper middle-income countries, such as China, Malaysia, and Brazil; lower middle-income countries, such as India, Nigeria, and the Philippines; and low-income countries, such as Haiti, Tanzania, and Bangladesh.[3] Most countries in Asia, Africa, and Latin America and the Caribbean are developing countries.

The rate of economic growth varies not only across countries but also across different periods. Table 1.2 breaks down the 1980–2010 period into three decades (the 1980s, 1990s, and 2000s), leading to the following observations. First, China's economic growth was the fastest in the world in all three decades. In addition, India had a much slower growth rate than China but still grew faster than other developing countries.

Second, the so-called BRICS countries (Brazil, Russia, India, South Africa, and China) had little in common other than the fact that they were relatively large economies among developing countries. Among these five countries, only China and India experienced fast economic growth, while Russia, Brazil, and South Africa only grew modestly. In addition, Russia's economy suffered negative

---

[3] In this book, unless stated otherwise, "China" refers to mainland China, excluding the Chinese territories of Hong Kong, Macau, and Taiwan.

Table 1.2 *GDP per capita growth rates in the world: 1980–2010 by decade*

Country or Region	Avg. Annual Growth Rate, 1981–1990	Avg. Annual Growth Rate, 1991–2000	Avg. Annual Growth Rate, 2001–2010
BRICS			
China	**7.8**	**9.3**	**9.9**
India	3.3	3.6	5.9
Russia	–3.4	–3.5	5.2
Brazil	–0.4	1.0	2.5
South Africa	–0.9	–0.4	2.2
Asian Tigers			
South Korea	7.5	5.2	3.7
Taiwan	6.2	5.3	3.5
Hong Kong	5.5	2.4	3.5
Singapore	5.3	4.3	3.3
Developing Regions			
East Asia and the Pacific	5.7	7.1	8.2
South Asia	3.0	3.2	5.3
Europe and Central Asia	–1.7	–1.7	4.7
Middle East and North Africa	0.2	1.8	2.6
Sub-Saharan Africa	–0.9	–0.4	2.2
Latin America and the Caribbean	–0.8	1.5	2.1
Grouped by Income			
High-Income Countries	2.6	1.9	0.9
Middle-Income Countries	1.1	2.3	4.8
Low-Income Countries	0.1	0.3	3.2

Table 1.2 (cont.)

Country or Region	Avg. Annual Growth Rate, 1981–1990	Avg. Annual Growth Rate, 1991–2000	Avg. Annual Growth Rate, 2001–2010
Developed Countries			
European Union	2.1	2.0	1.0
Japan	4.1	0.9	0.7
United States	2.3	2.2	0.6
World	1.5	1.4	1.3

Data source: World Development Indicators.

growth in the 1980s and 1990s. Its growth between 2001 and 2010 largely represented an economic recovery after a long recession and was more or less driven by oil and gas. Brazil's economic growth was even slower than the average growth rate of all developing countries. Its slightly more robust growth in the 2000s was also mainly due to the resource boom of the decade. With the end of the resource boom, Russia and Brazil have again stagnated in recent years.

Third, the four Asian Tigers grew relatively quickly in the 1980s, but by 1990, they were all high-income developed economies, and their growth rate slowed significantly. In the twenty-first century, their GDP per capita growth rate fell to around 3.5 percent, a growth figure still significantly higher than that of other developed economies.

Fourth, during these three decades, the overall economic growth of developing countries generally accelerated, while that of high-income developed economies (including the Asian Tigers) slowed over time. However, apart from countries in East Asia and the Pacific region (mainly China and Southeast Asian countries) and South Asia (mainly India), which had significantly higher growth than that of developed countries, other developing regions tended to grow more slowly than high-income developed countries in the 1980s and the

1990s. It was not until the twenty-first century that the growth of these regions started to outpace that of high-income countries. This was probably due to the resource boom brought about by rapid growth in China and India, as many developing countries are rich in natural resources.

HOW ACCURATE ARE CHINA'S GDP DATA?

Whether compared with its own past or with other countries, China's economic growth seems to have been too fast to be credible. Could this be due to China's official data overestimating or overstating the country's growth rate? Some twenty years ago, Thomas Rawski, an eminent scholar of the Chinese economy, published an article questioning the credibility of China's GDP data for 1998, the year of the Asian financial crisis, pointing out that the official GDP growth rate of 7.8 percent did not match electricity usage data and other relevant figures.[4] This article sparked great media interest and debate. In fact, China's current Premier Li Keqiang did not really trust the official GDP data when he was the party secretary in Liaoning Province, opting instead to trust the figures on power generation, railway freight, and bank loans. *The Economist* even created a "Keqiang Index" using these three indicators to measure the health of China's macroeconomy.[5]

GDP growth has always been a key performance measure in China for provincial and local officials, which means that they may have a strong incentive to falsify GDP reports, especially when the local economy is not doing well. As a result, China's national GDP growth may be overstated.[6] Local over-reporting is only one reason for the inaccuracy of China's GDP growth figures. Economists familiar with Chinese statistics have long recognized that underestimating inflation is another important reason for the overestimation of

[4] Rawski (2001).   [5] *The Economist* (2010).
[6] See, e.g., Young (2003) and Chen, Chen, Hsieh, and Song (2019).

Table 1.3 *Growth rates based on the Maddison Project and the Penn World Table: Compound annual growth rates of GDP per capita over the 1980–2010 period (%)*

Country	Maddison Project	Penn World Table 8.0
China	6.98	6.06
India	2.85	3.97
United States	1.67	1.64
United Kingdom	1.85	1.89
Nigeria	1.56	−0.85
Brazil	0.99	1.94
Chile	1.50	2.57

Note: The author made the calculations using data from the Maddison Project Database 2013 (www.rug.nl/ggdc/historicaldevelopment/maddison/releases/maddison-project-database-2013) and the Penn World Table version 8.0 (www.rug.nl/ggdc/productivity/pwt/pwt-releases/pwt8.0).

China's GDP growth.[7] Real GDP growth is equal to nominal GDP growth minus inflation. Thus, if inflation is underestimated, real GDP growth will be overestimated.

So, how much of China's GDP growth has been overstated? According to Angus Maddison and Harry Wu, two authorities on Chinese GDP statistics, China's annual growth between 1978 and 2003 was 7.85 percent, not 9.59 percent as in the official data.[8] Their research had an influence on the Penn World Table, a widely used data set of national income accounts based on PPP, which also lowered its estimates of China's GDP growth rate over the years. Table 1.3 shows the compound annual growth rate of China and other countries between 1980 and 2010 based on GDP figures from the

---

[7] See, e.g., Wu (2002), Young (2003), Maddison (2007), Holz (2014), and Lai and Zhu (2020).

[8] See Maddison and Wu (2008). Similarly, economist Alwyn Young (2003) found that due to the underestimation of inflation, the annual growth of China's nonagricultural economy during the 1978–1998 period was overstated by 2.5 percentage points.

Maddison Project and the Penn World Table.[9] These two data sets lowered China's growth rate by about 2 percent and 3 percent, respectively, from the official statistics. Yet even with these adjustments, China's economic growth was still far ahead of every other country.

Although China's GDP growth is very likely to have been overstated, its GDP level has probably been underestimated (Maddison 2007).[10] This statement may sound contradictory, but it is plausible for two reasons. First, China's overestimation of real GDP growth may be largely due to an underestimation of inflation, not to an overestimation of its nominal GDP levels.[11] Second, the value added of the service industry has been constantly underestimated due to poor coverage and other shortcomings in the national statistical system. For example, after the first national economic census in 2004, the NBS revised upward the GDP level for 2004 by 16.8 percent, with an increase in the service industry accounting for more than 90 percent of the total increase.[12] A 2009 report from Morgan Stanley's Asia Research department pointed out that the official value added of the service sector significantly underestimated housing costs and personal medical expenses.[13] My own research with Jun Zhang also showed that during the 2004–2011 period, the imputed rent of resident-owned housing alone, a component of GDP, was underestimated in official statistics by an amount equivalent to 4–5 percent of GDP.[14]

INFERRING GROWTH FROM ENGEL'S LAW

As a household's income level increases, the ratio of its food expenditure to total consumption expenditure will decrease. This is called Engel's Law, which was proposed by nineteenth–century German statistician Ernst Engel (1821–1896). The ratio is called the Engel

---

[9] These two data projects are now hosted in the same institution, the University of Groningen Growth and Development Centre.

[10] See, e.g., Maddison (2007), p. 64.

[11] See, e.g., Maddison and Wu (2008) and Young (2003).   [12] See Holz (2014).

[13] See Wang and Zhang (2009).   [14] Zhang and Zhu (2015).

coefficient. Engel's Law also applies at the national level: That is, the proportion of a country's household food expenditure in total consumption expenditure decreases as per capita income increases. Government officials in China may have incentives to falsify GDP figures, but not household consumption expenditure. By quantifying Engel's Law, linking the Engel coefficient with national income per capita, it is possible to use the change in the Engel coefficient over time to infer the change in income, that is, economic growth.

In a study published in 2011, Richard Anker of the University of Massachusetts collected the Engel coefficients of 207 economies around the world.[15] He divided these economies into ten deciles, classifying them from low income to high income by their GDP per capita (in constant 2005 PPP dollars) in the year the Engel coefficient was available. Each decile contained about twenty economies. Professor Anker then calculated the average Engel coefficient of all economies in each decile. The results are presented in the first two columns of Table 1.4. I added the third column, which divides all economies in the World Development Indicators data set into ten equal deciles by GDP per capita in 1998 and lists the range of GDP per capita for each decile for that year. I used 1998 because Anker collected data on the Engel coefficient over various years and the average data year was 1998. As GDP per capita here is measured in constant dollars, the year chosen should not have a significant effect on the results. My assumption here is that when a country's per capita GDP falls within a certain decile range in the third column, its Engel coefficient should be around the value in the corresponding decile, and vice versa.

In China, the relevant data to calculate the Engel coefficient as defined by Anker are only available from 1992 and only for urban households. I made the calculations for the years between 1992 and 2012. China's Engel coefficient was 43 percent in 1992 and 25 percent

---

[15] Anker (2011).

Table 1.4 *GDP per capita and Engel coefficients*

Decile Ranked by Income (i.e., GDP Per Capita) from Low to High	Decile Average of the Engel Coefficient (%)	Range of GDP Per Capita for Each Income Decile in 1998 (in Constant 2005 PPP Dollars)
1 (Lowest Income Decile)	50.1	(122–342)
2	53.7	(349–617)
3	45.4	(637–1,029)
4	40.2	(1,052–1,865)
5	40.0	(1,869–2,522)
6	33.7	(2,682–4,012)
7	28.8	(4,164–7,371)
8	21.4	(7,451–16,824)
9	16.7	(17,932–30,486)
10 (Highest Income Decile)	14.8	(30,612–116,108)

Note: The first two columns are reproduced from table 11 in Anker (2011), and the third column is based on data from the World Development Indicators published by the World Bank.

in 2012. Comparing these figures with the results in Table 1.4, we can see that the Engel coefficient for Chinese urban households in 1992 was between the third and fourth deciles. Based on the third column, the corresponding GDP per capita (in constant 2005 PPP dollars) should be around US$1,040. In 2012, China's Engel coefficient fell to 25 percent, between the seventh and eighth deciles in the table, with a corresponding GDP per capita in the third column around US$7,400. If the aforementioned inference is correct, GDP per capita in urban China increased sixfold between 1992 and 2012, implying an average annual growth rate of about 10 percent. Taking into account the slower growth rate of rural household income in China (about 1 percentage poin slower), the overall growth rate of GDP per capita in China over these two decades was just under 10 percent.

The correlation between the Engel coefficient and GDP per capita is of course not perfect. Therefore, using Engel's Law to infer economic growth may not be very accurate. Nevertheless, the fact remains that China's Engel coefficient went from a lower middle-income economy (about 30th percentile) to an upper middle-income economy (about 70th percentile) in twenty years, suggesting that China's economic growth during these twenty years was indeed very fast.

DISPOSABLE HOUSEHOLD INCOME GROWTH IN CHINA

The GDP growth rate is only one indicator of economic growth. The growth of disposable household income is another indicator, and it better reflects the improvement in the standard of living. China's disposable income data are collected through household income and expenditure surveys. Unlike GDP, until recently, household income was not part of the performance assessment of Chinese government officials; therefore, the likelihood of falsification was low. Some studies have shown that China's household income may have been significantly underestimated, mainly because high-income households are significantly underrepresented in income surveys.[16] However, as long as the degree of underestimation remains basically constant each year, the growth rate of household income should be fairly accurate.[17]

Table 1.5 shows in the second column that between 1982 and 2012, China's nominal disposable income per capita increased fifty-fold, with a compound annual growth rate of 14.01%.[18] Over the same period, the consumer price index increased by 5.56% per year. Therefore, after accounting for the rise in prices, the real growth rate

---

[16] I discuss this issue in more detail in the Appendix.

[17] As China's income inequality increased significantly between 1982 and 2012, the underestimation of income due to the underrepresentation of wealthy households may have been more severe in the 2000s than in the 1980s and the 1990s. As a result, real income growth may be even higher than the growth rate calculated in this section based on household survey data.

[18] For rural households, I used the net income value to replace disposable income, which until recently was a concept reserved for urban households in China.

Table 1.5 *Growth in disposable income per capita in China*

	RMB	Calculated in US$ with the Official Exchange Rate	Calculated in US$ with the World Bank's PPP–Adjusted Exchange Rate
Disposable Income Per Capita, 1982	326	194	200
Disposable Income Per Capita, 2012	16,669	2,641	4,003
Growth Factor	51.11	13.63	19.99
Nominal Compound Annual Growth Rate	14.01%	9.10%	10.50%
Inflation Rate (CPI), RMB, or US$	5.56%	2.93%	2.93%
Real Compound Annual Growth Rate	8.45%	6.17%	7.57%

Note: The author made these calculations using data from the CEIC Global Database and the World Development Indicators. The official exchange rates in 1982 and 2012 published by the Chinese government were US$1 for RMB1.68 and RMB6.31, respectively, while the PPP–adjusted exchange rates published by the World Bank were US$1 for RMB1.63 and RMB4.16, respectively.

should be around 8.45%, slightly lower than the growth rate of GDP per capita of 9.12% over the same period. Of course, China's inflation rate may also have been underestimated, so that real income growth may not have been as high as 8.45%. To avoid using the official inflation rate, in the third column of the table, I converted all income figures in RMB to US dollars based on the official exchange rate. China's disposable income per capita in 2012 was US$2,640.63, 13.63 times the 1982 figure of US$193.71. The compound annual growth rate should then have been 9.1% over this period. In other words, Chinese household income increased by 9.1% per year in US dollars. In comparison, the compound annual growth rate of disposable income of American households was only 3.14% over the same period, almost 6 percentage points lower than that of China. The inflation rate of the US dollar during this period was 2.93%, so the annual growth rate of income per capita in China measured by constant US dollars was 6.17%, while that of the United States was only 0.21%. As China's RMB exchange rate was overvalued in 1982 and generally considered to be undervalued in 2012, the growth rate of disposable income in China calculated with the official exchange rate is actually an underestimation.

In the last column, I used the PPP–adjusted exchange rate published by the World Bank to convert RMB income to US dollars. As a result, China's per capita income in 1982 was US$200 and reached US$4,003 in 2012, twenty times higher. In this calculation, the nominal compound annual growth rate would be 10.5%, and even adjusted for inflation, it would be as high as 7.57%.

Regardless of the data set we use, there is no doubt that China has indeed grown rapidly. The level and growth rate of China's GDP in any given year may not be reliable, and its long-term average growth rate may not have reached 10 percent per year, but the fact remains that China has experienced the fastest growth rate in the world in the past three to four decades. So, unless otherwise noted, I use the official growth figures in the rest of this book with the understanding that the debate over the accuracy of the figures does not qualitatively affect my arguments.

HOW UNIQUE IS CHINA'S GROWTH MIRACLE?

Although China's rapid economic growth in recent decades has been extraordinary, it should be noted that China was not the first country in history to sustain rapid growth for three decades or more. Using a compound annual growth rate in GDP per capita of 6 percent or more during any thirty-year period as a benchmark, seven other economies experienced similar growth miracles after WWII according to Angus

Maddison's data.[19] As shown in Table 1.6, these economies include Japan, South Korea, Taiwan, Singapore, and Hong Kong in East Asia, Botswana in Africa, and Saudi Arabia in the Middle East. The rapid growth of Japan and Saudi Arabia occurred between 1950 and 1980. The economic miracles of the Asian Tigers and Botswana took place ten years later, from the 1960s to the 1990s, while the Chinese economy took off twenty years after that. These eight economies have increased their GDP per capita fivefold or more in one generation.[20]

The growth miracles all happened in economies that were trying to catch up to countries at the technological frontier. In theory, an economy far from the technological frontier can potentially grow rapidly by adopting existing technologies instead of inventing new ones. This catch-up effect is also called "convergence" in economics. Table 1.7 shows that the United States, the world's largest economy and one of the most advanced economies, experienced a GDP per capita growth rate of about 2 percent per year between 1950 and 2010. The average growth rate of Western European countries between 1950 and 1970 exceeded 4 percent, much faster than that of the United States. This was largely due to the effect of Europe's postwar reconstruction and catching up to the United States. After 1970, the growth of developed countries in both Western Europe and the United States generally declined, and in the first decade of the new century, it fell below 1 percent. Table 1.7 also shows that the growth rate of developing countries in Latin America and Africa in general was not higher, but lower than that of developed countries. As a

---

[19] I used the Maddison Dataset here for the following reasons. First, it has the most comprehensive GDP data for the 1950–1960 period. Second, the data set does not overestimate China's growth. Third, later I use his historical GDP data, which is probably Professor Maddison's greatest contribution to economic research.

[20] A World Bank report in 2008 identified thirteen economies that had grown at an average rate of 7 percent per year or more for twenty-five years or longer since 1950, including Botswana, Brazil, China, Hong Kong, Indonesia, Japan, South Korea, Malaysia, Malta, Oman, Singapore, Taiwan, and Thailand. The report used a different indicator (GDP, not GDP per capita) and different data sources (World Development Indicators and other World Bank sources). See the Commission on Growth and Development (2008).

Table 1.6 *Growth miracles after WWII*

Economies	Fastest Growing 30 Years	Compound Annual Growth Rate	1950–1960	1960–1970	1970–1980	1980–1990	1990–2000	2000–2010
South Korea	1965–1995	7.4%	3.7%	5.9%	6.6%	7.8%	5.6%	3.8%
Botswana	1960–1990	7.3%	1.5%	4.9%	10.5%	6.5%	2.1%	2.0%
Taiwan	1962–1992	7.1%	4.0%	6.5%	7.6%	6.6%	5.3%	3.4%
Mainland China	1980–2010	7.0%	4.0%	1.6%	3.1%	5.8%	6.2%	8.9%
Japan	1950–1980	6.7%	7.6%	9.3%	3.3%	3.4%	0.9%	0.7%
Singapore	1964–1994	6.7%	0.4%	6.8%	7.4%	4.6%	4.1%	3.2%
Saudi Arabia	1950–1980	6.1%	5.2%	7.4%	5.7%	-3.8%	-0.1%	1.4%
Hong Kong	1958–1988	6.0%	3.5%	6.2%	6.3%	5.3%	2.3%	3.4%

Data source: Maddison Project Database 2013.

Table 1.7 *"Non-miracle" growth in GDP per capita worldwide: 1950–2010*

Country or Region	Fastest Growing 30 Years	Compound Annual Growth Rate	1950–1960	1960–1970	1970–1980	1980–1990	1990–2000	2000–2010
Western Europe	1950–1980	3.6%	4.2%	4.0%	2.6%	1.9%	2.0%	0.8%
Latin America	1950–1980	2.6%	2.3%	2.4%	3.2%	-0.7%	1.5%	1.4%
World	1950–1980	2.6%	2.8%	3.0%	1.9%	1.3%	1.6%	2.6%
United States	1958–1988	2.5%	1.7%	2.9%	2.1%	2.2%	2.2%	0.6%
Africa	1950–1980	1.8%	1.7%	2.4%	1.3%	-0.6%	0.6%	3.0%

Data source: Maddison Project Database 2013.

result, the gap between them did not decrease, but widened. This is in stark contrast to the miracle economies.

In class, I often ask my Chinese students to guess the annual growth rate of GDP per capita in the United Kingdom during the Industrial Revolution. First, a student may give an estimate of 30%, to which I say no, not that fast. Others may then answer 20%, 15%, or 10%, but I tell them those are still too optimistic. They may then propose 8%, 5%, and so on, with no one guessing 2% or less. Table 1.8 shows the estimated historical growth rate of selected large economies between 1500 and 1940. Unless you are an expert, you will be surprised to find that the annual GDP per capita growth rate of the United Kingdom during the Industrial Revolution (around 1750–1850) was actually less than 0.5%. You may wonder how such "slow" growth can be called a "revolution." But consider this: in the 250 years before the Industrial Revolution, GDP per capita in the United Kingdom grew at an annual rate of only 0.18% according to Maddison's data, while its growth rate before 1500 was almost 0. In fact, before the Industrial Revolution, the growth rate of per capita income of every nation in the world was close to 0. In 1940, China's GDP per capita was actually lower than in 1850. It is very possible that the living standard of Chinese people in 1940 was not much better than a thousand years earlier during the Song Dynasty.[21]

Now imagine that China had started to grow at a rate of 1 percent per year since the Song Dynasty, 1,000 years ago. How much higher would China's GDP be today? Without a calculator, you may guess ten, twenty, or even fifty times higher. However, the correct answer is 20,000 times! In other words, if, during the reign of Emperor Zhenzong in the Song Dynasty, China had a per capita income of US$300 measured in current currency, then with an average growth rate of 1 percent per year, it would have reached an incredible US$6

---

[21] According to the Maddison Historical Dataset, China's per capita GDP around 1000 AD was US$466 (in 1990 US dollars), and it was US$562 in 1940. These numbers are of course subject to debate and should not be taken too literally.

Table 1.8 *Economic growth from a historical perspective*

Country	GDP Per Capita (Measured in 1990 US Dollars)							Compound Annual Growth Rate of GDP Per Capita						
	1500	1750	1800	1850	1900	1940	1500–1750	1750–1800	1800–1850	1850–1900	1900–1940
United Kingdom	1,086	1,695	2,097	2,330	4,492	4,988	0.18%	0.43%	0.21%	1.32%	0.26%
United States			1,296	1,849	4,091	7,010			0.71%	1.60%	1.36%
Germany	1,146	1,050	986	1,428	2,985	5,403	-0.03%	-0.13%	0.74%	1.49%	1.49%
Japan		598	641	681	1,180	2,874		0.14%	0.12%	1.11%	2.25%
China				600	545	562				-0.19%	0.08%
India					599	686					0.34%
Brazil			683	683	678	1,250			0.00%	-0.01%	1.54%

Data source: Maddison Project Database 2013.

million today. Even with an annual growth rate of 0.4 percent, GDP per capita would have multiplied fifty times in 1,000 years. This is the power of compound growth.

Therefore, it is no exaggeration to say that the annual GDP per capita growth rate of 0.4 percent that the United Kingdom was able to achieve between 1750 and 1800 was truly the greatest leap forward in economic history. The term "revolution" is indeed well deserved. The total size of the world economy before the Industrial Revolution had certainly increased over time with population growth, but income per capita had never been able to sustain steady growth before this point. In economic jargon, the world was stuck in the "Malthusian trap," named after the great classical economist Thomas Robert Malthus (1766–1834), who believed that population growth will always catch up with economic growth, thereby bringing income per capita to subsistence level.

Before WWII, the average annual growth rate of GDP per capita in Western countries never exceeded 2 percent. As a latecomer, Japan developed rapidly after the Meiji Restoration, with a growth rate of 2.25 percent between 1900 and 1940, surpassing that of Europe and the United States. This was due to the catch-up effect mentioned earlier. Japan benefited from "the advantage of backwardness," meaning that a country with a relatively backward economy does not need to reinvent the wheel to develop, but can simply learn and absorb technologies from more advanced countries to achieve faster growth. The Industrial Revolution started relatively late in Germany and the United States compared with the United Kingdom, but their economic growth after 1800 exceeded that of the United Kingdom.

After WWII, economic growth in Western developed countries accelerated and average GDP per capita growth exceeded 2 percent for much of the fifty years before 2000. Third World countries also began to industrialize, but most did not grow faster than developed countries, indicating their inability to achieve the catch-up effect of latecomers. As shown, Japan and the four Asian Tigers sustained a growth rate of over 6 percent for more than thirty years. Outside East Asia,

Saudi Arabia and Botswana were exceptions. Saudi Arabia's economic growth was driven by its abundant oil reserves. Between 1980 and 2010, its real GDP per capita not only failed to grow but actually contracted. Similar to Saudi Arabia, Botswana's economic development relied heavily on its abundant diamond reserves. When its GDP per capita was still below US$3,000 in 1990, the Botswanan economy lost momentum and slowed considerably. After 1990, its GDP per capita growth returned to a more modest level of around 2.5 percent per year.

Thus, only six economies in the Maddison Dataset, all from East Asia, maintained rapid growth for more than thirty years in the absence of abundant natural resources.[22] Apart from China, which had a late start in 1978, the other five economies (i.e., Japan and the four Asian Tigers) all joined the ranks of high-income economies and crossed the finish line in the race to catch up with developed economies. This leads to three questions. First, how did Japan become the first non-Western country to achieve successful industrialization? Second, why did the Asian Tigers manage to catch up with developed countries through sustained rapid growth after WWII? Third, why has China been the fastest growing economy in the past four decades? These three questions constitute what I call the "East Asian growth puzzle," and the Chinese growth puzzle is only one part of it. The answer to the third question should help answer the first two.

---

[22] Macau, another Chinese territory, would have made the list, but it was not included in the Maddison Dataset.

2 Explaining China's Rise
Some Popular Views

In this chapter, I evaluate three popular explanations of China's rapid economic rise over the past forty years, including its low-income base and cheap labor, demographic dividend, and export promotion, and leave various institutional explanations such as market reform and strong government for the next chapter.

DOES A LOW INCOME BASE MAKE A COUNTRY GROW FASTER?

When asked why China has grown faster than other countries, most of my students answer that it is because China had a very low per capita income base to start with. In this case, the "other countries" they have in mind are most likely developed countries: Growing from a per capita income of US$1,000 to US$2,000 should be much easier than going from US$20,000 to US$40,000. However, this overlooks the fact that developed countries are a minority in the world, while developing countries are the majority. China's economic growth has not only been faster than that of developed countries but also faster than that of other developing countries. The cheap labor explanation is similar to that of the low income base: The cost of labor in low-income countries is cheap. Low income base and cheap labor may explain why China has grown faster than high-income and some upper middle-income countries, but not why it has grown faster than low-income or lower middle-income countries – not just a little faster, but much faster.

Generally, will a country with low income and cheap labor naturally grow faster? The answer is not as simple as one might imagine. Low income can mean absolute low income or relative low income. Absolute low income does not always mean faster growth; in

33

fact, it often means the opposite. Take the example of a developed country like the United States.[1] In 1850, GDP per capita in the United States was only US$1,849 in 1990 dollars, lower than that of some African countries today. Its annual growth rate between 1850 and 1900 was only 0.71 percent (still one of the fastest growth rates for this period). In 1950, GDP per capita in the United States reached US$10,000 in 1990 dollars, several times higher than in 1850. Its annual growth rate between 1950 and 2000 was more than 2 percent, much faster than that between 1850 and 1900, when income in the Untied States was much lower. In fact, the US economy doubled from a per capita income of US$20,000 to US$40,000 much faster than it did from US$1,000 to US$2,000. The former took little more than thirty years, while the latter took more than 100 years!

Relative low income can theoretically lead to faster economic growth due to the catch-up effect, so a developing country can narrow the relative income gap with developed countries. However, the catch-up effect implies that as the income level of a fast-growing country approaches that of the most developed countries, its growth rate will begin to decline. For instance, after a few decades of rapid growth, Japan and the Asian Tiger economies have slowed considerably. However, this slowdown in growth has nothing to do with the absolute size of these economies. Hence, China's growth will not slow down simply because it is already the world's second largest economy, but it will slow down considerably when its GDP per capita exceeds a certain level of relative income, for example, 40 percent of the US level. I come back to this point in Chapter 9.

The catch-up effect, or convergence, is only a theoretical possibility and may not necessarily play out in the real world. In fact, economists have found that convergence is not a rule, but an exception.[2] Figure 2.1 shows that the growth rate of GDP per capita

---

[1] The following historical figures are taken from the Maddison Dataset already used in Chapter 1.

[2] See, e.g., McGrattan and Schmitz (1999) and Barro and Sala-i-Martin (2003).

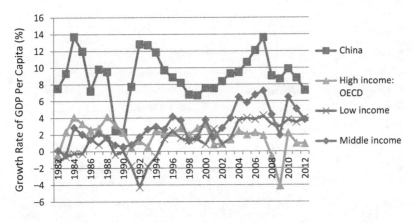

FIGURE 2.1 Economic growth by income group
Data source: World Development Indicators

in low-income countries on average was significantly lower than that of high-income countries before 2000. It was not until 2001 that the economic growth of low-income countries began to outpace that of high-income OECD countries. In addition, middle-income countries on average did not grow faster than high-income countries before 1990, but began to grow faster after, mainly because China belongs to this group and carries significant weight due to its size and rapid growth. Figure 2.1 also shows that although China's economic growth has fluctuated significantly over time, it always stands out. Even its relatively modest growth (by China's standard) of 7.3 percent in 2012 was still much faster than that of most other countries.

Figure 2.2 paints an even clearer picture. It shows no apparent correlation between the annual growth rate of a country during the 1982–2012 period and its initial income level measured by GDP per capita in 1982. It can be said that all developing countries with a growth rate of more than 2 percent in these thirty years converged with developed countries, the growth rate of the most developed countries being generally less than 2 percent, but these countries were in reality a minority. In addition, all countries with a growth rate of more than 4 percent can be considered to have converged rapidly, but

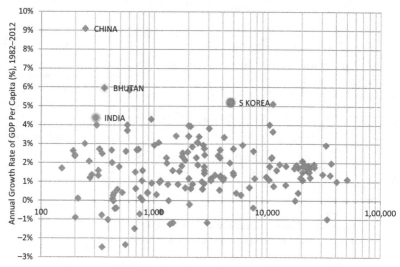

FIGURE 2.2 Economic growth and initial income level: 1982–2012

Note: In this scatterplot, each point represents a country (or economy), the vertical axis represents the compound annual growth rate of GDP per capita between 1982 and 2012, and the horizontal axis is a country's initial GDP per capita in 1982 (in 2005 PPP dollars). A logarithmic scale is used, with grids between US$100 and US$1,000 representing US$100; grids between US$1,000 and US$10,000 representing US$1,000; and grids between US$10,000 and US$100,000 representing US$10,000. All data are from the World Development Indicators.

these countries were even rarer. China's growth rate was the fastest, 3 percentage points faster than Bhutan, ranked second, and twice as fast as India, with a growth rate of 4.41 percent per year.[3] Conversely, developing countries with a growth rate of less than 2 percent were the majority. They had different levels of income per capita and did not converge with developed countries.

In Figure 2.3, I plotted the thirty-year trajectories in GDP per capita of China, South Korea, and other country groups by income or geography. The figure shows that China and South Korea were catching up very quickly. In 1982, China was extremely poor and its GDP

---

[3] Equatorial Guinea is not included in Figure 2.2.

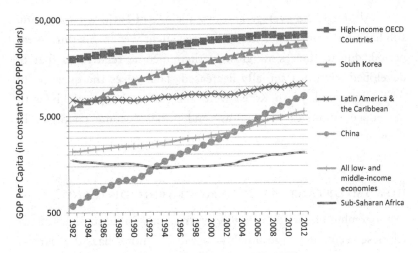

FIGURE 2.3 Growth in GDP per capita: 1982–2012

Note: The vertical axis represents GDP per capita in 2012 (in constant 2005 PPP dollars) on a logarithmic scale. Each grid between US$500 and US$5,000 represents US$500, and each grid between US$5,000 and US$50,000 represents US$5,000. All data are from the World Development Indicators.

per capita was only one third of the average sub-Saharan African level. During these thirty years of rapid growth, China went from one of the poorest countries to one of the richest poor countries in the world. In contrast, sub-Saharan Africa barely grew at all. China could still be considered a poor country in 2012, as its GDP per capita was below the average for Latin America and the Caribbean and less than a quarter of that of high-income OECD countries.

In 1982, South Korea's GDP per capita was below the average for Latin American countries, but with its subsequent growth, it quickly left these countries behind. The 1998 Asian financial crisis did not stop South Korea's growth for long, and in 2012, South Korea had an income level close to that of the most developed countries. Its GDP per capita jumped from 31 percent of that of high-income OECD countries to 80 percent. In contrast, GDP per capita in Latin America during the same period fell from 38 percent of that of high-income countries to just 31 percent.

Although the average absolute income of Latin American and sub-Saharan African countries increased slightly over this thirty-year period, due to their slow growth, their income relative to that of developed countries actually decreased. This raises the question of why China and South Korea were able to catch up quickly with developed countries, while low- and middle-income countries in Latin America and Africa were not. This is the puzzle I try to address in this book.

HOW IMPORTANT IS THE DEMOGRAPHIC DIVIDEND?

Demographic factors often figure prominently in discussions of the Chinese economy, presumably because China has the largest population in the world and implemented a draconian one-child policy for more than thirty years. However, neither the size nor the growth rate of the population has a direct effect on economic growth measured per capita.[4] There are both stars and laggards of economic growth among large and small countries. Population control may appear to have contributed to China's economic growth, but it is important to note that over the past four decades, coastal provinces in China, such as Guangdong, Fujian, and Zhejiang, have attracted large numbers of migrant workers from inland provinces and have therefore experienced faster population growth, but they have also had a faster growth rate of GDP per capita.

"Demographic dividend" is a phrase used by demographers, but it has become almost a household term in China. In mass media and casual conversations, one often hears the following statement: Until recently, China's rapid growth has been largely driven by a demographic dividend, but now this dividend has disappeared, and China must look for new engines of growth. The truth is that very few people outside academia understand the concept of demographic dividend.

Simply put, a demographic dividend is a growth benefit resulting from an increase in the share of a country's working-age

[4] See, e.g., Kelley and Schmidt (1995).

population or, equivalently, a decrease in the dependency ratio (i.e., the number of dependents divided by the number of working-age people). When a country's fertility rate declines, the proportion of dependent children in the total population decreases, and the proportion of working-age adults increases. When this happens, even if productivity (i.e., output per worker) remains unchanged, GDP per capita (i.e., output per person) will increase. This increase in GDP per capita can be described as a direct demographic dividend. In addition to this direct benefit, a lower dependency ratio may increase household savings, which can then be used to invest in productive fixed capital and can help improve education for children (i.e., human capital), both leading to an increase in labor productivity.[5] This second type of growth benefit can be described as an indirect demographic dividend. However, the demographic dividend is not permanent. A lower fertility rate and a longer life expectancy will eventually lead to an increase in the proportion of the elderly population, which will lead to an increase in the dependency ratio at some point. In fact, China's dependency ratio reached its trough in 2010, apparently killing its demographic dividend.

China's declining fertility rate and the resulting demographic dividend before 2010 are usually attributed to its strict one-child policy. However, the fertility rate in China began to drop before the policy was implemented, and the fertility rate in many developing countries without such a policy also fell significantly. Therefore, the one-child policy may not be the only reason for China's declining fertility rate. In fact, it may not even be the most important reason.[6] As such, although the policy has been abandoned, China's fertility rate may not increase significantly and may even continue to decline.

Demographers do not seem to agree on how to measure the total (i.e., direct plus indirect) demographic dividend and its contribution to

---

[5] See Bloom, Canning, and Sevilla (2003) and also Naughton (2018), who called the direct demographic dividend a "mechanical effect" on growth (p. 280).
[6] See Wang and Mason (2008).

economic growth. According to various estimates, the demographic dividend accounted for between 15 and 25 percent of China's economic growth in the last two decades of the twentieth century.[7] One study showed that the drop in the dependency ratio between 1982 and 2000 in China led to a growth rate of GDP per capita 1.3 percent higher than it would have been otherwise, suggesting that the contribution of the demographic dividend to China's economic growth was 15 percent.[8] Another study found that the sum of the direct demographic dividend and the human capital effect accounted for about 20 percent of China's growth between 1990 and 2005.[9] In a well-known study published in Chinese, Fang Cai, one of the main advocates of the concept of demographic dividend in China, and his collaborators estimated that the demographic dividend for the 1982–2000 period was 2.3 percent of GDP growth, explaining about a quarter of China's total growth.[10] These are, of course, very significant effects. However, they still only explain a relatively small part of the Chinese growth puzzle. After all, China's GDP per capita growth rate was about 7 percentage points higher than the average growth of other developing countries during the 1982–2012 period before its demographic dividend turned to zero toward the end of the period.

It is also important to note that China is not the only country to have benefited from a demographic dividend. In many other developing countries, the growth of their working-age population has outpaced that of their total population, leading to a drop in their dependency ratio. Table 2.1 compares *direct* demographic dividends around the world. The working-age population refers to people aged fifteen to sixty-four. The direct demographic dividend in the table is equal to the compound annual growth rate of GDP per capita minus that of GDP per working-age person.[11] It reflects the direct effect of

---

[7] Ibid.   [8] Ibid.   [9] See Zhang, Zhang, and Zhang (2015).
[10] See Wang, Cai, and Zhang (2004).
[11] This is also equivalent to the annual change in the dependency ratio.

Table 2.1 *GDP, population growth, and demographic dividend: 1982–2012 (%)*

Country or Region	GDP Growth	GDP per Capita Growth	Population Growth	Growth of the Working-Age Population	Growth of GDP per Working-Age Person	Direct Demographic Dividend
China	10.15	9.07	0.98	1.59	8.56	0.50
Middle East and North Africa	3.67	1.30	2.32	3.05	0.61	0.68
Latin America and the Caribbean	2.71	1.09	1.59	2.09	0.62	0.47
Europe and Central Asia (Developing Countries)	2.26	1.78	0.59	0.91	1.35	0.44
South Asia	5.92	3.97	1.86	2.32	3.61	0.37
Sub-Saharan Africa	3.04	0.28	2.75	2.88	0.16	0.12
European Union	2.02	1.75	0.26	0.32	1.69	0.05
United States	2.78	1.75	1.02	1.03	1.75	0.00

Data source: World Development Indicators.

the faster growth of the working-age population on GDP per capita growth, excluding the indirect benefit of higher savings and investment and the improvement in education that may be brought about by the fall in the dependency ratio.

Table 2.1 shows that China's direct demographic dividend accounted for 0.5 percentage point of its annual GDP per capita growth between 1982 and 2012, a very small fraction of the growth rate of 9.07 percent. Importantly, China's direct demographic dividend was not so different from that of most other developing regions. It was very similar to that of the developing regions of Latin America and the Caribbean and Europe and Central Asia, and was actually below the level of the developing regions of the Middle East and North Africa, excluding the oil-rich countries. Yet amazingly, all of these regions had an average GDP per capita growth of less than 1.8 percent, implying that their indirect demographic dividend must be very small. If a similar direct demographic dividend is accompanied by a much bigger indirect dividend in China, this latter growth effect has not panned out much in these developing regions. That is, lower dependency ratios in these regions have not led to much higher savings and more or better education, in stark contrast to China. To foreshadow the argument in Chapters 4 and 5, it may be Confucian culture's emphasis on thrift and education that is responsible for the disparity in the indirect demographic dividend between China and these developing regions.[12] In other words, it may not be China's demography per se but its culture of savings and education that has made a bigger difference.

Aside from China, other previously fast-growing East Asian economies enjoyed similar demographic dividends during their period of rapid economic growth, and these benefits were also insufficient to explain their extraordinary growth performance. Table 2.2 presents

[12] I thank an anonymous reviewer for pointing out to me the link between Confucian culture and the demographic dividend.

Table 2.2 *Demographic dividends in East Asia and other regions: 1965–1990 (%)*

Region	Average Growth Rate of GDP Per Capita	Average Population Growth Rate	Average Growth Rate of the Economically Active Population	Estimated Demographic Dividend: Effect on the Average Growth Rate of GDP Per Capita
Asia	3.33	2.32	2.76	0.73–1.64
East Asia	6.11	1.58	2.39	1.37–1.87
Southeast Asia	3.8	2.36	2.9	0.91–1.81
South Asia	1.71	2.27	2.51	0.41–1.34
Africa	0.97	2.64	2.62	–0.07–1.1
Europe	2.83	0.53	0.73	0.33–0.52
South America	0.85	2.06	2.5	0.74–1.54
North America	1.61	1.72	2.13	0.69–1.34
Oceania	1.97	1.57	1.89	0.53–1.14

Data source: Table 7 in David E. Bloom and Jeffrey G. Williamson (1998), pp. 419–455. The "economically active population" in the table is defined according to the UN's definition of labor supply. "East Asia" only includes mainland China, Taiwan, Hong Kong, Japan, South Korea, and Singapore.

the results of a study conducted by two Harvard economists, David Bloom and Jeffrey Williamson (1998). It shows that between 1965 and 1990, the economic growth rate of East Asia led the world, with an average annual growth rate of GDP per capita of 6.11%. Not only was this rate much higher than that of Europe (2.83%) and North America (1.61%), which can be attributed to the catch-up effect, but it was also higher than that of all other developing regions, especially South Asia (1.71%), Africa (0.97%), and South America (0.85%). To what extent can demographic dividends explain the difference in economic growth between regions? Table 2.2 shows that with the exception of Africa, all other regions benefited from a demographic dividend, the growth rate of their working-age population exceeding that of their total population. East Asia had the most demographic dividend, followed by Southeast Asia. In this sense, the demographic dividend may explain part of the rapid economic growth in East Asia, but almost all countries benefited from a demographic dividend, and the demographic dividend in East Asia was less than 1 percentage point higher, while the growth rate of GDP per capita in East Asia was between 4.4% and 5.26% higher than those of South Asia, Africa, and South America. The conclusion is clear: The demographic dividend has played a positive role in the economic growth of East Asia (including China), but it explains only a fraction of the region's extraordinary growth.

As a country's population ages, its demographic dividend eventually turns into a demographic debt, having a negative impact on future economic growth. However, they are two sides of the same coin. If the effect of the demographic dividend on economic growth is limited, then the effect of the demographic debt will also be limited. It is true that China will face a rapidly aging population. Many developed countries have already faced this problem, and even with a GDP per capita growth rate of 1–2 percent, these countries have not experienced any unmanageable crisis due to aging. According to popular opinion, rich countries have the means to face the problem of aging, while China will soon be old but not yet rich. Nevertheless, as long as China is still in the development stage of being "not yet rich," its economy will generally grow faster than that of rich countries due to the catch-up effect. A higher growth rate of just 1 percentage point may be enough to deal with the problems caused by an aging population. "Old but not yet rich" may soon be China's reality, but this does not mean that Chinese people will not continue to get rich after they start to age.

AN EXPORT-LED GROWTH MODEL?

It is often said that China's rapid economic growth has been propelled by an export-led growth model, riding on the wave of globalization. According to this view, with the reform and opening up policy, China has taken advantage of a large and cheap labor force to participate in the international division of labor. It has mass-produced and exported low- to mid-end consumer goods to the rest of the world, especially to developed countries. This explanation for China's rapid growth seems to be so self-evident that it requires no further proof. However, there is an obvious problem with this explanation once we take a global comparative perspective. China has certainly benefited from trade and globalization over the past few decades, but, in theory, trade and globalization should have worked for all countries.[13] In particular, all developing countries with cheap labor could have participated in the globalization of trade and production and exported their way to economic prosperity, but few have been able to do so.

It is true that China's exports have grown at the fastest rate in the world, but this may very well be due to the fact that the Chinese economy has grown the fastest; therefore, the causality may run the other way. A country's openness and the world trade regime as institutional factors apparently affect its economic growth.[14] However, as I explain in Chapter 4, exports per se, whether their growth or share in GDP, are not an engine of a country's long-term growth. It is the ability to increase production capacity for export (or domestic demand) that matters for growth.

On the demand side, an economy's dependence on exports, measured by the ratio of exports to GDP, depends on many factors, but this ratio is unrelated to a country's long-term economic growth. In fact, China's ratio of exports to GDP has been quite average, although it has increased significantly over the past few decades. China's export value ranks first in the world, not because China is

---

[13] See, e.g., Lamy (2013).
[14] See Sachs and Warner (1995) and Frankel and Romer (1999).

Table 2.3 *Export-to-GDP ratio around the world (%)*

Country	1982	1992	2002	2012
South Korea	33	27	36	57
Germany	23	24	23	52
Mexico	15	15	27	33
World	19	20	25	30
China	12	19	25	27
Turkey	12	14	25	26
India	6	9	14	24
Japan	14	10	11	15
United States	8	10	9	14

Data source: World Development Indicators.

more export-oriented than other countries, but because China has the second largest economy in the world. For example, in 2018, the value of China's total exports was 3.7 times that of South Korea, but its GDP was 8.4 times that of South Korea. Thus, the Korean economy is far more dependent on exports than the Chinese economy in terms of aggregate demand. Table 2.3 presents the export-to-GDP ratio of selected countries between 1982 and 2012. For China, this ratio was 27 percent in 2012, lower than the world average. Based on this measure, China is just an ordinary exporter that is no more dependent on exports than other large developing economies like India, Mexico, and Turkey. Table 2.3 also shows the trend in the globalization of trade during these three decades: The export-to-GDP ratio for the world as a whole increased from 19 percent in 1982 to 30 percent in 2012, and the importance of trade for both developed and developing economies increased significantly, perhaps with the exception of Japan.

Figure 2.4 shows that China's share of exports in GDP started at a very low 6.6% in 1978 and increased rapidly after 2001, peaking at 39% in 2006, probably due to China's accession to the WTO in 2001. After the global financial crisis in 2008, China's export growth slowed

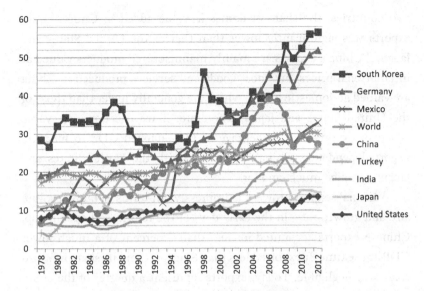

FIGURE 2.4 Export-to-GDP ratio (%): 1978–2012
Note: The trajectories are ordered according to the value of the export-to-GDP ratio in 2012, from high to low. All data are from the World Development Indicators.

sharply, and in 2009, its share of exports returned to a relatively normal level of around 27%. It is important to note that India and Turkey started with equally low export shares in 1978, 6% and 4%, respectively. In 2012, their export shares reached 24% and 26%, respectively, also close to that of China (27%). Mexico, a more export-oriented large developing economy, started with an export share of 10% in 1978 and reached 33% in 2012. Clearly, these three countries rode the wave of globalization to the same degree as China during the 1982–2012 period, but their economic growth rates were very different (the average growth rates of GDP per capita were 4.4%, 2.8%, and 0.7% for India, Turkey, and Mexico, respectively), all much lower than that of China.

In terms of dependence on exports, Figure 2.4 shows that Germany and South Korea led the pack by a large margin. The export shares of the United States and Japan were among the lowest in the world. Although China had a much higher export share than these two countries, the share of domestic value added in China's gross exports was significantly lower than that of the United States and Japan.[15] China's exports are mainly manufactured products valued at international prices, but most goods and services produced in China are valued at domestic prices, which are generally lower than those of the United States and Japan. Therefore, if we use domestic value added in exports as a percentage of PPP-adjusted GDP to measure export dependence, China's difference with the United States and Japan would be much smaller.

China's export prowess is impressive in terms of both absolute size and growth rate. In the early days of the reform and opening up, Chinese exports accounted for less than 7 percent of a much lower GDP at the time. It exported less than Singapore and its share in world trade was negligible. Today, exports represent a quarter of the country's GDP, which is not remarkable in relative terms, but a quarter of the second largest GDP makes China the largest exporter in the world. Thus, China's extraordinary export growth should be seen as a result, not the cause, of its rapid economic growth. Indeed, if export orientation can produce a growth miracle, almost all countries could have produced such a miracle, especially small countries, which are naturally more export-oriented and less likely to be subjected to foreign protectionist measures. However, in reality, it is China and India, the two largest developing countries that have achieved the fastest growth in recent decades.

Some American critics have attributed China's rapid rise to its unfair trade practices, unfair competition, IP theft, and poor labor and environmental protection. Peter Navarro, Director of the Office of Trade and Manufacturing Policy in the Trump administration, called these China's "Weapons of Job Destruction."[16] China is certainly no model for fair trade, good protection of IP rights, or strict environmental protection. However, if these "weapons" have made China the fastest growing economy in the world in the past few decades, we

---

[15] See Koopman, Wang, and Wei (2014).   [16] See, e.g., Navarro and Autry (2011).

have found the magic bullet for economic development: subsidizing domestic companies, undervaluing currencies, not protecting IP rights, and sacrificing the environment. If economic development were that simple, at least many small developing economies would have gotten rich a long time ago.

3   Do Institutions Rule?

In Chapter 2, I showed that China's low income base, direct demographic dividend, and export orientation are not special Chinese characteristics that have produced the country's growth miracle. The keys to the Chinese growth puzzle are elsewhere. Professional economists and political scientists have typically looked for answers from a policy and institutional perspective. Many of my Chinese students also give more credit to China's reform and opening up policy and its strong government, which is presumably authoritarian but efficient. Whatever policy or institutional advantages are attributed to China, they must be subject to global comparisons between China and other countries, especially developing countries.

A pioneer of the institutional approach to economic growth and development was the late Nobel laureate Douglass North, whose 1990 book, *Institutions, Institutional Changes and Economic Performance*, is widely influential. He defined institutions very broadly as "the rules of the game in a society" including both formal constraints – such as the rules that human beings devise – and informal or cultural constraints – such as conventions and codes of behavior.[1] North acknowledged the role of both formal institutions (e.g., the rule of law and private property rights) and informal institutions (e.g., cultural beliefs) in determining economic performance.[2] Most economists, however, generally use the term institutions more narrowly to refer only to formal rules established by government or legal authorities. For example, in a highly cited article, "Institutions Rule," Dani Rodrik of Harvard University and his coauthors identified institutions as the rule of law and the protection of private property

---

[1] North (1990), pp. 3–4.   [2] Also see North (2010).

rights in a country.[3] They showed that the quality of institutions thus defined trump geography and trade openness in explaining the large income disparities between nations. Unfortunately, too many economists have not only adopted a narrower definition of institutions but also neglected the important role that informal constraints such as culture, which are part and parcel of North's definition of institutions, play in a country's economic performance.

In this book, I also use the term "institution" in a narrow sense to distinguish it from culture. Specifically, institutions refer to a country's political system (e.g., democratic versus authoritarian); economic system (e.g., market system versus central planning, and private ownership versus state ownership of enterprises); and broad policy orientation of the economy (e.g., free trade versus protectionism, export promotion versus import substitution, and laissez-faire versus active industrial policy). In this sense, policy reforms lead to institutional changes. As a point of departure from existing studies of the Chinese economy, culture plays a major role in this book. Culture, like institutions, is a common word that has many meanings. I define culture as beliefs, values, and codes of conduct shared by a community of people.[4] A big difference between institutions (formal constraints) and culture thus defined, as North pointed out, is that formal rules may change overnight as the result of political or judicial decisions, but cultural constraints are much more impervious to deliberate policies.[5] Based on this distinction between institutions and culture, do institutions rule in explaining economic performance around the world and China's growth miracle in particular? The answer is not as clear-cut as Professor Rodrik and his coauthors would have us believe. Institutions are clearly an important determinant of

---

[3] Rodrik, Subramanian, and Trebbi (2004).

[4] This definition is similar to that of economists Luigi Guiso, Paola Sapienza, and Luigi Zingales (2006, p. 23), who defined culture as "those customary beliefs and values that ethnic, religious, and social groups transmit fairly unchanged from generation to generation."

[5] North (1990), p. 6.

economic performance, but not necessarily the most important. What Rodrik and his coauthors demonstrated is the positive relationship between a country's income level (GDP per capita) and the quality of its institutions (particularly the rule of law). To be sure, most rich economies have high-quality institutions, and their outcome may have been largely driven by this fact. What about the relationship between economic growth and the quality of the rule of law in developing countries? Do fast-growing China and India have higher institutional quality than other developing economies? The answer to the latter turns out to be negative.

MARKET REFORM: MYTHS AND FACTS

Both economists and the Chinese public attribute China's rapid economic growth to the market reform officially launched at the end of 1978. There is no doubt that without the reform and opening up policy, the Chinese growth miracle would not have happened. However, market reform can only explain why China grew faster after 1978 than before, but not why China grew faster than other developing countries, unless all have maintained a state-dominated, centrally planned economy like North Korea, which is certainly untrue. Most developing countries never implemented a Soviet-style central planning system, but many, if not most, had considerable state ownership and tight government control before the 1980s. Driven by the global wave of marketization reform in the 1980s, both developed and developing countries around the world, with a few exceptions, moved toward privatization, deregulation, and liberalization to varying degrees. This is why Harvard economist Andrei Shleifer called the period after 1980 the age of Milton Friedman, the best-known defender of the free market.[6]

However, market reforms do not seem to have helped most countries, developing or developed, to improve their economic growth by much, if at all. Table 3.1 compares the average annual growth rates

---

[6] Shleifer (2009).

Table 3.1 *Annual growth rates of GDP per capita between two twenty-five-year periods (%)*

Country or Region	1961–1985	1986–2010
China	4.69	8.91
India	1.61	4.62
United States	2.53	1.65
OECD Members	3.14	1.78
Latin America and the Caribbean	2.40	1.25
Middle East and North Africa	2.99	1.67
Sub-Saharan Africa	0.97	0.60

Data source: World Development Indicators.

of GDP per capita worldwide between two twenty-five-year periods: 1961–1985 and 1986–2010. Overall, the growth rate of Latin America and the Caribbean declined from an annual average of 2.4% to 1.25%; that of the Middle East and North Africa (excluding oil-rich countries) fell from 2.99% to 1.67%; and that of sub-Saharan Africa fell from 0.97% to 0.6%. I do not cite these data to argue that market reforms caused the economic slowdown in these developing regions; after all, economic growth in developed OECD countries also fell from 3.14% in the twenty-five years before 1985 to 1.78% in the twenty-five years after. Nevertheless, these data at least show that marketization and liberalization did not lead to economic miracles in most developing countries during these two periods, while China's growth rate increased from 4.69% before 1985 to 8.91% after 1985, and that of India increased from 1.61% to 4.62%.

Why have market reforms worked wonders in China and India but not in most other developing economies? Could it be that other developing countries have not carried out economic reforms as thoroughly as China and India? On the contrary, according to the two well-known country rankings of the degree of economic freedom produced by the Heritage Foundation in the United States and the Fraser Institute in Canada, China and India rank far below the world average, even after decades of reform; not only lower than almost all Latin American countries but also lower than many African countries.

Table 3.2 presents three 2017 rankings of selected countries by economic freedom from the Heritage Foundation and the Fraser Institute, and the World Bank's ease of doing business index. Hong Kong and Singapore, two prominent examples of free markets, were naturally at the top of the three rankings. North Korea and Venezuela understandably ranked lowest. China's ranking in the economic freedom indices was comparable to that of Nigeria and Tanzania, not only far behind middle-income countries such as Mexico and Jamaica but also behind low-income countries such as Cambodia and Uganda. China's ranking on a more objective ease of doing business index was much better, but it was still barely above average and below some slow-growing developing countries such as Colombia and Mexico. India performed even worse than China in two of these indices despite its rapid growth.

Based on the standards of these rankings, China clearly has no advantage over many developing countries in terms of the thoroughness of its market reform. In fact, there seems to be a consensus inside and outside the country that China is still a long way from being a true market economy. Even Chinese leaders acknowledged that the country needed to broaden and deepen its structural market reform and drew up a blueprint for it at the third plenum of the 18th CCP Congress held in 2013, with the aim of letting the market play a decisive role in the allocation of resources.

Economists firmly believing in the fundamental importance of the free market for economic development may challenge the validity of the indices used for the above rankings, that is, whether they reflect the real quality of a country's market institutions. It is of course reasonable to question the quality of these indices, but ironically, the organizations that produced them are precisely those that firmly believe in the free market. Their goal is to promote economic freedom to improve growth performance around the world. If the indices

Table 3.2 *Economic freedom and business environment around the world*

Economy	The Heritage Foundation's 2017 Index of Economic Freedom Ranking	The Fraser Institute's 2017 Economic Freedom Ranking	The World Bank's 2017 Ease of Doing Business Ranking
Hong Kong	1	1	4
Singapore	2	2	2
Switzerland	4	4	31
United States	17	5	8
Mauritius	21	9	49
South Korea	23	33	5
Colombia	37	94	53
Jamaica	41	61	67
Philippines	58	53	99
Mexico	70	76	47
Uganda	91	48	115
Cambodia	94	43	131
Tanzania	105	87	132
China	**111**	**112**	**78**
Nigeria	115	81	169
D. R. Congo	117	157	184
India	143	79	130
Venezuela	179	162	187
North Korea	180		

Note: Economic freedom indices are from the Heritage Foundation (www
.heritage.org) and the Fraser Institute of Canada (www.fraserinstitute.org).
Both are well-known conservative think tanks advocating laissez-faire
economic policies. They rank the economic freedom of countries around
the world each year. These two indices have similar definitions, including
a country's rule of law and property rights, government size, regulatory
efficiency, market openness, and macro stability. The World Bank's ease
of doing business index (www.doingbusiness.org/rankings) attempts to
measure the business environment of each country with objective
indicators, such as the complexity, time spent, and cost of project
approval procedures.

produced by these organizations are not really correlated with economic growth, perhaps the correlation between economic freedom and economic growth is not as strong as they believe it to be.

Some degree of market liberalization is clearly necessary for a growth miracle, but a free market alone does not seem to be sufficient. Market reform may have been a prerequisite for China's takeoff over the past forty years, but not a reason for China's much faster growth than that of other developing countries, many of which appear to have a freer market than China.

A free market proponent can use the rankings in Table 3.2 to argue for greater economic freedom in China, but those who disagree with laissez-faire economics can use the same rankings to draw precisely the opposite conclusion, that too much freedom is bad for economic development. So, could it instead be the strong role played by the Chinese government in the economy that has enabled China to achieve its rapid growth?

HOW REFORM WORKED IN CHINA

After forty-some years of reform, China's economic freedom is still ranked below average in the world. In fact, the United States and the European Union still do not recognize China as a market economy today. Mainstream economists have found it difficult to explain China's apparent economic success despite the fact that China's market economy has been far from free, and private property rights have been far from secure. In standard economic theory, a free market and private property rights are the cornerstones of a market economy and essential for the efficient allocation of resources at any given time. Institutional economists go even further by claiming that they are also the conditions for sustained economic growth over time.

China's double-digit growth in the 1990s presented an especially stark contrast to the economic failures of countries emerging from the former Soviet Union, some of which implemented more reforms in the areas of price and trade liberalization and privatization than China. This fact stimulated a large body of research trying to understand why market reform, however incomplete it was, had succeeded in delivering sustained economic growth in China but not in the former Soviet Union. There was a heated debate on the merits of the strategy of gradualism versus big bang or shock therapy to push forward market reform. This led to the birth of a field of research called the economics of transition.[7]

So, how did the reform work in China? Yingyi Qian of Tsinghua University, who has probably contributed the most to our understanding of China's transition from a planned to market economy, published an article with this question as the title in 2003.[8] In that influential article, Qian argued that China's reform succeeded precisely because it did not try to emulate "best practice institutions" (i.e., conventional Western-style free market and private property rights) at the early stage of market reform. Instead, China experimented with a series of novel, second-best "transitional institutions" such as the famous "dual track" price reform, collectively owned rural township and village enterprises (TVEs), and fiscal contracting between the central and local governments. These institutions worked because they unleashed the standard forces of incentives and competition in a country with high growth potential. After all, a developing country with a very inefficient economy may only need to remove some institutional barriers to achieve substantial growth. Perhaps more importantly, transitional institutions were acceptable to those in power, such as government officials, bureaucrats, and SOE managers, because the reforms also provided financial incentives to these powerholders.

In China's semi-reformed market economy, government plays a much more important role than in a typical market economy, so the incentives of government officials are crucial in determining economic performance. However, financial incentives can be too weak or even distortionary under transitional institutions. Are there other

---

[7] See Roland (2000).

[8] Qian (2003). Also see Qian (2017) for a recent book with the same title.

incentives for government officials? Chinese economists have offered a number of theories on this question. At the central government level, Yang Yao of Peking University proposed a hypothesis that the Chinese government is an "autonomous government" in the sense that it neither represents a specific social class nor is it captured by a specific social group, and that being autonomous enables the central government to adopt highly inclusive economic policies that favor long-term economic growth of society as a whole.[9] For some historical reasons, Yao argued, China had a relatively egalitarian social structure during the first two decades of its market reform, which together with the encompassing nature of the CCP, helped to produce an autonomous government. This is plausible, but Yao did not offer much empirical evidence to support his idea.

With regard to incentives for local governments, Hongbin Li and Li-An Zhou showed in a highly cited article that China's personnel control system links the promotion of local government officials directly to local economic performance, providing career incentives for local officials to promote economic growth.[10] However, local governments need to work with business enterprises to achieve growth. How can they help private companies and give them confidence to invest and do business in their localities when formal institutions are not so hospitable to private enterprises? According to Chong-En Bai, Chang-Tai Hsieh, and Zheng Michael Song, Chinese local governments take advantage of their strong political power and administrative capacity to offer "special deals" for their favorite private companies. These special deals enable firms to either break formal rules, which are often cumbersome and inefficient, or gain favorable access to resources, which are otherwise not generally available to private companies. They argued that overall, the benefits of these special deals in the Chinese context have outweighed their costs; as a result, China's extraordinary economic growth may have come from these special deals that have helped efficient private

9 Yao (2018).   10 Li and Zhou (2005).

companies to overcome the country's lack of business-friendly formal institutions.[11]

All of these arguments sound like cleverly designed schemes, but they are not. According to the late Nobel laureate Ronald Coase, a founding father of institutional economics, and his coauthor Ning Wang, "the series of events that led China to become capitalist was not programmed and ... the final result was entirely unexpected."[12] Moreover, of course, not all scholars agree with the narrative described in this section. For example, Yasheng Huang of MIT did not believe that China's economic success contradicts mainstream economic theory that emphasizes private property rights and the rule of law. He argued that most TVEs in China were actually private companies, not collective firms as is widely believed, and that "Chinese policy makers in the early 1980s strongly, directly, and self-consciously projected policy credibility and predictability."[13] In addition, Huang lamented the slow pace of market-oriented reforms in China after the 1990s. In contrast, Coase and Wang suggested that China has come a long way and quite rapidly down the unintended path to capitalism.

There is a vast literature (and much disagreement) on China's institutional changes and their economic consequences, too large to summarize in a few paragraphs.[14] However, it has mostly focused on the question of how economic growth is *in theory* even possible under a weak rule of law and insecure private property rights. The literature has often looked for nonstandard, transitional, or informal institutions in China that may be more or less effective substitutes for Western-style institutions, the standard point of reference. It has rarely addressed the causes of China's economic growth per se nor discussed the question examined in this book, that is, why China has

---

[11] Bai, Hsieh, and Song (2020).   [12] Coase and Wang (2012), preface.
[13] Huang (2008), p. xiv.
[14] See Xu (2011) for a partial synthesis of institutional perspectives on China's reform and chapter 5 of Naughton (2018), arguably the best textbook on the Chinese economy, for an overview of China's forty-year process of institutional reform. For a standard reference in Chinese, see Wu (2018).

grown so much faster than all other countries, especially less developed ones, despite its average if not poor institutional quality.

THE MYTH OF A STRONG GOVERNMENT: IS THERE A CHINA MODEL?

China's economic success in the past few decades has led some to believe that the country has created a unique political and economic system (the "China model" or "Beijing consensus") that can achieve economic growth and technological advances better than the Western system of liberal democracy and free market (or "Washington consensus").[15] The China model supposedly features a mixed economy in which SOEs and private firms coexist, and a strong authoritarian government that actively intervenes in the economy through regulations, subsidies, protectionist trade policies, and other means of developing certain targeted companies and industries.[16] Yet, is this authoritarian, state-centered development model truly unique and really conducive to economic growth?

The link between the political system and economic development is a venerable topic. Whether in academia, in the media, or in casual conversations, there are generally two conflicting views. One view holds that political democracy is a positive factor, if not a necessary condition, for a country to achieve long-term sustainable growth. Indeed, today, almost all countries with the most developed economies in the world are democracies, while most authoritarian countries have less developed economies. A recent influential expression of this democratic view is a book written by two prominent economists, Daron Acemoglu and James Robinson, titled *Why Nations Fail*.[17] The authors divided political institutions into two

---

[15] For a representative view by a Chinese author, see Zhang Weiwei (2011). For a Western view, see Bremmer (2017). For a debate on the Beijing consensus versus the Washington consensus, see Yao (2011).

[16] See, e.g., Naughton (2010), Zhao (2010), Breslin (2011), and Bell (2016).

[17] Acemoglu and Robinson (2012). I come back to their prediction for China's growth prospects in Chapter 9.

categories: inclusive or extractive. A democracy is an inclusive institution, while an autocracy is usually an extractive institution. They argued that only an inclusive political institution can sustain long-term economic growth. Although they admitted that a country may be able to achieve relatively rapid economic growth for some time, this growth will eventually falter. They used the former Soviet Union as an example. Naturally, the authors predicted that China's economic growth is not sustainable in the long term and that unless the country becomes a democracy, its growth will inevitably stagnate.[18] Although their theory allows the possibility of a growth miracle for a limited time in an autocracy, it does not explain why this possibility has materialized in China in recent decades and not in most developing countries.

An opposite view, which was once prominent in the modernization literature, holds that premature democracy in a Third World country is not conducive to economic development. With China's rapid rise, this view is gaining popularity. The late American political scientist Samuel P. Huntington was a major proponent.[19] According to this view, for Third World countries, economic development and Western–style liberal democracy cannot be achieved at the same time. In other words, liberal democracy is a luxury that economically backward countries cannot afford.[20] Supposedly, democracy in a poor developing country can lead to populist and redistributive economic policies, resulting in too much consumption and too little investment. It is ineffective in dealing with ethnic and social conflicts and in policymaking and resource mobilization. Conversely, some modernization theorists have suggested that economic development will lead to eventual democratization.[21] These theories seem to have been confirmed by the experience of South Korea, Taiwan, and Chile, which all developed their economies first under an authoritarian

[18] For critiques of this view, see, e.g., Glaeser et al. (2004).
[19] See Huntington and Nelson (1976).   [20] See also Zakaria (2003).
[21] The best-known expression of this view is that of Lipset (1959).

regime and then democratized. However, the experience of a few countries is not sufficient to prove a general rule. Many Western observers have certainly been disappointed by the lack of political liberalization in China after its rapid economic development.

When discussing the effect of democracy or lack thereof on economic development, China and India are often compared. Forty years ago, China's GDP per capita was still lower than that of India. Today, it is more than double that of India in PPP terms. If calculated with the market exchange rate, China's GDP per capita is more than four times that of India. Many people use this comparison as evidence that an authoritarian government is more conducive to economic development than a democratic one, yet such a simple comparison with only two countries can be very misleading. As a popular Chinese proverb originated from a Buddhist parable says, a blind man who feels only one part of an elephant's body may think he knows, but does not really know, what an elephant looks like. The fact is that in the past two or three decades, India has been one of the fastest-growing economies in the world. Therefore, the most interesting question is not why India has not grown as fast as China – after all, no country has – but why India has grown faster than other developing countries.

Political scientists and economists have conducted hundreds, if not thousands, of quantitative studies on the link between democracy and economic development. Some have found that democracy is good for economic development and growth, some have reached the opposite conclusion, and others have found no simple relationship.[22] As all studies carry the risk of having poor-quality data or methodological flaws or both, it is difficult to determine which of these studies to trust. Therefore, some scholars have conducted so-called meta-analyses using quantitative methods to summarize the results of all relevant published studies. According to a meta-analysis published in a top political science journal, democracy has no direct effect on

---

[22] See Przeworski et al. (2000) for an excellent introduction to the issue.

economic growth.[23] However, the authors of this study also found that democracy seems to help a country improve its human capital, lower inflation, reduce political instability, and increase economic freedom. In this sense, democracy has indirect positive effects on economic growth. The authors also found indirect negative effects, including that democratic governments tend to be larger and that there is often less freedom in international trade. These conclusions are of course average results and do not apply to a specific country or region. In the end, the authors could only draw a very modest conclusion: Considering all direct and indirect effects together, democracy does not seem to be harmful to economic growth.[24]

Here I use a scatter plot to illustrate why there is no apparent link between democracy and economic growth. Each point in Figure 3.1 represents a developing country or economy. The vertical axis represents the average annual growth rate of GDP per capita over the 2000–2010 period and the horizontal axis is a quantitative indicator of democracy ("democracy index"). The lowest score is –10 (extremely autocratic) and the highest score is +10 (completely democratic). The average score assigned to each country between 2000 and 2010 is used. The figure reveals that the economic growth rate of a developing country has little to do with its degree of democracy or autocracy. Among the autocratic countries are Azerbaijan and China, which experienced rapid economic growth over the decade, but also Zimbabwe and Eritrea, which suffered negative average growth. Among the democratic countries, there is Armenia with relatively fast economic growth and Jamaica with negative growth.[25]

---

[23] See Doucouliagos and Ulubasoglu (2008).

[24] However, whether or not democracy is beneficial to economic development, political freedom is, according to Sen (1999), an important end in itself.

[25] Savvy readers may note that China's economic growth rate in Figure 3.1 is not the highest. The reason is that during the 2000–2010 period, developing countries generally grew faster, largely benefiting from the increase in world prices for natural resources brought about by the rapid economic growth of China and India. The oil-rich countries of Azerbaijan and Equatorial Guinea grew especially fast, faster than China. Some former Soviet republics, such as Armenia, Kazakhstan, Turkmenistan, Belarus, and Georgia, also began to recover in the 2000s after experiencing a decade

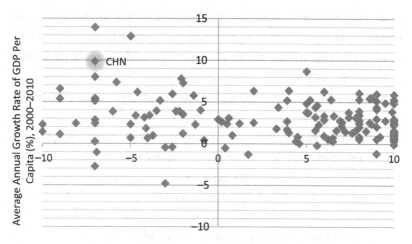

FIGURE 3.1 Democracy and economic growth: 2000–2010

Note: The "democracy index" comes from a project called Polity IV, which assigns each country a score ranging from –10 to +10. See www.systemicpeace.org/polityproject.html for more details. This scatter plot only includes developing countries as defined by the World Bank.

Perceptive readers may object that measuring a government system in a one-dimensional index of democracy or autocracy is too simplistic to be a useful analysis: There are good democracies and bad democracies and good autocracies and bad autocracies.[26] Perhaps what really matters is not whether a political system is democratic or autocratic, but whether it can achieve political order and stability and whether the government is effective. China may be an autocracy, but it may have greater political stability and a stronger, more effective government than most countries in the world. However, global comparisons do not seem to support this argument either.

Since 1996, the World Bank has published the World Governance Indicators every year to measure the quality of political institutions

of negative growth in the 1990s. The growth of these economies all slowed considerably to modest rates after the 2008 global financial crisis.

[26] See, e.g., Che, Chung, and Qiao (2013) and Bell (2016).

and governments around the world. It contains six indicators: voice and accountability; political stability and absence of violence; government effectiveness; regulatory quality; rule of law; and control of corruption. Table 3.3 presents the ranking of the political stability and absence of violence indicator and that of the government effectiveness indicator, both averaged over twenty years between 1996 and 2016, for a selection of countries or territories. In China, the government and the general public are very proud of the country's political stability and its low level of violence, but surprisingly, China only ranked 151st on this indicator among 214 countries and territories in the world. One can always challenge the quality of this type of indicator, but my interpretation of this result is that most countries, including China and India, which was ranked even lower (188th), enjoyed political stability during these two decades. Only a small number of countries, such as Somalia and the Democratic Republic of the Congo, suffered from political instability and violence. In other words, China was very stable, but not necessarily more stable than most other countries.

China is supposed to have a strong government, but in terms of government effectiveness, it ranked 92nd, only slightly above the world average. China was ranked lower than developing countries such as Malaysia, Costa Rica, and Mexico, and comparably with countries such as Jamaica, the Philippines, and India. Again, one can discuss the validity of the data used and ranking methodology, but I have not seen any solid evidence that the Chinese government is the most effective in the developing world. The country's superior economic performance should not be used to infer the quality of its government.

In summary, there is no clear evidence that China has a distinct advantage in its political system or government quality over many, if not most, developing countries, and the "China model" of active government, if there is one, may not be so unique or particularly effective to be the main reason behind the country's rapid economic growth. More generally, the effect of political systems on economic development, positive or negative, seems to have been greatly overestimated.

Table 3.3 *Ranking for political stability and governance effectiveness*

Country or Territory	Political Stability and Absence of Violence Indicator (1996–2016, Average)	Government Effectiveness Indicator (1996–2016, Average)
Greenland	1	46
Finland	3	2
Switzerland	7	4
Singapore	19	1
Mauritius	50	54
Costa Rica	72	75
Italy	77	61
Chile	78	33
United States	83	19
South Korea	92	42
Malaysia	103	41
Ghana	119	100
Jamaica	121	86
North Korea	128	210
Tanzania	142	137
Cambodia	148	174
China	**151**	**92**
Bolivia	152	129
Mexico	158	82
Venezuela	184	182
India	188	97
Philippines	194	96
Columbia	202	103
Nigeria	205	181
D. R. Congo	210	209
Somalia	214	212

Note: The ranking is based on the average values of the two indicators between 1996 and 2016 from the World Governance Indicators data set.

CHINA'S RISE AS PART OF THE "EAST ASIAN MIRACLE"

As noted in Chapter 1, China is not the only country to have experienced a growth miracle. Five other resource-poor East Asian economies, Japan and the four Asian Tigers, experienced similar, if not more remarkable, growth before China between the 1950s and the 1990s, successfully becoming high-income, developed economies. Their success has been called the "East Asian miracle," and rightly so.[27] What contributed to this miracle? Is there an "East Asian model" of economic development? What are the characteristics of this model?

To explain the East Asian miracle, mainstream economists have tended to argue that the East Asian model is essentially an export-oriented market economy dominated by private enterprises.[28] However, this "free market" view overlooks the great variations in policy orientation between these economies. It also cannot explain why only a handful of East Asian economies have succeeded in adopting the "correct" export-promoting, market-oriented policies, while other developing countries somehow have failed to do so. What is even more puzzling is that many developing countries abandoned the protectionist policy of "import substitution industrialization" and adopted pro-market reforms from the 1980s onward, but few countries have accelerated their growth, let alone matched the performance of East Asia.

Departing from this dominant economic view, political economy scholars have emphasized the key role played by active government policies in the economic development of East Asia. According to them, the core of the East Asian model is a "developmental state" promoting an industrial policy in line with local conditions.[29]

---

[27] Some people are more impressed by China's rapid growth than by that of the four Asian tigers because they mistakenly believe that it is easier for a small economy to grow quickly. If they were right, China would have grown faster if it had been broken up into dozens of smaller economies, and many small African and Latin American countries would have become rich.

[28] See, e.g., World Bank (1993) and Edwards (2010).

[29] See Wade (1990), Evans (1995), Woo-Cummings (1999), Kohli (2004), and Chang (2006).

Prominent Chinese economists Justin Lin and Yi Wen also advocated a similar view in the context of China's rapid economic development.[30] However, like the free market view, the active government or developmental state view also ignores the great diversity of policy orientations among the East Asian economies. Japan, South Korea, and Taiwan may fit this model, while Singapore and Hong Kong, two models of a free market economy, do not. This school of thought also cannot explain why many developing countries have engaged in active government intervention in their economies, but only a few East Asian countries have done so successfully. One may argue that the problem is not whether there is more or less government intervention, but whether the intervention is right or appropriate. Yet how is it that only a few East Asian economies have intervened wisely, but not most developing countries?[31]

Both the free market view and the active government view are institutional in nature. However, it should be clear by now that institutions may not be the differentiating factor for the East Asian growth miracle. After all, the political and economic systems of Japan, the Asian Tigers, and China during their respective periods of rapid development were quite diverse. If they had discovered growth-promoting institutions and industrial policies, at least some other developing countries should have been able to imitate and learn from them. It is hard to imagine that in the seventy-some years since WWII, out of about 150 developing countries and territories in the world, only a few in East Asia have managed to find the most favorable institutions and policies for their economic development, while almost all others have failed not only to identify the right institutions and policies, but also to learn from the East Asian examples.

For many years since the end of WWII, economists have sought solutions to the problem of economic development in Third World countries, but so far the quest for sustained growth has been elusive to

---

[30] See Lin (2014) and Wen (2016).   [31] See Summers and Thomas (1993).

say the least.[32] Whether it is infant industry protection, foreign aid and investment, export orientation, market liberalization, or institutional reforms, none of these policy prescriptions, in vogue at one time or another, have worked their magic.[33] Ironically, East Asia has produced few internationally renowned development economists, but it has nonetheless developed well.

While economists and political scientists have tended to view the East Asian miracle from an institutional perspective, many sociologists have attempted to explain it from a cultural perspective. According to them, certain characteristics of Confucian culture, such as strong motivation for achievement, work ethic and thrift, and an emphasis on education, were key factors in the successful development of East Asian economies.[34] The cultural view was popular in the 1980s, but the Asian financial crisis of 1998 weakened its impact. However, if institutional factors cannot satisfactorily explain the growth miracle of East Asia between the 1950s and the 1990s and that of China over the past four decades, then it becomes necessary to consider culture as a legitimate differentiating factor. It seems unlikely to be just a coincidence that these miracle economies happen to share traditional Confucian culture. From a cultural perspective, therefore, it is not any particular politico-economic model, but Confucian culture that may be at the heart of the East Asian miracle of rapid catch-up in the seventy-some years since WWII.

The cultural view, however, seems to have its own problems. As will become clear later, hard work only determines the level, not the rate, of growth in output. A culture of thrift implies high savings and thus more funds for investment, presumably leading to faster economic growth. However, it has often been said that the Chinese save too much and consume too little; as a result, China's

---

[32] See, e.g., Mankiw (1995), Easterly (2001), Collier (2007), and Banerjee and Duflo (2011).

[33] See, e.g., Williamson (2000) and Rodrik (2006 and 2008).

[34] See, e.g., Berger (1988), Hofstede and Bond (1988), and King (1992).

economic growth has become too unbalanced and unsustainable, also contributing to global economic imbalances. If so, a culture of thrift would not be an advantage but a weakness for the Chinese economy. Chinese culture may emphasize education, but that does not mean that China has an excellent education system or educational performance. Many affluent Chinese families have sent their children to study abroad (mainly to the United States and the United Kingdom), precisely because they have no confidence in China's education system. Furthermore, if Chinese culture is so good for economic development, how come China's rapid growth has occurred only in the past four decades, but not earlier? Perhaps more importantly, how do we prove that there are indeed major cultural differences between nations and that these differences matter to economic development? I try to answer these questions in the following chapters.

GEOGRAPHY AND ETHNIC DIVERSITY

Before delving into the cultural argument, let us examine some other explanations of cross-country disparities in economic performance around the world. In an article entitled "Institutions Don't Rule," Jeffrey Sachs of Columbia University strongly advocated a geographic view of economic development.[35] In a series of papers, Professor Sachs and his collaborators argued that geographic and climatic conditions have directly hindered the development of tropical and landlocked countries in Africa and that of tropical island countries disconnected from other regions due to their effects on transport costs, disease burden, agricultural productivity, and so on.[36] Indeed, in his influential book *Guns, Germs, and Steel*, Jared Diamond of UCLA demonstrated vividly how geographic factors affected the economic and technological development of the different continents of the world before 1500. He showed quite convincingly that the differences in the shape of the continents and their indigenous species could explain

---

[35] Sachs (2003).   [36] See, e.g., Gallup, Sachs, and Mellinger (1999).

why Eurasia had been much more developed than sub-Saharan Africa, the Americas, and Oceania in 1500.[37]

Geography may even explain why Europe, not China or India, discovered the New World (due to its relative proximity to the Americas) and why Britain, not China or any other country, industrialized first (due to its abundance of coal and the exploitation of resources, especially primary goods, from the New World).[38] If so, geography could even explain, to a large extent, the differences in the level of economic development in different regions of the world up to seventy years ago: Europe's geographic advantages allowed it to industrialize before other continents, and the resulting first-mover advantage was enormous and made it easier for Europeans to conquer and colonize most of the rest of the world. It was not until the end of WWII that most developing nations in Africa and Asia gradually gained independence and began the process of industrialization.

However, it is much more difficult to use geography to explain vastly different cross-country development performances after WWII, especially in the past four decades, the age of globalization. In a world with modern medicine, air conditioning, and modern transport and communication technologies, geography as an independent factor should only have a limited effect on contemporary economic growth for many, if not most, developing countries. The economic miracle of East Asia is clearly not due to superior geographic conditions. A tropical climate is generally considered unfavorable to economic development, but this has not prevented Singapore from becoming a developed economy. In mainland China, there are great disparities in geographic and climatic conditions between its thirty-one provincial regions, but economic growth in all of these regions has been very rapid over the past forty years, even in the landlocked mountainous provinces of Yunnan, Guizhou, and Sichuan. If any Chinese province had been an independent country, it would have been one of the fastest growing countries in the world. In fact, Shanghai, China's most

---

[37] Diamond (1997).   [38] See Pomeranz (2000).

developed coastal city, has experienced the slowest GDP per capita growth in the past forty years of all provincial level economies. In addition, the economic growth of many inland provinces has outpaced that of the coastal provinces in the last decade or so.

Natural resources can be viewed as a geographic factor, and the East Asian economies have few natural resources compared with most developing countries in Africa and Latin America, many of which have abundant oil and mineral reserves or are rich in cash crops. However, according to the resource curse theory, the lack of natural resources may have been a blessing in disguise for the East Asian economies. Also known as the Dutch disease, the resource curse indicates that an abundance of resources is bad for the development of manufacturing industries and hinders a country's long-term growth. In Third World countries, the abundance of natural resources can lead to too much redistributive politics, ethnic conflicts, or even civil wars. However, is the abundance of natural resources really a curse for economic development? No consensus has been reached on this question.[39] Even if there is a resource curse, it cannot be used to explain the growth miracle of China (or more generally East Asia), as most developing countries are not really rich in natural resources.

Geography sometimes has implications for the demographic structure of a country. Unlike Europe and Asia, the geography of Africa is special, in the sense that the national borders of most African countries are often linear and not "natural" boundaries, as most of them were arbitrarily drawn by the colonial powers. The consequence is that most African countries are made up of many ethnic groups, leading to pronounced ethnic, linguistic, and religious divisions. For different historical reasons, most Latin American countries are also made up of very diverse ethnic groups. In comparison, almost all East Asian countries and territories, with the exception of Singapore, have a much more homogeneous population. Some economists have argued that a high degree of ethnic diversity is a major

---

[39] See Sachs and Warner (2001) and Frankel (2010).

cause of ethnic conflicts, political instability, poor public policy, and the poor quality of institutions in many African and Latin American countries.[40] However, ethnic diversity can only explain a fraction of the difference in growth rates between countries. According to the empirical analyses by these economists, a difference of 2 to 3 percentage points in the average annual GDP per capita growth rate between sub-Saharan Africa and Latin America and the rest of the world (including East Asia) still cannot be accounted for by their explanatory variables, including ethnic diversity. As East Asia's growth rate is several percentage points higher than the world average, a much larger gap between East Asia and the regions of sub-Saharan Africa and Latin America cannot be explained purely by ethnic diversity. In fact, Singapore is also ethnically diverse with a mixed population of ethnic Chinese, Malays, and Indians, but this did not stop the country from becoming one of the richest in the world.

[40] See Easterly and Levine (1997) and Alesina et al. (2003).

4 Savings and China's Investment-Led Growth

In Chapter 3, I examined the fundamental causes of economic growth, namely institutions, culture, and geography, and I argued that institutions and geography are not the differentiating factors for the East Asian miracle in general and the Chinese growth miracle in particular. I then suggested that Confucian culture may be the fundamental factor that distinguishes China and the other East Asian miracle economies from the rest of the developing world. In the next three chapters, I evaluate the three proximate causes of growth (i.e., investment, education, and technological progress), and in the process, I try to show why culture, not institutions, may be the more distinctive fundamental cause of China's rapid growth compared with other developing economies. The analyses in these three chapters help to prepare the synthesis and defense of the cultural perspective of China's rise in Chapter 7.

ECONOMIC GROWTH VERSUS ECONOMIC FLUCTUATIONS

Before proceeding, it is important to distinguish between economic growth and economic fluctuations. In economics, a country's economic growth is typically defined as "a long-term rise in capacity to supply increasingly diverse economic goods to its population."[1] The economic theory of growth is concerned with how an economy can sustain the increase in the supply, not the demand, of goods and services year after year. The underlying assumption is that in the long term, supply will create its own demand.[2] In contrast, economic

---

[1] Kuznets (1973).

[2] This is often called Say's Law, named after the French classical economist, Jean-Baptiste Say (1767–1832). See Baumol (1999).

fluctuations refer to the variation in short-term (annual or quarterly) GDP growth rates along a long-term trend rate of growth.

Almost by definition, economic growth is determined by factors that influence the expansion of productive capacity. Standard analytical frameworks are based on the famous Solow model or its variants and various so-called endogenous growth theories, which all look at the supply side only. However, in the short term, a country's productive capacity can be considered fixed, so GDP growth for a given year or quarter is largely determined by demand. Therefore, to analyze economic fluctuations, economists have mainly focused on demand. The most commonly used analytical frameworks are based on Keynesian theory (old and new).[3] Many journalists and commentators have failed to distinguish between long-term growth and short-term fluctuations and have often mistakenly applied Keynesian theory to discuss issues related to long-term growth.

Whatever the fundamental causes of a country's economic growth, whether institutional, cultural, or something else, there are only three channels through which an economy can grow over time: (1) the accumulation of physical capital such as machinery, equipment, and buildings, that is, investment; (2) the accumulation of human capital such as knowledge and skills, that is, education, including on-the-job training; and (3) productivity growth resulting mainly from technological progress.[4] For a developing economy like China and India, productivity growth can also be generated by reallocating resources from low productivity to higher productivity activities.[5] One such reallocation of particular importance to China is urbanization, which includes the movement of labor from agriculture to industry or services and the conversion of rural land to urban and industrial use. However, presumably, higher productivity economic activities use different and generally more advanced technologies. As a result, the economy-wide technological level increases due to this

---

[3] See, e.g., Romer (2001).   [4] See, e.g., Barro and Sala-i-Martin (2003).
[5] See Bosworth and Collins (2008).

reallocation. Therefore, the reallocation effect can be broadly seen as a kind of technological progress of the whole economy.

The three channels through which an economy grows are also called the proximate causes or factors of growth. The quantity of labor as a factor of growth has been ignored in this book, because I use the growth of GDP per capita as the main indicator of economic growth. After all, it is GDP per capita, not GDP, that measures a country's income level. All other things being the same, labor force growth will lead to GDP growth, but if the labor force grows at the same rate as the general population, it will have no effect on the growth of GDP per capita. It is only when the labor force grows faster than the population that the growth of GDP per capita will increase accordingly. This is called the direct demographic dividend, as discussed in Chapter 2. However, as we saw in that chapter (Tables 2.2 and 2.3), the difference between the growth of the general population and the growth of the working-age population or the labor force (the economically active population) is quite small around the world. Moreover, differences in labor force growth among nations play only a minor role in explaining cross-country disparities in terms of GDP per capita growth. Therefore, ignoring the quantity of labor as a factor of growth has no qualitative impact on our analysis. However, if labor force growth diverges significantly from population growth, its impact will then need to be considered. I discuss this possibility and its implications for China's current slowdown and future growth prospects in Chapters 8 and 9.

It is of the utmost importance to note that the three proximate factors of economic growth are not the troika of consumption, investment, and exports often mentioned in the popular press. These are three demand factors that, with the exception of investment, only determine short-term growth rates, but not the long-term growth trend. The confusion caused by the failure to distinguish between the causes of long-term growth and the determinants of short-term fluctuations has contributed to the general misunderstanding of the Chinese economy as well as the global economy for that matter, an issue I discuss later in this chapter and also in Chapter 8. Investment occupies a special position because it creates both short-term demand and long-term supply. In summary, investment, education, and technological progress are the three real engines of growth.

INVESTMENT VERSUS PRODUCTIVITY GROWTH

Although economists have debated which of the three engines contributes most to economic growth, there is basically a consensus that all three play a role in any sustained economic growth. In fact, they are not separable from each other. Human capital, be it the current level or its accumulation over time, is essential to technological progress, which not only requires but also stimulates investment in human and physical capital. Therefore, it is not really possible to unambiguously identify the independent contributions of each of the three engines of growth. Nevertheless, a vast literature has endeavored to do just that.

To quantify the contribution share of each proximate engine of growth, economists have tended to group investment and education together as factor accumulation (physical and human capital are called factors of production), and the residual portion of GDP growth that cannot be explained by factor accumulation is said to be due to the increase in the so-called total factor productivity, or TFP. TFP growth is generally seen as the result of technological progress and, to a lesser extent, of improved efficiency in resource allocation (e.g., workers leaving agriculture for higher productivity jobs in manufacturing and services).[6]

In the case of China, no definitive conclusion has yet been reached regarding the respective contributions of factor accumulation and productivity growth. Most researchers have found that the accumulation of physical capital (i.e., investment in fixed assets) has contributed the most to China's rapid economic growth, while productivity has also increased significantly over the years. According to

[6] See, e.g., Bosworth and Collins (2008).

an authoritative estimate, between 1978 and 2005, during which China's average annual GDP growth rate was 9.5%, the annual growth of TFP was 3.8%.[7] That is to say, 40 percent of China's economic growth was brought about by increased productivity, while the rest was due to factor accumulation, mainly fixed capital investment.[8]

Contrary to the opinions of most scholars, economist Alwyn Young did not believe that the rapid growth of China or East Asia should be called a miracle. In a 2003 article published in the prestigious *Journal of Political Economy*, Professor Young stated that China's TFP between 1978 and 1998 only grew at an annual rate of 1.4%, which is nothing special. At the time, Young was famous for his earlier research on the economic growth of the four Asian Tigers. In a 1995 article, he reached the surprising conclusion that the economic growth of the four Asian Tigers was essentially driven by capital accumulation, while their productivity improvement was very limited. Even more shockingly, he found that Singapore's productivity even declined.[9] These findings were publicized by outspoken economist and later Nobel Prize winner Paul Krugman, who wrote an article in *Foreign Affairs* based on Young's work, disparaging East Asia's economic achievement. In this article, Professor Krugman claimed that their rapid growth was achieved through heavy capital investment, making it similar to the Soviet growth model, not at all a miracle. He then predicted that East Asia's investment-led growth

---

[7] See Perkins and Rawski (2008). Their estimate was close to the results reported by Bosworth and Collins (2008), Chow and Li (2002), and Zheng, Bigsten, and Hu (2009).

[8] Using a different growth accounting method, Xiaodong Zhu (2012) attributed 78 percent of China's GDP per capita growth between 1978 and 2007 to TFP growth; 15 percent to human capital growth; and almost 0 to physical capital investment. The idea behind this method is that physical capital accumulation itself may be induced by TFP growth. My reading of Zhu's result compared with that of the standard growth accounting method is that we cannot really separate the contribution of capital investment from that of TFP. Also see chapter 5 of Knight and Ding (2012).

[9] Young (1995). In fact, other economists have obtained similar results before Young. See Kim and Lau (1994).

would not be sustainable and would slow down sooner than expected.[10] When it was published in 1994, the article sparked much debate, but the Asian financial crisis that followed in 1998 seemed to prove Krugman's prescience. However, since then, China and the four Asian Tiger economies have continued to significantly outperform other economies at similar income levels. Singapore, used by Krugman and Young as a case study of an investment-led growth model without increased productivity (i.e., without technological progress), is now one of the richest countries in the world. In addition, according to official statistics, it has exceeded the US per capita GDP in both nominal and PPP terms.

Alwyn Young's findings on East Asia's economic growth may sound disparaging, but if his numbers are correct, they simply demonstrate that factor accumulation, especially fixed capital investment, is the most important engine of rapid catch-up growth (i.e., the growth of less developed economies trying to catch up with advanced economies).[11] Being able to explain the rapid growth of East Asia by physical capital accumulation does not prove that it is not a miracle. If a country can achieve rapid growth and get rich quickly through the accumulation of physical capital, how many poor developing countries would not want to be in this situation? The real question is why only a few East Asian economies have been able to achieve this. So, if Young's findings are valid, the Chinese growth puzzle and the East Asian growth puzzle become the following: Why did China and other East Asian economies accumulate capital so much faster than other developing countries?

SAVINGS AND INVESTMENT AROUND THE WORLD

A country's GDP can be broken down into final consumption, domestic investment, and net exports (i.e., exports minus imports) on the

---

[10] Krugman (1994).
[11] See also Collins and Bosworth (1996) for a similar conclusion based on conventional growth accounting.

expenditure side. Final consumption includes both household consumption and government consumption. Table 4.1 presents the average shares of these three components of GDP for selected countries and regions during the 1982–2012 period. It shows that China had the highest domestic investment rate by far, with an average of 40.2 percent of GDP for the 1982–2012 period. In comparison, the world average was only 23.8 percent. In general, developed countries had slightly higher investment rates than developing countries: The United States and the European Union invested on average 22 percent of GDP, but Latin America and sub-Saharan Africa invested 20 percent or less. In the Appendix, I show that China's official investment rate may have been overestimated by as much as 10 percent of GDP for the 2004–2011 period when it officially reached an average level of over 44 percent. Yet, even taking this into account, China's investment rate was still one of the highest in the world, and thus the possible overestimation will not affect our following argument qualitatively.

In Table 4.1, economic growth appears to be positively correlated with domestic investment in physical capital, which is exactly what economic theory predicts. In a widely cited article in cross-country growth studies, economists Ross Levine and David Renelt (1992) found that the positive correlation between GDP per capita growth and the investment rate was one of the very few robust relationships that withstood rigorous empirical tests. Indeed, fast-growing countries, such as China, Singapore, South Korea, and India, all had relatively high investment rates, while the slow-growing regions of Africa and Latin America had low investment rates. However, this correlation was not perfect as other factors may confound the positive relationship between investment and growth. For countries already at the technological frontier such as Switzerland and Japan, more investment did not seem to generate higher growth. Moreover, Chile enjoyed relatively high growth but had an average investment rate. However, compared with the Latin American average, Chile's investment rate was 2.5 percentage points higher.

Table 4.1 *Savings, investment, and economic growth: 1982–2012*

Country/Region	Final Consumption (% of GDP)	Domestic Investment (% of GDP)	Net Exports (=100–Final Consumption–Domestic Investment)	GDP Per Capita Growth (Annual %)	Gross Domestic Savings (=100–Final Consumption)
China	57.5	40.2	2.3	9.1	42.5
Singapore	51.8	32.0	16.1	4.2	48.2
South Korea	66.8	31.3	1.8	5.8	33.2
India	74.7	27.4	-2.1	4.5	25.3
Switzerland	68.4	26.6	5.0	1.1	31.6
Japan	72.6	26.0	1.4	1.7	27.4
Greece	84.2	24.7	-9.0	0.8	15.8
World	76.1	23.8	0.0	1.5	23.9
Chile	74.5	22.5	3.0	3.9	25.5
United States	80.7	22.1	-2.8	1.9	19.3
European Union	77.5	22.0	0.6	1.8	22.5
Latin America and the Caribbean	79.0	20.0	1.0	1.2	21.0
Low-Income countries	90.0	19.7	-9.7	1.3	10.0
South Africa	78.5	18.8	2.7	0.3	21.5
Brazil	80.1	18.8	1.2	1.4	19.9
Sub-Saharan Africa	81.7	18.4	-0.1	0.4	18.3

Note: All rates are simple averages of thirty annual rates from 1983 to 2012. Gross domestic saving in the last column is equal to GDP minus final consumption; that is, everything that is not consumed is saved. These savings are then invested domestically. If savings are greater than domestic investment, the rest is invested in foreign countries, which is equivalent in value to the trade surplus (i.e., the value of net exports). All data are from the World Development Indicators.

As investment is one of the most important factors in economic growth, the question is why all countries have not invested as much as China. For developed countries, long-term growth seems to depend more on technological progress than on capital investment. In these countries, the capital stock per worker is already at a high level, too high an investment rate would yield a low rate of return without really stimulating economic growth. However, for developing countries, the capital–labor ratio is very low and there is plenty of room for more investment. So why do all developing countries not invest more? A simple answer is that there is not enough money. All investments must be financed either by domestic savings or by foreign sources. In theory, a developing country can attract foreign capital to supplement its domestic savings. However, international capital is far from perfectly mobile, and due to cross-country differences in human capital, productivity, and various market imperfections, domestic savings and investment rates are strongly positively correlated in almost all countries, and this relationship is stronger for large countries.[12]

One can argue that the reason many developing countries fail to attract enough foreign capital is the poor quality of their institutions, so the cause of their low investment rate is not low savings per se but poor institutions.[13] However, as shown in Chapter 2, China's institutional quality is not much better than that of many developing countries. Moreover, even with relatively good institutions as ranked by think tanks like the Heritage Foundation, a developing country can still find it difficult to attract as much foreign investment as it wants. Think about it: How much can a country borrow from foreigners year after year without eventually getting into a debt crisis? A typical Latin American or sub-Saharan African country would need to attract foreign investment equivalent to at least 10–20 percent of its GDP each year to be able to reach China's rate of investment.

---

[12] See Lucas (1990), Frankel (1992), and Baxter and Crucini (1993).
[13] See, e.g., Alfaro, Kalemli-Ozcan, and Volosovych (2008).

As a result, for most countries, especially large ones, domestic savings remain the main source of funding for domestic investment. Therefore, it is a great advantage for China to have one of the highest gross domestic savings rates in the world, as shown in the last column of Table 4.1. In fact, China has saved more than it has invested domestically for most years in the past four decades and, therefore, has been a net exporter of capital, which is very unusual for a developing country. Most countries seem to save around 20 percent of GDP. Again, like the investment rate, China's savings rate is considerably overestimated, especially after 2004, as I show in the Appendix, due to the underestimation of its consumption rate. Nevertheless, even correcting that, China's savings rate remains one of the highest in the world. So why do some countries save more than others? Why does China save so much more? The answer may lie in cultural rather than institutional or other differences.

EXPLAINING CHINA'S HIGH SAVINGS RATE

A country's gross domestic savings are made up of the savings of households, corporations, and the government. In China, based on average ratios over the 1992–2012 period, households contributed 50%; corporations contributed 42%; and the government contributed 8% of domestic savings. As a percentage of GDP, household, corporate, and government savings rates were 22%, 18%, and 3%, respectively.[14] These ratios have more or less remained stable. Compared with most OECD countries, China's corporate savings rate is high, but it is not as unusual as some economists have claimed.[15] What makes China special are mainly its unusually high household savings and, to a much lesser extent, its positive government savings.

The fact that China has one of the highest savings rates in the world may not be surprising to many noneconomist readers. After all, Chinese people are known to be thrifty, and saving is part of Chinese

[14] These numbers were calculated by the author based on data from the CEIC data set.
[15] See Kuijs (2005), Wolf (2006), and Bayoumi, Tong, and Wei (2009).

culture. Economists, however, are by profession typically averse to cultural explanations. For example, the late Nobel laureate Franco Modigliani, inventor of the famous life-cycle theory of consumption, and his coauthor Shi Larry Cao (2004) dismissed the "thrifty Chinese" explanation offhandedly by pointing out that the Chinese only saved 5.3% between 1958 and 1975, even less than the supposedly profligate Americans who saved 7.6% of their disposable income during the 1990–1994 period. According to life-cycle theory, people try to smooth consumption over their lifetime regardless of their income level, and the working-age population saves for retirement. As a result, the theory predicts that the rate of savings is not affected by absolute income, but by the growth rate of income and the demographic composition. Therefore, the authors concluded that China's high and rising savings rate during the reform period was not related to its culture, but to its rapid economic growth and declining dependency ratio (i.e., demographic dividend).

However, China's low household savings during the 1958–1975 period do not prove that culture played little role in the country's current high savings rate. Modigliani and Cao failed to appreciate the fact that China was one of the poorest countries before 1975, with a per capita GDP ranging from US$130 to US$270 (in constant 2010 US dollars) during the 1960–1975 period, which was near or even below subsistence level. During the same period, the average GDP per capita of sub-Saharan Africa was over US$1,000.[16] I personally knew how poor China was back then as I grew up in the 1960s and 1970s. Even as a "privileged" urban resident, I barely had enough to eat, not to mention my relatives in the rural areas of now prosperous Jiangsu Province. To expect people to save on such a low income is too much to ask. In Table 4.2, we can see that the savings rates of China's urban households increased sharply during the 1985–2012 period across all income groups, but the rates of savings were strongly correlated with income, and the wealthiest households had much higher savings rates

---

[16] All figures are taken from the World Bank's World Development Indicators.

Table 4.2 *Urban household savings rates by income group (%)*

Income (high to low)	1985	1990	1995	2000	2005	2010	2012
90th percentile	16.0	23.8	26.7	30.9	38.7	43.7	46.1
80th percentile	12.3	18.7	22.7	25.1	35.2	38.7	40.7
60th–80th percentile	11.2	17.1	18.4	21.7	30.8	36.7	39.5
40th–60th percentile	10.1	14.4	15.4	19.2	26.1	33.4	35.9
20th–40th percentile	9.4	13.3	12.8	15.1	22.3	30.9	33.2
20th percentile	8.0	10.8	9.4	10.5	17.4	28.2	30.0
10th percentile	5.6	9.0	5.4	5.2	7.9	18.4	20.7

Note: The figures in the table are calculated by the author based on data from the CEIC data set. The savings rates are calculated as one minus the consumption rate, which is the ratio of per capita consumption expenditure to per capita disposable income.

than the poorest. The lowest income group (10th percentile) had a savings rate not much higher than 5 percent before 2000. The standard of living of China's average urban households during the 1958–1975 period was even lower than that of the lowest income households in 2000. Being able to save 5 percent of their income back then should be viewed as an "achievement." Indeed, even the highest income households (90th percentile) had a lower savings rate in 1985, when China was still very poor, than the lowest income households (10th percentile) in 2010, when China was much richer. It is amazing that China's poorest 20th percentile households managed to save 30 percent of their income in 2012. If not culture, how else can we explain it?

Although most economic research on China's household savings rate has been motivated by the fact that it is much higher than that of virtually any other country, almost all noteworthy studies on the issue have focused solely on China, trying to explain why

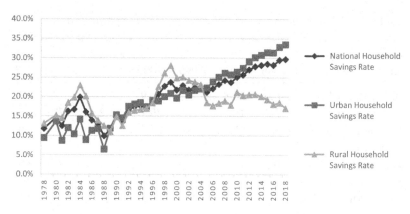

FIGURE 4.1 China's household savings rates: 1978–2018
Data source: CEIC data set

Chinese household savings increased so much after the 1980s.[17] As shown in Figure 4.1, the national household savings rate increased from 10% in 1988 to 30% in 2018. The savings rates of urban households rose especially rapidly from 6.5% to 33.5%, while the savings rates of rural households increased from 11% in 1989 to 28% in 1999, then fell to 17% in 2018.[18] The catalyst for the changing patterns of China's urban and rural household savings obviously cannot be cultural factors, because culture is not expected to change much in a few decades. It must have been the economic forces unleashed by market reforms and population control policies that have propelled the rapid increase in China's household savings, especially among urban residents. Nevertheless, culture may still have played an important mediating role in the sense that the same economic forces may lead to

[17] For concise summaries of these explanations, see Yang (2012), Yang, Zhang, and Zhou (2012), chapter 8 of Knight and Ding (2012), and chapter 19 of Naughton (2018).

[18] I have not seen a satisfactory explanation for the apparent differences in savings patterns between China's urban and rural households, especially after 2000. See Horioka and Wan (2007) for an educated guess as to why China's rural households had a higher savings rate than urban households before 2004. They argued that rural incomes may be more volatile and rural price levels lower. Also see Pan (2016) for a study covering the period between 1995 and 2002.

different savings outcomes in different cultures. However, it is difficult to see the role of culture purely on Chinese data.

Some economists have attempted to show that conventional economic theories can explain China's high savings. For example, life-cycle theory predicts that the savings rate increases with an increase in economic growth and a decrease in the dependency ratio, which is exactly what happened in China after the 1980s.[19] However, others have argued that conventional theories cannot fully explain China's savings patterns (e.g., both the young and the elderly in China save a lot). Some have mentioned habit formation (or consumption inertia) as an alternative theory that may explain the rise in savings across age cohorts and income groups in China.[20] According to this theory, current consumption depends not only on income but also on past consumption ("habit"), which means that there is a kind of consumption inertia that causes consumption growth to lag behind income growth, leading to higher savings under rapid economic growth.[21] This theory appears to be compatible with a culture-based explanation of China's high savings in the sense that consumption habit may be culturally determined.[22]

Other popular explanations for the increase in household savings in China after the 1980s include the increased risk of unemployment and other uncertainties introduced by economic reforms; the growing private burden of expenditures on housing, education, and health care; and the country's underdeveloped social welfare system and financial market. All of these factors combined may have created greater financial insecurity and induced precautionary savings in China despite anticipated increases in future incomes due to economic growth.[23] These are plausible explanations for why Chinese households may have wanted to save more in the 1990s and the 2000s than in the 1980s. However, China's social welfare system

---

[19] Modigliani and Cao (2004).   [20] See, e.g., Horioka and Wan (2007).

[21] Carroll, Overland, and Weil (1994).   [22] See Yang, Zhang, and Zhou (2012).

[23] See, e.g., Meng (2003), Chamon and Prasad (2010), and Chamon, Liu, and Prasad (2013).

has improved significantly over the last ten to fifteen years, but, as shown in Figure 4.1, China's urban household savings rate has continued to increase.[24]

The popular claim that a low level of social safety net leads to high savings seems reasonable in theory. But does it explain China's higher savings compared with other countries? Probably not. From a global comparative perspective, there is simply no simple relationship between a country's level of social welfare and its savings rate. For example, Singapore has a sound social welfare system compared with most countries, but it has one of the highest savings rates in the world. In Europe, Switzerland has the highest household savings rate among all OECD countries (averaging 15 percent during the 1995–2015 period), while Greece has the lowest rate (averaging –3 percent during the same period).[25] It is certainly not due to Switzerland's poor social welfare system, as the opposite is true.

THE CULTURE OF SAVINGS

Studies that have focused solely on China can only explain the economic forces behind the rise of its savings rate, but not why China's savings rate is higher than that of other countries. They cannot tell us whether or not similar forces would have led to a similar increase in the savings rate of other economies. In other words, they do not prove that cultural factors have played no important role. For example, it is entirely possible that a similar demographic change has led to a higher savings rate in China than in other developing countries for cultural reasons. As discussed in Chapter 2, the indirect demographic dividend

---

[24] Shangjin Wei and Xiaobo Zhang (2011) proposed an interesting culture-related son preference theory to explain China's rising savings rate. According to these authors, due to its strong son preference culture, China's strict family planning policy led to a very imbalanced gender ratio and consequently to a super competitive marriage market. Because a young man who owns a home is more competitive in the marriage market, house prices are bid up, resulting in (somewhat forced) high savings, especially among households with a son.

[25] These figures were calculated by the author from official data from the OECD website https://data.oecd.org/hha/household-savings.htm.

operating through the effect of savings and education during the 1982–2012 period was much higher in China than in developing regions with a similar direct demographic dividend.

To understand differences in the savings rate between countries, a global comparative perspective is needed. In cross-country studies of the determinants of savings, economists have looked at demographic factors, income levels and their growth rates, social welfare systems, tax systems, interest rates and inflation, and the development of financial markets.[26] However, according to some researchers, even after controlling for differences in these economic and policy factors, much of the differences in savings rates across societies remains unexplained; therefore, culture must be considered as an importance source of differences in savings behavior.[27]

To test the relevance of culture for savings, some economists have studied the savings behavior of immigrants in one host country to see whether savings rates vary systematically by place of origin. Presumably, all immigrants face the same institutional and economic environment in the host country, therefore any systematic differences in the savings behavior of immigrants across their places of origin could be attributed to culture. One early study found that the savings patterns of immigrants did not vary systematically according to their place of origin.[28] A very recent study pointed out that data limitations may have led to the conclusion of this early study that culture did not matter.[29] The authors of the new study used a better data set from the United Kingdom to analyze the savings behavior of up to three generations of immigrants in the country, and found that cultural differences are an important determinant of savings behavior and that their relevance persists for up to three generations.

All other things being equal, those who work hard and spend little will have a higher savings rate. Chinese people are generally

---

[26] See, e.g., Edwards (1996), Higgins (1998), Masson, Bayoumi, and Samiei (1998), and Bandiera et al. (2000).

[27] See Costa-Font, Giuliano, and Ozcan (2018).   [28] Carroll, Rhee, and Rhee (1994).

[29] Costa-Font, Giuliano, and Ozcan (2018).

proud of their hard work and thrift ethics, but are the Chinese particularly hardworking and thrifty? Is there any evidence supporting this claim? If we have data on the number of hours people work each week and the fraction of their income people save in all countries, we could use them to partially answer this question. However, the number of hours worked per week and the savings rate in each country are not necessarily indicators of cultural differences, as they also depend on many factors other than culture, such as national policies and economic situations.

Some social scientists have attempted to measure cultural values directly through questionnaire surveys. Two widely used databases on national cultures generated from these surveys are the World Values Survey (WVS) developed by a global network of social scientists under the leadership of Ronald Inglehart of the University of Michigan, and the multidimensional measures of national culture associated with the late Dutch social psychologist Geert Hofstede.[30]

According to the results of a recent WVS wave (2010–2014), Chinese people in general encourage their children to learn the quality of hard work and thrift more than their counterparts in most countries. The WVS includes the following question: "Here is a list of qualities that children can be encouraged to learn at home. Which, if any, do you consider to be especially important?" The list contains eleven qualities: independence, hard work, feeling of responsibility, imagination, tolerance and respect for other people, thrift (saving money and things), determination and perseverance, religious faith, unselfishness, obedience, and self-expression. The respondents are asked to choose five of these eleven qualities. Column A1 of Table 4.3 shows that 75.3 percent of the respondents from mainland China chose hard work as an important quality that children should learn, which was higher than the average percentage of the sixty countries surveyed (59.8%). However, China was only ranked sixteenth (see column A2) in this value, indicating that one in four

---

[30] See Hofstede, Hofstede, and Minkov (2010).

Table 4.3 *Do Chinese people value hard work and thrift more than others?*

Country or Territory	A1 Number of Respondents Choosing Hard Work as an Important Quality to Encourage in Children (%)	A2 Ranking of the Percentage of Respondents Choosing Hard Work as an Important Quality	B1 Number of Respondents Choosing Thrift as an Important Quality to Encourage in Children (%)	B2 Ranking of the Percentage of Respondents Choosing Thrift as an Important Quality
China (mainland)	75.3	16	50.7	12
South Korea	64.3	26	65.1	3
Singapore	60.8	29	47.4	17
Hong Kong	58.0	32	43.7	20
Taiwan	40.4	46	54.1	8
Japan	35.1	50	47.8	15
Average of the Sixty Countries or Territories Surveyed	59.8		39.1	

Note: Based on data obtained from the official website of the World Values Survey (www.worldvaluessurvey.org).

countries (or territories) surveyed had a higher percentage of people recognizing the importance of hard work compared with China, and almost all of them were developing countries, such as India, Ghana, and Nigeria. In addition, South Korea, Singapore, and Hong Kong were only average in terms of the importance given to hard work among the respondents, while Taiwan and Japan ranked well below the average. The survey data in Table 4.3 are certainly subject to measurement errors. For example, the fact that Japanese people were ranked lower in this quality does not necessarily mean that they are one of the least hard-working people. Nevertheless, this survey at least shows that hard work is not a value unique to East Asian cultures.[31]

It is important to note that hard work alone only affects the level of output, not the growth rate of output. To illustrate this, consider a hard-working farmer who produces 2,000 kg of grain in the first year, while his lazier neighbor produces only 1,000 kg. If nothing else changes in the second year, each farmer will produce the same amount of grain as in the first year. Therefore, although the two farmers have different output levels, their growth rate of output is zero. However, saving can help both farmers achieve positive growth. If the hard-working farmer consumes only half of his production each year, sells the rest (a savings rate of 50 percent), and uses his savings over time to buy more land and farming tools and to hire additional workers, then his production will grow year by year. If the lazy farmer also consumes half of his grain and saves the rest, then he will achieve the same growth rate of output. Taking it a step further, at least in theory, if the lazy farmer has a higher savings rate, his growth rate will actually be faster than that of his hard-working neighbor. However, in reality, it is more likely that the lazy farmer will not be inclined or able to save at the same rate as the hard-working farmer, needing to

---

[31] The late American sinologist Lucian Pye (2000) argued that in China's traditional belief systems, Confucianism is actually contemptuous of hard physical labor, while Taoism emphasizes inaction or non-effort. According to him, Chinese people have traditionally placed more emphasis on the importance of good luck, exploiting opportunities, and *guanxi*.

consume a greater proportion of a much lower level of output to subsist. As a result, the output growth of the lazy farmer is likely to be lower than that of the diligent farmer.

This example demonstrates that hard work will lead to growth only when it is combined with thrift. Savings, not hard work per se, drive growth. In the Chinese language, hard work (qin) and thrift (jian) are often mentioned together as one word (qinjian), suggesting that they are two inseparable virtues.[32] Thrift is considered an important element of Confucian culture. There is a well-known statement in the Confucian classic Zuo Zhuan: "Thrift is a great virtue, while extravagance is a great evil." However, do Chinese people today really value thrift more than people in other developing countries? According to the WVS results, China and other Confucian societies do indeed seem to place more emphasis on thrift than most other societies. Column B1 of Table 4.3 shows that among the respondents from mainland China, the percentage choosing thrift as one of the five most important qualities that children should learn was 50.7 percent, while the average of the sixty countries surveyed was 39.1 percent. All East Asian societies ranked in the top third for this measure. A hardworking and thrifty nation is likely to have a relatively higher national savings rate, and its capital accumulation will be faster, leading to faster economic growth.

Some readers may argue that if a culture that values hard work and thrift is conducive to economic growth, why did China or any other country with a similar culture not achieve sustained (even if slow) economic growth before modern times? Were premodern people not frugal enough? The answers to these questions are actually quite simple. Before the Industrial Revolution, technological progress was extremely slow by modern standards, and the fruit of any small technological advance was eventually offset by population growth, leading to stagnant per capita income and very low savings. More

---

[32] Another common Chinese word chiku (literally "eat bitterness") also contains both meanings of working hard and being frugal.

importantly, in an agrarian society, the accumulation of wealth through savings mainly took the form of land ownership, but the amount of land was naturally limited, which constrained the amount that a society could produce. In contrast, the economic growth of modern industrial societies is not based solely on the quantitative expansion of current products, but also on the expansion of the variety of products, the upgrading of current products, and the continuous improvement of production methods. Therefore, sustained economic growth is only possible in an industrial society, in which a savings culture can play an important role in the accumulation of produced physical capital.

In Geert Hofstede's famous multidimensional measures of national culture, there is one dimension that is related to thrift and probably hard work as well: long-term orientation (LTO) versus short-term orientation. In the data set, the LTO index, ranging from 0 to 100, measures the importance a society places on thrift and perseverance.[33] Table 4.4 presents the LTO index for selected countries or economies. It shows that all East Asian economies, including China, rank high in the table. Other countries with high savings, such as Switzerland and Germany, also rank high, while the United States and many Latin American and African countries rank low on the LTO index.

For most economists, the idea that the high savings rates of East Asian economies are due to their thrifty culture is still controversial. Whereas culturalists tend to believe that East Asia's strong propensity to save has led to its rapid growth, economists tend to believe the opposite, that is, that the rapid growth of East Asia has led to its high savings rate. For example, Christopher Carroll and David Weil pointed out that in the East Asian economies of Japan, Korea, Hong Kong, and Singapore, rapid economic growth preceded high savings, not the other way around, and that higher savings rates did not subsequently lead to faster growth between the 1950s and the 1980s.[34] However,

---

[33] Hofstede and Minkov (2013).   [34] Carroll and Weil (1994).

Table 4.4 *Hofstede's long-term orientation (LTO) index*

Country or Economy	LTO Index	Country or Economy	LTO Index
South Korea	100	Brazil	44
Taiwan	93	Malaysia	41
Japan	88	Poland	38
China (mainland)	87	Israel	38
Germany	83	Canada	36
Russia	81	Saudi Arabia	36
Switzerland	74	Denmark	35
Singapore	72	Tanzania	34
Netherlands	67	South Africa	34
France	63	New Zealand	33
Indonesia	62	Thailand	32
Italy	61	Portugal	28
Hong Kong	61	Philippines	27
Vietnam	57	United States	26
Sweden	53	Mexico	24
Romania	52	Algeria	26
United Kingdom	51	Australia	21
India	51	Argentina	20
Pakistan	50	Venezuela	16
Spain	48	Zimbabwe	15
Turkey	46	Iran	14
Greece	45	Nigeria	13

Data source: https://geerthofstede.com/research-and-vsm/dimension-data-matrix.

this result does not prove that the culture of thrift had no effect on the savings rates and economic growth of these economies. First, the magnitude of the increase in the rate of savings after the increase in economic growth may be affected by culture. In fact, Carroll and Weil's own results showed that the effect of growth on the rate of savings of OECD countries was more than three times that of all countries (including mostly developing countries), and that excluding the four East Asian economies from the sample would reduce the effect by 40 percent. In other words, the same increase in economic growth would lead to larger increases in savings rates in some countries (especially East Asian economies) than in others. Indeed, in a cross-country study, Luigi Zingales of the University of Chicago and his coauthors showed that the percentage of people who choose thrift as an important quality for children to learn in the WVS affects the national savings rate, even after controlling for the rate of economic growth.[35]

Second, it is true that higher savings rates did not subsequently lead to faster growth in the four East Asian economies in the 1970s and the 1980s, and the same goes for China's economy in the 2000s and the 2010s. However, this does not mean that high savings rates did not contribute to their rapid economic growth during these decades. In fact, as an economy reaches a relatively more developed stage, it requires a higher rate of investment and therefore a higher rate of savings to maintain the same economic growth rate. The incremental capital–output ratio (ICOR), which is the ratio of investment rate to GDP growth, is generally higher for more developed economies than for less developed ones (excluding very poorly performing economies).[36]

IS THERE A CONSUMPTION-DRIVEN GROWTH MODEL?

I just argued that high savings and investment have been a key advantage of the Chinese economy. However, a widely held view in recent years has been that China's economic growth is unbalanced, unhealthy, and unsustainable precisely because of its high savings and investment, and consequently, low consumption. China's consumption rate at around 50 percent of GDP is not only much lower than that of the rest of the world but also significantly lower than that of twenty years ago when it exceeded 60 percent of GDP. According to this popular view, because of its low consumption and high savings, China has been forced to rely too much on investment and exports for

---

[35] Guiso, Sapienza, and Zingales (2006).   [36] See Table 4.6.

its growth, contributing to global trade imbalances. Therefore, the argument goes, China must shift from an investment-driven and export-oriented growth model to one driven by domestic consumption, which would not only contribute to the rebalancing of global trade but would also make China's own growth more sustainable.[37]

Despite its popularity, the aforementioned view is actually a myth based on a misapplication of Keynesian theory to economic growth and a misplaced faith in official statistics.[38] Its underlying theory is that economic growth is driven by the troika of consumption, investment, and exports. As I explained earlier, these are the three demand factors that, with the exception of investment, affect a country's current or short-term growth when production is significantly lower than productive capacity, according to Keynesian theory. However, this theory should not be applied to a country's long-term economic growth, which fundamentally depends on the accumulation of physical and human capital, that is, investment and education, and the speed of its technological progress. There is no such thing as "consumption-driven growth" in any respectable economics textbook.

Although on the expenditure or demand side, GDP can be divided into three components of consumption, investment, and net exports, it still refers to the value of all final goods and services that are *produced* in an economy. A country can increase its GDP over an extended period not by increasing its consumption or net exports, but by increasing its productive capacity and improving its production efficiency. Consider this analogy. The human body is made up of three parts: the head, the limbs, and the body. The weight of a person is the sum of the weight of each part. So how does a lean person increase her weight? Is it by increasing the weight of the head, body, or limbs individually? Obviously not. To gain weight, her choice is to

---

[37] See, e.g., Lardy (2006, 2011), Pettis (2010), Wolf (2011), and Yao (2014).

[38] Yukon Huang of Carnegie Endowment for International Peace, a former World Bank country director for China, was one of the few prominent voices to challenge this popular view and other misconceptions about the Chinese economy. See Huang (2017).

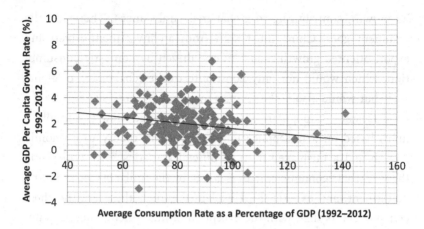

FIGURE 4.2 Consumption and economic growth

Note: In this scatter plot, each point represents a country or economy. There are 172 data points after eliminating the countries or economies with missing or incomplete data. All data are from the World Development Indicators data set.

increase her food intake and improve the efficiency of her digestion and absorption. As the person gains weight, the weight of her head, body, and limbs naturally increases.

If consumption were a growth engine, countries with a high consumption rate would grow faster. This is certainly not the case in Figure 4.2, a scatter chart of the average consumption rate and the growth rate of GDP per capita between 1992 and 2012. If anything, the two may have a negative rather than a positive correlation. Table 4.5 seems to confirm this negative relationship. All of the countries with a relatively low consumption rate (i.e., government and household final consumption expenditure as a percentage of GDP) during the period, such as China, India, South Korea, and Singapore, experienced fast GDP per capita growth, whereas those with a high consumption rate, such as Greece and many sub-Saharan African countries, experienced slow GDP per capita growth.

China's low consumption rate does not necessarily imply, as Paul Krugman suggested, that Chinese people have made a big

Table 4.5 *Consumption rate and consumption growth (%): 1992–2012*

Country or Region	Final Consumption Rate	Gross Domestic Savings Rate	Average Annual Growth of GDP Per Capita	Average Annual Growth of Final Consumption Per Capita
Singapore	50.00	50.00	3.71	2.46
China	54.90	45.10	9.51	7.80
South Korea	66.24	33.76	4.37	3.52
India	73.07	26.93	5.09	4.68
World	76.37	23.63	1.42	1.34
European Union	77.55	22.45	1.48	1.39
Latin America and the Caribbean	79.86	20.14	1.74	1.90
United States	81.50	18.50	1.58	1.63
Sub-Saharan Africa	82.42	17.58	1.14	1.26
Greece	86.17	13.83	0.79	1.05

Data source: World Development Indicators.

sacrifice in consumption for the sake of economic growth.[39] In fact, as Table 4.5 shows, China's per capita consumption increased at an average rate of 7.8% per year between 1992 and 2012. Although it was lower than the GDP per capita growth of 9.51%, it was already the fastest in the world. During the same period, annual global growth in consumption per capita was only 1.34%. Other countries with a relatively low consumption rate, such as Singapore, South Korea, and India, also enjoyed faster consumption growth than countries with a high consumption rate, such as Greece. The reason is quite simple.

[39] Krugman (1994).

A low consumption rate implies a high savings rate, which means that there is more money for investment, resulting in faster capital accumulation and faster GDP growth. Given a constant consumption rate, the amount of consumption will increase at the same rate as GDP. Therefore, consumption growth is a result of economic growth, not its cause.

Even in Keynesian theory, consumption does not occupy a special place among the troika of demand factors. When an economy is in recession, stimulating consumption, investment, or exports will help the recovery. However, because investment and exports typically fluctuate more than consumption during a business cycle, stimulating investment or exports may be more effective than stimulating consumption in a downturn. Moreover, in the Keynesian framework, stimulating consumption aims to increase the absolute quantity of consumption demand, not to increase the relative share of consumption in aggregate demand (i.e., the consumption rate). A Keynesian policy package in an economic downturn will try to stimulate consumption, investment, and net exports all at once, not increase their relative share. After all, the three shares cannot all be pushed up at the same time.

If a country is underdeveloped, it is not because its people are reluctant to consume, but because its capacity to produce is low: It has a low level of fixed capital per worker, a poorly educated labor force, and backward technological capability. Investment in physical and human capital rather than consumption is the real driving force for a developing country to continuously increase its per capita output and move closer to developed countries. Indeed, the continuous increase in GDP per capita is a prerequisite for the continuous improvement of per capita consumption, not the other way around. Technological progress is equally, if not more, important for economic growth. However, for a developing country, striving for technological progress without sufficient investment in physical and human capital is like attempting to build a house without a foundation.

IS CHINA'S INVESTMENT EFFICIENCY TOO LOW?

Those who are familiar with growth economics may readily agree with the aforementioned criticism of a consumption-driven growth model, but some may still point to the fact that China's consumption rate is unusually low, while its investment rate is unusually high.[40] It seems that few economies have had such a low consumption and high investment rate in history for an extended period, not even the current high-income East Asian economies during their own periods of rapid growth. In other words, China's investment efficiency may be too low, presumably due to too much investment.

Some economists have used the ICOR to show the decline in China's investment efficiency over time. As mentioned, the ICOR measures the amount of investment (as a percentage of GDP) required for each percentage increase in the GDP growth rate. Table 4.6 shows that China's ICOR increased over time from 3.6 during the 1983–1992 period to 4.3 during the 2003–2012 period. The reason is that China's investment rate increased significantly between 1982 and 2012, while the GDP growth rate barely increased. Some economists have used this as evidence that China's investment efficiency has declined significantly.[41]

However, Table 4.6 shows that China's ICOR was similar to that of India, another rapidly developing country, and significantly lower than that of the United States and all high-income OECD countries in general. As a country's level of economic development and per capita income increase, its ICOR will generally increase. Moreover, the ICOR of developed OECD countries during these three decades increased more significantly than that of China, especially during the 2003–2012 decade, during which the greatest post–WWII financial crisis hit economic growth in the developed world the hardest. In general, it seems preferable not to use a simple ICOR measure to judge the level of investment efficiency of a country.

---

[40] See, e.g., Perkins (2012).   [41] See, e.g., Huang (2010).

Table 4.6 *Comparative investment efficiency: ICOR (%)*

Country	1983–1992 Average			1993–2002 Average			2003–2012 Average		
	Investment Rate	GDP Growth	ICOR	Investment Rate	GDP Growth	ICOR	Investment Rate	GDP Growth	ICOR
China	36.8	10.3	3.6	39.0	9.9	4.0	44.9	10.5	4.3
India	23.0	5.3	4.4	24.2	5.8	4.2	35.0	7.8	4.5
United States	22.9	3.6	6.3	22.5	3.4	6.6	20.9	1.8	11.8
High-Income	24.2	3.3	7.3	22.9	2.6	8.7	21.6	1.5	14.1
OECD Countries									

Note: The ICOR for each decade was calculated as the ratio of the decadal average investment rate to the decadal average annual GDP growth. Investment and growth rates are from the World Development Indicators.

Even if one insists on using this indicator, China's investment efficiency remains among the best in the world.[42]

Still, there are concerns that China's high investment rate has resulted in waste, overcapacity, and low return on capital. The law of diminishing returns teaches us that as the stock of capital per worker increases, the rate of return on capital will eventually fall. In fact, some economists were already worried about China's extraordinary investment rate in the early 2000s, which they feared would lead to significant declines in the return on capital. However, subsequent studies did not find strong evidence for this.[43] The return on capital at the macro level is notoriously difficult to estimate with precision. Nevertheless, according to estimates from the latest version of the Penn World Table (introduced in Chapter 1), China's return on capital (measured by the real internal rate of return) has declined over the last decade. However, as Figure 4.3 shows, it is not unusually low and is comparable to that of the United States and Taiwan and much higher than that of Japan and Germany.

Moreover, China's capital stock per worker is still low compared with that of developed countries. According to the Penn World Table (version PWT 9.1), it is only about 30% of the German level; 34% of the United States level; and 40% of the South Korean level. Therefore, China still has a long way to go in the accumulation of physical capital.

So far in this chapter, all comparisons have been based on official Chinese statistics. However, as previously mentioned, China's investment rate may be significantly lower than official statistics indicate. Therefore, China's investment efficiency may be higher than just suggested. The reason for the inflated investment statistics is that China's consumption rate has been underestimated by official statistics. According to my own research with Jun Zhang, China's

---

[42] China's ICOR is probably much lower than shown here because, as I will demonstrate shortly, China's investment rate may be significantly overestimated by official statistics.

[43] See Bai, Hsieh, and Qian (2006).

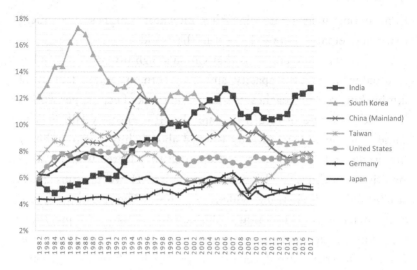

FIGURE 4.3 Return on capital: 1982–2017
Note: Return on capital data are based on the "real internal rate of return" from the Penn World Table data set (version 9.1 www.rug.nl/ggdc/productivity/pwt).

consumption rate may be one of the lowest in the world, but it is not as low as the official figures indicate.[44] We showed that the actual consumption rate between 2004 and 2011 may be 10 percentage points higher than the official figures. As a result, the domestic savings rate and investment rate may be overestimated by 10 percentage points. For more details on our estimations, interested readers can find them in the Appendix.

In summary, this chapter cast strong doubt on the popular view that China needs to shift from an investment-led growth model to a consumption-driven model. Long-term economic growth is driven by investment, education, and technological progress, not by consumption. Even in the short term, investment is just as important if not more important than consumption in determining the magnitude of fluctuations in aggregate demand. Empirically, China's true investment rate, 30–40 percent of GDP, is one of the highest in the world,

[44] Zhang and Zhu (2015).

but is comparable to the level recorded by other East Asian economies during their years of rapid growth. There must be investment inefficiencies at the firm level or sectoral level in China, but given its high rate of GDP growth, there is no strong evidence that China is suffering from macro-level investment inefficiencies. Its comparatively high savings and investment rates are not a weakness but a strength of the Chinese economy. There is no compelling reason for China to deliberately reduce the role of investment in its future economic growth. How many governments of developed and developing countries hope that their people would be willing to increase their savings and investment rate – that is, to reduce their consumption! Those who naively call for the Chinese economy to switch to a consumption-driven growth model have probably misunderstood economic theories or have been misled by distorted official statistics.

5   The Role of Education

Quantity and Quality

Education is another engine of growth, as a more educated labor force is more productive. There are two channels through which education can promote economic growth. First, the increase in a country's education level in a given year can have a direct effect on its economic growth in that year.[1] However, this effect will be small because the annual change in a country's education level is generally very small. Second, the level of education in a country can affect its economic growth in subsequent years through its effect on technological progress and investment incentives.[2] This, as I will show, is a more important effect.

It is widely acknowledged that Confucian culture places education at the top of its value system, but what does this really mean? If education is important for economic development, wouldn't all countries value education? Are Chinese people really more and better educated than people in other developing nations?

THE QUANTITY OF EDUCATION

First, let us examine whether China has made more progress in educating its people in the past few decades. Table 5.1 presents the average years of schooling attained by the adult population over fifteen years old in a selection of countries in 1980 and 2010, and the corresponding annual growth rates in years of schooling. It shows that almost all countries have improved the average years of schooling of their population during these three decades. In general, developing countries had a low initial level of education in 1980 and made more

---

[1] See, e.g., Mankiw, Romer, and Weil (1992).
[2] See, e.g., Nelson and Phelps (1966), Benhabib and Spiegel (1994), and Barro (2001).

Table 5.1 *Average years of schooling of the adult population over fifteen years old*

Country	Average Years of Schooling (1980)	Average Years of Schooling (2010)	Total Increase in Years of Schooling (1980–2010)	Annual Growth in the Average Years of Schooling (%) (1980–2010)	Rank in Annual Growth (out of 146 Economies)
Yemen	0.23	3.73	3.50	9.73%	1
Nepal	0.99	4.02	3.03	4.78%	2
Botswana	3.12	9.56	6.44	3.80%	7
Brazil	2.77	7.55	4.78	3.40%	10
Haiti	1.99	5.13	3.14	3.21%	16
Pakistan	2.15	5.53	3.38	3.20%	17
Tunisia	3.25	7.30	4.05	2.73%	27
India	2.34	5.20	2.86	2.70%	29
Jordan	4.58	9.17	4.59	2.34%	40
Zimbabwe	3.85	7.70	3.85	2.34%	41
Mexico	4.89	9.06	4.17	2.08%	45
Bolivia	5.47	9.87	4.40	1.99%	48
Kenya	3.79	6.65	2.86	1.89%	52
Singapore	5.24	9.13	3.89	1.87%	53
Swaziland	4.44	7.69	3.25	1.85%	55
China	**4.75**	**8.11**	**3.36**	**1.80%**	**56**
South Africa	5.11	8.48	3.37	1.70%	62
Paraguay	5.20	8.51	3.31	1.66%	64

Table 5.1 (cont.)

Country	Average Years of Schooling (1980)	Average Years of Schooling (2010)	Total Increase in Years of Schooling (1980–2010)	Annual Growth in the Average Years of Schooling (%) (1980–2010)	Rank in Annual Growth (out of 146 Economies)
Jamaica	6.05	9.75	3.70	1.60%	67
Ghana	4.94	7.26	2.32	1.29%	81
Chile	6.97	10.17	3.20	1.27%	84
South Korea	8.29	11.94	3.65	1.22%	89
Peru	6.22	8.93	2.71	1.21%	91
Ukraine	7.92	11.10	3.18	1.13%	95
Philippines	6.63	8.95	2.32	1.01%	101
Argentina	7.30	9.42	2.12	0.85%	112
Japan	9.25	11.59	2.34	0.75%	119
Sweden	9.42	11.48	2.06	0.66%	125
Finland	8.27	9.96	1.69	0.62%	129
Vietnam	5.29	6.34	1.05	0.61%	132
United States	12.03	13.09	1.06	0.28%	142
New Zealand	11.83	12.68	0.85	0.23%	144
Switzerland	10.29	9.92	−0.37	−0.12%	146

Note: Data on the average years of schooling come from Barro and Lee (2013). Available at www.barrolee.com.

progress in education over the next three decades. In contrast, developed countries generally had a higher initial level of education, with less room for improvement. In terms of annual growth in years of schooling, China did not stand out among all developing countries, ranking fifty-sixth out of 146 economies. Other fast-growing economies such as India, South Korea, Singapore, and Vietnam also did not stand out.

In the early 1990s, the Nobel laureate Robert Lucas pointed out in a seminal paper that the annual accumulation of human capital through schooling alone cannot explain the East Asian miracle.[3] In a provocative article published twenty years ago, the then–World Bank economist Lant Pritchett found that between the 1960s and the 1980s, a significant improvement in educational attainment did not accelerate growth in developing countries in general.[4] These economists did not mean to suggest that education is useless, but that the direct effect of an annual increase in years of schooling on contemporaneous economic growth is quite limited, and that the great cross-country disparities in the rate of economic growth cannot be explained by the very limited differences in the growth rates of years of schooling.

Although the relationship between the increase in years of schooling and contemporaneous economic growth is weak, some economists have argued that a country's current education level will have a significant effect on its economic growth in the years to come. More specifically, they have found that the ability of an economically backward country to achieve catch-up growth over an extended period depends to a large extent on its initial level of human capital (i.e., education level).[5] Indeed, a country with a less developed economy and cheap labor but a relatively higher level of human capital is better able to digest and imitate the technologies of more developed countries, thereby achieving faster technological progress. Moreover, a relatively higher level of human capital increases the return on

---

[3] Lucas (1993).   [4] Pritchett (2001).
[5] See, e.g., Barro (1991) and Barro and Sala-i-Martin (2003).

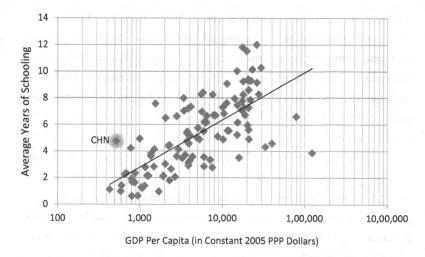

FIGURE 5.1 Average years of schooling and GDP per capita in 1980
Note: Each dot in the figure represents a country. The horizontal axis represents the level of GDP per capita in 1980 (in constant 2005 PPP dollars) on the logarithmic scale. The vertical axis represents the 1980 human capital level measured by the average years of schooling of the adult population over fifteen years old in a country from the same Barro-Lee data set as in Table 5.2. GDP data are from the World Development Indicators.

investment in physical capital, which will attract more domestic and foreign investment, thereby accelerating the accumulation of physical capital.[6]

The case of China seems to confirm this hypothesis. As shown in Figure 5.1, China was one of the poorest countries in the world in 1980. However, the average years of schooling of the adult population aged fifteen and over was already similar or close to that of middle-income countries at the time. If education is indeed an important driver of economic development, why did the Chinese economy not develop well before 1980? The answer seems clear: Central planning and bad policies during most of the thirty years before 1980 hampered China's development. Once the reform and opening-up policy was

[6] See, e.g., Barro (2001).

adopted in the late 1970s, China's relatively high level of education became a great advantage for subsequent catch-up growth. In fact, the Nobel laureate Amartya Sen even argued that the whole East Asian miracle was, to a large extent, based on the expansion of basic education before the economic takeoff.[7]

So, why did China have a relatively high level of education or human capital in 1980? One explanation is that in the thirty years after the founding of the People's Republic, China accumulated considerable human capital through the promotion of universal primary education and the expansion of secondary education. In 1952, only half of all school-aged children in China attended primary school. In 1978, that number was 98 percent.[8]

However, China's apparent advantage in the education level of its labor force in 1980, with an average of 4.75 years of schooling, is far from sufficient to explain its growth puzzle. According to Robert Barro, a pioneer in the cross-country study of economic growth, the growth rate of a country increases by 0.44 percentage points for each additional year of schooling that its adult men receive beyond primary education.[9] This is not a small effect. However, according to the Barro-Lee data set, Chinese people on average only received 0.93 year of secondary education or above in 1980. Indeed, by 2005, as shown in Figure 5.2, China's advantage in terms of average years of schooling had all but disappeared, and there were quite a few countries with lower per capita income but more years of schooling than China. Nevertheless, China's subsequent economic growth has remained strong compared with the rest of the world.

Some economists have suggested that China's initial advantage in human capital cannot be captured by using only the number of years of formal schooling. They have argued that before 1978, China had already laid a basic foundation for its industry sectors. Although not very efficient, Chinese industries already covered most sectors, and the number of industry and mining workers in China exceeded

[7] Sen (1999), pp. 40–41.   [8] See Yao (2014).   [9] Barro (2001).

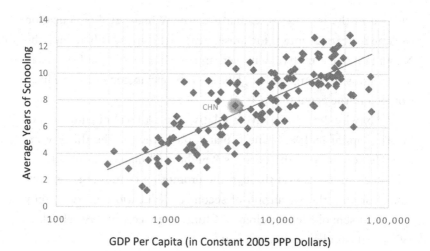

FIGURE 5.2 Average years of schooling and GDP per capita in 2005
Data sources: Barro-Lee data set and World Development Indicators

the total number of workers in all other Third World countries. During the pre-reform years, China was more concerned about its heavy industries, which did not help improve people's livelihoods. However, these sectors trained many professionals and technicians, who played an active role in China's industrialization process after the reform.[10] Some scholars have even gone further in history, arguing that before the rise of modern industries, China had already developed a relatively sophisticated economic system for an agricultural society. New technologies were invented in agriculture, industry, and transportation, and domestic trade was relatively well developed. These historical conditions were passed on to become China's human capital in the twentieth century.[11]

So, can China's historical advantage in human capital explain much of its growth miracle over the past four decades? Probably not. If China's long history and industrialization efforts in the three decades after 1949 were only reflected in its relatively high level of human

---

[10] See Brandt, Rawski, and Sutton (2008).   [11] See, e.g., Perkins (2010).

capital at the start of the reform and opening-up policy, and if human capital is reflected in skills that can be learned through formal education or informal training, it should not take too long for a country with no historical advantage to acquire these skills and knowledge. Perhaps China's rich history is embedded not only in human capital in terms of skills but, more importantly, in people's worldviews, values, and behavioral norms, that is, culture.[12]

THE QUALITY OF EDUCATION

The quantity of education measured by the average years of schooling does not seem to have a strong effect on economic growth, and it can neither explain the failure to catch up of most developing countries nor the growth miracle of East Asia, including China. For this reason, some economists have started to look into the quality of education and its effect on economic growth. Education economist Eric Hanushek of Stanford University is a pioneer in this endeavor.[13] Professor Hanushek and his coauthors noted that a quantitative increase in education may not be useful if the quality of education is low. Simply sitting in class does not mean that students actually acquire useful cognitive skills. They found that a country's economic growth has more to do with the quality than the quantity of education. This finding makes theoretical sense, as high-quality education makes it easier for workers to accumulate on-the-job knowledge and skills that cannot be captured by quantitative measures of education, such as years of schooling.

So, how did they measure the quality of education? Hanushek and his coauthors used the test scores of twelve international student achievement tests in math and science between 1964 and 2003 taken

---

[12] Gregory Chow of Princeton University, one of the few prominent economists to give culture an important role in China's economic growth, argued that in addition to formal education, human capital should include what one has learned growing up and living in a given society, and that the work habit of workers and the resourcefulness of entrepreneurs in China are part of the country's human capital, influenced by its history and cultural tradition. See Chow (2012), chapter 2.

[13] See Hanushek and Kimko (2000).

by primary and secondary school students to construct a "cognitive skills" index for more than seventy countries or territories. These internationally comparable test scores measure the knowledge and skills acquired by students of the same age in each country and can therefore be used to measure the quality of education in each country.[14]

The best known of these tests is PISA (Program for International Student Assessment) organized by the OECD, which also has the largest number of participating countries or economies. The purpose of PISA is to assess the quality, equity, and efficiency of the education systems of the participating countries and to use the results as a reference to improve education, especially for underperforming countries. The test has been conducted every three years since 2000. It measures the level of reading, mathematics, and science literacy of fifteen-year-old students and emphasizes the functional skills acquired by students. Shanghai and a few coastal provinces in China participated in the 2012, 2015, and 2018 rounds, but PISA 2018 had not been published at the time of writing this chapter.

Table 5.2 presents the "cognitive skills" index for a selection of countries or economies compiled by Eric Hanushek and Ludger Woessmann and the results of PISA 2015. It shows that the two measures were not identical but strongly correlated. For both measures of the quality of education, the East Asian economies influenced by Confucian culture were not only among the best but also far ahead of all other developing economies. Mainland China ranked high in both measures and exceeded the average scores of OECD countries, which are mainly developed economies. Based on the PISA 2015 results, China and Vietnam were the only developing economies to outperform OECD countries.

So, what is the magnitude of the effect of the quality of education measured by the "cognitive skills" index on economic growth? According to Hanushek and Woessmann's estimates using GDP data

---

[14] See Hanushek and Woessmann (2012).

Table 5.2 Measures of education quality around the world

Country/Economy	Cognitive Skills Index	PISA 2015 Math Average Score	PISA 2015 Science Average Score
Taiwan	5.452	542	532
South Korea	5.338	524	516
Singapore	5.33	564	556
Japan	5.31	532	538
Macau	5.26	544	529
Hong Kong	5.195	548	523
Estonia	5.192	520	534
Switzerland	5.142	521	506
Finland	5.126	511	531
Australia	5.094	494	510
France	5.04	493	495
Germany	4.956	506	509
United Kingdom	4.95	492	509
China, mainland	4.939	531	518
Vietnam	N/A	495	525
Russia	4.922	494	487
OECD Average	N/A	490	493
United States	4.903	470	496
Italy	4.758	490	481
Israel	4.686	470	467

Country/Economy	Cognitive Skills Index	PISA 2015 Math Average Score	PISA 2015 Science Average Score
Thailand	4.565	415	421
Romania	4.562	444	435
Swaziland	4.398	N/A	N/A
Uruguay	4.3	418	435
India	4.281	N/A	N/A
Jordan	4.264	380	409
Columbia	4.152	390	416
Turkey	4.128	420	425
Zimbabwe	4.107	N/A	N/A
Chile	4.049	423	447
Lebanon	3.95	396	386
Mexico	3.998	408	416
Argentina	3.92	456	475
Indonesia	3.88	386	403
Tunisia	3.795	367	386
Philippines	3.647	N/A	N/A
Brazil	3.638	377	401
Peru	3.125	387	397
South Africa	3.089	N/A	N/A
Dominican Republic	N/A	328	332

Note: "Cognitive skills" index data are from Hamushek and Woessmann (2012). The results of PISA 2015 are from www.oecd.org/pisa.

between 1960 and 2000, after controlling for the initial level of education and GDP per capita, for every one point difference in the "cognitive skills" index, the annual growth rate of GDP per capita will differ by about 2 percentage points.[15] This is a significant effect. For example, China's "cognitive skills" index is about two points higher than that of Peru and South Africa. As a result, *ceteris paribus*, China can grow by almost 4 percentage points faster than these two countries each year based on this factor alone. If this result holds, given the high quality of education (primary and secondary) in China and the rest of East Asia, the economic miracle of the region is no longer difficult to understand.

Some readers, especially those familiar with the Chinese education system, may laugh at the idea that China has a higher quality system than many developed countries, such as the United States. However, note that we are not talking about the quality of education at all levels, but the quality of primary and secondary education. Based on Hanushek and Woessmann's index or the PISA results, Chinese secondary school students have on average more cognitive skills than those from the United States. However, as the average number of years of schooling in the United States (13.09 in 2010) is much higher than that of China (8.11 years), the overall level of education in the United States is obviously higher. Moreover, the quality of higher education, especially at the doctoral level, in the United States may be much higher than that of China.

Still, one may question the use of exam results to measure the quality of education. Chinese students may simply be better at taking tests without actually having acquired superior knowledge and skills, let alone being more creative. Carly S. Fiorina, former CEO of Hewlett Packard, said during her unsuccessful presidential campaign in 2015: "I have been doing business in China for decades, and I will tell you

---

[15] Even when controlling for more factors that can affect economic growth, the effect of a one-point increase in cognitive skills is still greater than that of a 1.2 percentage–point increase in the annual growth of GDP per capita, also a significant effect.

that yeah, the Chinese can take a test, but what they can't do is innovate. They are not terribly imaginative. They're not entrepreneurial, they don't innovate, that is why they are stealing our intellectual property."[16] Ms. Fiorina seems to suggest that test scores are not correlated with creativity and innovation. It is certainly true that good test scores do not guarantee a great ability to create or innovate and that low test scores do not necessarily imply low creativity. However, test scores and abilities are strongly positively correlated. There are far fewer students with high scores and low abilities than students with low scores and low abilities. After all, Table 5.2 shows that students from more innovative developed countries in Europe and the United States performed better on international tests on average than those from all developing countries, except China and Vietnam.

Ms. Fiorina also underestimated the difficulty of stealing someone else's IP. If a country could produce a growth miracle by just stealing technology from other countries, there would have been many more growth miracles than those observed. Naturally, IP protections are weaker in developing countries than in developed countries, but there is evidence that as a developing country, China's record on IP rights is actually better than what one would expect from its income level. As Shang-jin Wei of Columbia University and his coauthor pointed out, China's total IP payments to foreigners increased from US$1.3 billion in 2000 to US$28.7 billion in 2017, implying an average annual growth rate of 20 percent compared with a 9.5 percent median annual growth rate of IP payments across all countries during the same period.[17] In any case, learning and imitating existing technologies from advanced countries is necessary for a developing country to achieve catch-up growth. This raises an interesting question: How is it that China has imitated Western technologies, in one way or another, more successfully than other developing countries in the past four decades? The answer may very well lie in

---

[16] Quoted in Huddleston (2015).   [17] See Wei and Yu (2019).

the relatively high quality of basic education in China. It is precisely because a developing country can adopt current technologies without reinventing the wheel that it can potentially achieve faster technological progress, a topic I discuss in the next chapter.

Critics of the Chinese education system have used China's current scientific and technological achievements to judge the quality of its education, but this is a simplistic and static comparative perspective. As a middle-income country, China is naturally behind the most developed Western countries in science and technology. The problem is not necessarily that exam-oriented education strangles the innovative abilities of Chinese students, but that China is still behind many developed countries in terms of average years of schooling; the ratio of research staff to the overall population; and per capita R&D (research and development) expenditure. The problem is not that China's primary and secondary education or even undergraduate college education is poor, but that its postgraduate education, especially at the doctoral level (no longer at the exam-oriented education stage), is on average of lower quality than that of most developed countries.

Once Chinese students enter Western universities for postgraduate education, they are no less creative and innovative than students from any other country. According to a study by the World Intellectual Property Organization (WIPO), China contributes the largest number of immigrant inventors to other (mostly developed) countries.[18] The term "immigrant inventor" refers to a researcher who applies for a patent in a country where he or she is a resident but not a citizen. For example, a Chinese citizen working in the United States who applies for a patent as a US resident is considered an immigrant inventor. The data from the study showed that between 2006 and 2010, developed countries attracted 97 percent of the world's immigrant inventors. About half of these immigrant inventors came from developing countries, and the other half were from other

---

[18] World Intellectual Property Organization (2013), pp. 21–38.

Table 5.3 *Origin of immigrant inventors*

Country or Region of Origin	Percentage Share of Total Immigrant Inventors (2006–2010)	Immigrant Inventors per Million People
Africa	1.7	3
Asia	41.9	21
– China	16.3	25
– India	12.1	20
Europe	41.9	117
– United Kingdom	7.4	242
Latin America and the Caribbean	2.7	9
North America	9.7	58
– Canada	6.4	387
Oceania	2.1	118

Data source: World Intellectual Property Organization, *2013 World Intellectual Property Indicators*, WIPO Publication No. 941E, 2013. "Immigrant Inventors per Million People" were calculated by the author based on WIPO data and 2010 population figures.

developed countries (e.g., Canada and the United Kingdom). As Table 5.3 shows, immigrant inventors from China accounted for the highest proportion of immigrant inventors in the world with 16.3%, followed by India with 12.1%. Only 2.7% came from Latin America and the Caribbean (a total population of around 600 million), and only 1.7% came from Africa (a total population of over 1 billion). Thus, even on a per capita basis, China contributed far more immigrant inventors than Africa and Latin America.

The fact that China is at the top of this WIPO list suggests that the country faces a serious brain drain. However, it also means that its education system is capable of nurturing talented individuals valued by developed countries. After all, almost all of these immigrant inventors must have received primary, secondary, and more likely than not, undergraduate education in China, and its exam-oriented education apparently did not adversely affect their creativity. China's education system may leave a lot to be desired, but the quality of its basic education is not at all low, quite the opposite.

ARE CHINESE STUDENTS JUST SMARTER?

The fact that Chinese students and other East Asian students have higher test scores may not necessarily be due to high-quality education or a cultural emphasis on education. When I show the results presented in Table 5.2 in class, many students argue that it is because Chinese people are simply smarter. I have not seen such an overtly racial argument from reputable economists in scholarly work, but what interests me here is not whether this explanation is politically correct, but whether there is credible evidence that Chinese people are indeed smarter than others. Is the average IQ of Chinese people higher, for example? Even if this is true, are there any causal links between a nation's average IQ and its economic development? A British researcher, Richard Lynn, answered yes to both questions.[19] His work is definitely controversial. However, as this opinion seems popular, at least among Chinese people, I think it is important to address the issue head-on.

In their studies, Richard Lynn and his coauthors assembled a sample of IQ scores for over 100 nations or economies, with the UK average IQ score set at 100 as a benchmark, and used the difference in "national IQs" to explain the great disparities in per capita income and economic growth rates between countries. According to one version of their data (see Table 5.4), the average IQ of Chinese people is 105, while that of Japan and the four Asian Tigers is also higher than that of both developed and developing countries around the world.

At a glance, it seems that the IQ scores in Table 5.4 can indeed explain the growth miracles of China and East Asia. However, it cannot explain the economic development of many other countries. Ireland, for example, has been one of the fastest growing countries in

---

[19] See Lynn and Vanhanen (2002) and Lynn and Meisenberg (2010).

Table 5.4 *"National IQs" according to Lynn and Meisenberg*

Country/Economy	IQ	Country/Economy	IQ
Hong Kong	108	Turkey	90
Singapore	108	Mexico	88
South Korea	106	Brazil	87
China	105	Indonesia	87
Japan	105	Philippines	86
Taiwan	105	Iran	84
Switzerland	101	Egypt	83
United Kingdom	100	Papua New Guinea	83
Germany	99	Qatar	83
France	98	Yemen	83
Spain	98	India	82
United States	98	Lebanon	82
Russia	97	Saudi Arabia	80
Uruguay	96	Syria	79
Israel	95	Uganda	73
Argentina	93	Kenya	72
Greece	92	South Africa	72
Ireland	92	Botswana	71
Malaysia	92	Nigeria	69
Thailand	91	Mozambique	64
Chile	90	Malawi	60

Source: Lynn and Meisenberg (2010).

Europe for the past two decades. Its GDP per capita is already higher than that of the United Kingdom, but its IQ of 92 is near the bottom of the list among European countries, along with Greece. If IQ is primarily determined by genetics, it is also equally difficult to explain why the IQ of Greece, the cradle of Western civilization, is the lowest in Europe. In Latin America, Chile has been the fastest growing economy in the region for the past thirty years, but its IQ is only 90 in this table, lower than that of Uruguay at 96, which has experienced much slower economic growth. In Asia, India has been one of the fastest growing countries in the past two decades, but its IQ is only 82, lower than that of many economically backward, slow-growing Asian and Latin American countries. In Africa, Botswana is one of the most developed and politically stable democracies in the region. It is also one of the few countries in the world that once sustained rapid growth for more than thirty years, and it is often studied by development economists as a model for Third World countries. Yet, Botswana's IQ at 71 is even lower than that of slow-growing Uganda and Kenya. Certainly there are exceptions to every rule, but with too many exceptions that are too outrageous, including the cases like India, which represents more than one sixth of the world's population, we have no recourse but to doubt that the rule really exists.

Explaining the level and speed of economic development using the national IQ theory poses many problems. The extent to which IQ tests can reflect natural cognitive abilities is already highly controversial at the individual level, so measuring the average IQ at the national level is even more controversial.[20] In fact, critics have pointed out the many gaps in the work of Richard Lynn and his coauthors. Their IQ scores for many countries were based on IQ tests whose sample size was either too small or not representative of the general population. Some were erroneous extrapolations from neighboring countries, and people of the same racial or ethnic group from different countries had different IQs.[21] Moreover, the scores of many countries changed drastically without explanation in the two iterations of their national IQ scores, one in the 2002 book and the other in the 2010 article, both cited. For example, China's IQ was 98 in the 2002 book, but 105 in the 2010 article, a very significant increase.

Even without data quality issues, the statistically positive correlation between a country's IQ and its level and speed of economic development does not mean that the former is the cause of the latter. It is entirely possible that the level of economic development is the cause, and the average national IQ the effect. In fact, the famous Flynn

---

[20] See, e.g., Nisbett (2009) and Lee (2010).
[21] See Richardson (2004) and Unz (2012).

effect indicates that the average IQ of many countries (or ethnic groups) is not a constant, but increases over time as income and education levels increase.[22] Richard Lynn himself recognized this possibility, but did not take it seriously, concluding from the particular circumstances of several East Asian economies that the level of economic development does not affect national IQ scores. He pointed out that both China and the Asian Tiger economies had high IQ levels while their income was low.

However, the seemingly unchanged high IQ scores in East Asian economies may be an exception, not the rule.[23] This does not necessarily indicate that economic development has no effect on IQ scores, nor can it prove that people's IQ determines the speed of economic development. Instead, a common third factor, namely Confucian culture, may have affected both average IQ scores and the speed of economic development in East Asia. It may be Confucian culture that has led East Asians to pay more attention to education (resulting in high IQ scores) regardless of economic situations.

THE CULTURE OF EDUCATION

Why do China and the other East Asian economies influenced by Chinese culture have high-quality basic education? Is it because their governments have invested more in education than those of other countries or because East Asians culturally care more about education?

The importance of education for economic development is evident. So, which government would choose not to invest in their schools? Indeed, as Table 5.5 indicates, many developing countries, such as Botswana, South Africa, and Mexico, spend more public money as a percentage of total government expenditure or as a percentage of GDP or both, on education than China. From this perspective, China does not seem to value education more than other countries.

---

[22] See Flynn (1987).   [23] See Unz (2012).

Table 5.5 *Government expenditure on education*

Country/ Economy	Government Expenditure on Education (% of Government Expenditure)	Government Expenditure on Education (% of GDP)	Country/ Economy	Government Expenditure on Education (% of Government Expenditure)	Government Expenditure on Education (% of GDP)
Zimbabwe	30.02	6.14	Switzerland	15.53	5.11
Iran	21.15	3.96	Israel	15.45	5.85
Indonesia	20.5	3.58	China	14.31	4.04
Botswana	20.48	9.63	India	14.05	3.84
Singapore	19.96	2.9	United Kingdom	13.83	5.49
Thailand	19.13	4.12	United States	13.59	4.96
South Africa	18.87	6.16	Philippines	13.21	2.65
Hong Kong	18.79	3.32	Jordan	12.07	3.6
Peru	18.24	3.92	Egypt	10.94	3.76
Paraguay	18.15	3.44	France	9.6	5.43
Mexico	17.94	4.91	Japan	9.09	3.59
Brazil	16.15	6.24	Italy	7.81	3.83

Note: All figures are for the most recent years with relevant data in the World Development Indicators data set at the time of writing this book.

Table 5.6 *Pressure on children to do well in school: Global comparison*

Country	Too Much Pressure	Not Enough Pressure	Right Amount of Pressure	Don't Know/Refused
China	68	11	14	7
India	44	24	21	10
Kenya	42	33	24	1
Pakistan	32	21	35	12
Turkey	30	35	27	8
Germany	28	33	37	2
Mexico	20	42	36	2
Brazil	18	49	31	2
Indonesia	13	39	46	2
United States	11	64	21	4
Spain	8	52	37	3

Note: The data are from Pew Research Center, "Pew Global Attitudes Project Spring 2011" (www.pewresearch.org/global/dataset/spring-2011-survey). The respondents were asked to answer Question 86 of the Pew survey: "In general, do you think (survey country's) parents put too much pressure on their children to do well in school, not enough pressure, or about the right amount of pressure?"

However, government expenditure on education only reflects the importance a government places on education, not necessarily the value that families place on the education of their children. The latter is likely to be more important for increasing the quality of education in China. Indeed, Chinese parents seem to value the education of their children more than parents in other countries, putting more pressure on their children to do well in school.

According to the results of a multicountry survey (twenty-one countries) conducted by the Pew Research Center in 2011 (Table 5.6), 68% of the Chinese respondents believed that Chinese parents put too much pressure on their children to do well in school, the highest of all countries surveyed. Conversely, only 11% believed that Chinese parents did not put enough pressure on their children. In the United States, only 11% of the respondents believed that American parents put too much pressure on their children, while 64% thought the opposite. This is not necessarily because China is still a developing country where a large and dense population makes life more competitive. If this were the case, parents in other densely populated developing countries would put as much pressure on their children as their Chinese counterparts. However, Table 5.6 shows that the percentages of respondents from other densely populated countries, such as Pakistan, Mexico, and Indonesia, who believed that parents put too much pressure on their children to do well in school were only 32%, 20%, and 13%, respectively. Although Japan became a developed country a long time ago, 59% of the Japanese respondents believed that Japanese parents put too much pressure on their children to study hard, according to a similar survey conducted by the Pew Research Center in 2006.

The fact that Chinese and other East Asian students have distinguished themselves in international examinations may very well be related to their parents' high expectations and pressure. Asian students living in Western countries, in particular students of Chinese, Indian, and Korean descent, also tend to perform well in school. Are Asian students smarter, or do they just study harder? In a study published in 2014, sociologist Yu Xie of Princeton University and his coauthor, Amy Hsin, found that the main reason for the better academic performance of Asian-American students than white students is not higher intelligence but more diligence.[24] According to their analysis, the difference in cognitive abilities of Asian and white American students (measured by standard test scores) was greatest in kindergarten and elementary school, but disappeared when they started high school (ninth grade). In terms of academic performance, Asian students had no advantage in kindergarten, but their advantage was greatest by the time students were in the second year of high

[24] Hsin and Xie (2014).

school (tenth grade). This was also the time when the gap in diligence between the two groups was at its highest. Why do Asian students study harder? The authors suggested that Asian parents are more likely than white parents to believe in the importance of hard work rather than natural talent, and they therefore have higher standards for their children's grades and attitudes toward learning.

A culture that emphasizes hard work is ultimately reflected in the pressure that parents put on their children to study hard and do well in school. Professors Hsin and Xie also found that while parents' high expectations and pressure made Asian-American students study harder and get better grades, they were also less happy and less mentally healthy than white students and had much less close relationships with their parents.

Apparently, the culture of attaching great importance to education is a double-edged sword. It may have helped China's rapid economic growth over the past four decades, but it also has a dark side. Alas, there is no free lunch. Excessive attention to the academic subjects of math, science, and languages has reduced attention to the arts, sports, music, and various extracurricular activities beneficial to the physical and mental health of students. Chinese students have also sacrificed their leisure and entertainment activities and youthful enjoyment to focus exclusively on school work. The same can be said of overseas Chinese students and school children in South Korea and Japan who are influenced by Confucian culture.

Why do Chinese families and other East Asian families care so much about their children's education? It seems universally accepted that investment in education is the best type of investment, benefiting both individuals and their country economically. However, if education is so beneficial, wouldn't all governments and their citizens be equally committed to education for their own benefits? China and its East Asian neighbors would not have been so unique in this regard.

Economists generally believe that education has "positive externalities," that is, individuals do not receive the full benefits of their education, as a considerable part of the benefits spill over to others in society. For example, a student may become an accomplished scientist through long years of education and hard work, but the benefits she derives personally as a scientist are often insignificant compared with the benefits of her scientific work to society. Because education has such positive externalities, people would acquire less education than is socially optimal in the absence of public subsidies or other benefits. Governments around the world subsidize or provide free education, in large part because they want to reduce the cost of education for families so as to encourage them to send their children to school. However, as the private benefits of education will only materialize in the future, even free education may not be enough to motivate parents to send their children to school beyond a certain point, let alone motivate the students themselves to study hard now. Students' attitudes toward learning largely determine the amount of knowledge and cognitive skills they acquire, but this is not something governments can impose on them or buy with money. Most governments make a certain number of years of education compulsory for school-aged children. Yet although you can force students to go to school, you cannot force them to learn.

Therefore, to increase the quantity and quality of education beyond a certain suboptimal level, motivation beyond economic incentives may be necessary. A culture that values education not only for its economic benefits but also for other purposes will provide this additional motivation.

Historically, cultures known to prioritize education have not done so because education brings economic benefits to individuals or societies. In the case of Confucian culture, its emphasis on education was not utilitarian to begin with, but was to cultivate the virtues of educated individuals. The most influential book in East Asian civilization is the *Analects*, a collection of teachings from Confucius. The first sentence of the *Analects* concerns learning and education: "To learn something and regularly practice it: is it not a joy?"[25] For Confucius, learning is good not because it is profitable but because it is

---

[25] See Huang (1997).

a joy. The purpose of learning or education is to become a virtuous person, not to gain wealth or power. The *Three Character Classic* (*San Zi Jing*), a popular Chinese textbook used from the Song Dynasty to teach children literacy and Confucian values, clearly defined the purpose of education from the beginning: "Men at their birth are naturally good. Their natures are much the same; their habits become widely different. If foolishly there is no teaching, the nature will deteriorate."[26] The purpose of Confucian education was the promotion of virtuous action and the cultivation of a moral character.[27] The great Chinese historian and philosopher Qian Mu (or Ch'ien Mu) said it well: "In the Chinese cultural system, education shouldered the responsibilities that in other nations were shouldered by religion."[28]

Like Confucian culture, Jewish culture is known for its extraordinary devotion to education.[29] The Jews were the most literate people before modern times and account for a disproportionate percentage of Nobel Prize winners. Although education may have benefited Jewish people economically, the initial impetus was not economic. Let me quote a passage from an article on Jewish economic history by economists Maristella Botticini and Zvi Eckstein.[30]

> After the destruction of the Second Temple in 70 CE when the power in the Jewish community shifted from the Sadducees to the Pharisees. The new religious leadership transformed Judaism from a religion based on sacrifices in the Temple in Jerusalem to a religion whose main rule required each male Jewish individual to read and to teach his sons the Torah in the synagogue. This reform was implemented in Eretz Israel, Babylon, and other locations where most Jews were farmers who would not gain anything from investing in education. In other words, this educational reform was not prompted by economic motives but was the outcome of an

---

[26] See Giles (2014).   [27] See Yao (2000).
[28] Translated by the author from Qian (2001), p. 218.   [29] See, e.g., Harrison (2012).
[30] Botticini and Eckstein (2005), pp. 923–924.

exogenous change in the religious leadership after the destruction of the Temple.

Almost 2,000 years ago, Judaism already prescribed that all fathers must send their sons to school at the age of six or seven so that they could learn to read the Hebrew Bible. The idea that the father has the duty to educate his sons is also contained in the *Three Character Classic*: "To feed without teaching is the father's fault. To teach without severity is the teacher's laziness."[31] In an agrarian society, sending children to school brought few economic benefits. Instead, it was a financial burden on the family, and according to Professors Botticini and Eckstein, many Jews throughout history had converted to other religions for this very reason.[32]

Protestant Christians historically also attached great importance to education. When he launched the Reformation 500 years ago, Martin Luther explicitly demanded that every child go to school to learn how to read the Holy Scriptures, in particular the Gospel. More Protestants became literate than Catholics. Some economists have argued that the rise of capitalism and economic prosperity in the Protestant parts of Europe in the nineteenth century was due less to the industrious and frugal ethics suggested by Max Weber and more to the importance given by Protestants to education.[33]

Despite the emphasis of traditional Confucian culture on education as a means of cultivating benevolence, righteousness, and virtue in people, this does not mean that education did not benefit individuals. China traditionally selected the most educated to join the government through the imperial civil examination system for more than 1,000 years. This tradition allowed children from ordinary families to enter the ruling class through education. If successful, the children brought immense honor to their families and ancestors. However, the chances of receiving the palace degrees (*jinshi*) in the

---

[31] See Giles (2014).

[32] For more historical details, see Botticini and Eckstein (2012).

[33] See Becker and Woessmann (2009) and Schaltegger and Torgler (2009).

civil examinations, which all but guaranteed a position in government officialdom, were extremely low. During the Ming and Qing Dynasties, only about 300 of the millions of local candidates passed the triennial palace examinations.[34] If this was the sole purpose of educating children, it would be very irrational, almost like wanting to get rich by buying lottery tickets today. Nevertheless, this long tradition of civil examinations reinforced the importance that Confucian culture attached to education by enhancing the prestige of being an educated and learned person: Only the most learned scholars had the honor and privilege of occupying the most powerful and prestigious positions in the imperial government.

Even during the Cultural Revolution, when colleges were closed, years of schooling were shortened, and more education meant lower political status in the Maoist social stratification system, traditional respect for knowledge and education was not lost. Many urban youths sent to the countryside as farmers did not completely give up their studies, but taught themselves high school or even college courses. Some also read banned books by Western authors in secret. There was apparently no extrinsic gain for them but the intrinsic love of knowledge. Today, with abundant educational opportunities, having only an undergraduate degree can no longer make someone feel proud. Master's degrees and doctoral degrees have become sought after. Many high-ranking government officials and successful business people have been keen to seek doctoral degrees in certain soft subjects through part-time programs, the quality of which may have been very uneven to say the least. In this case, a doctoral degree probably does not generate economic gain or domain expertise, but confers some prestige on the recipient of the title of Doctor. In a twisted way, this reflects the fact that Chinese society gives prestige to those who have acquired the highest educational credentials whether or not they have apparent economic value.

---

[34] See Elman (2013).

However, the traditional emphasis on education did not make China the birthplace of modern science. On the contrary, the civil examination system and its narrow and exclusive focus on Confucian classics and poetry may have been one of the reasons why China did not develop modern science despite its sophisticated culture and advanced premodern technology.[35] However, once China's attention turned to the study of modern science and technology, its educational tradition began to show its constructive effects, enabling the country to make great strides in just a few decades. This is similar to the case of Jewish involvement in modern science. As mentioned, Jewish education was historically focused on religious studies, not secular knowledge. Jewish scholars contributed little to the scientific revolution of the sixteenth and seventeenth centuries. However, once integrated into Western society, their enthusiasm for learning began to turn to secular modern science. In one generation, they started to make important contributions to science and eventually produced many leading scientists.[36] It is entirely possible that in a few decades, there will be many more world-class Chinese scientists than today.

Traditional Confucian, Jewish, and Protestant cultures all valued education intrinsically beyond its economic benefits, making these societies treasure education more than others. Although historically not motivated by economic considerations, the passion for education in these cultures actually helped to promote their economic development in the industrial and post-industrial age. In contrast to the East Asian economies, most developing economies did not even have their own written languages before being colonized by Europeans, let alone a long tradition of education.[37]

---

[35] See Fei (1953). The eminent economic historian Joel Mokyr (1990) suggested that China's imperial civil examination system focused the nation's intellectual resources exclusively on bureaucratic activities rather than economic or technological activities. As a result, the technological progress of Imperial China was too dependent on the support of the state, which could change its priority at will.

[36] See Shillony (1992) and Ruderman (1995).   [37] See, e.g., Rogers (2005).

Therefore, from the perspective of the quality of education in East Asian societies traditionally influenced by Confucian culture, it is no longer difficult to understand why Japan was the only country outside the West to achieve successful industrialization before WWII; why in the forty years after the war, with the exception of a few southern European countries, Israel, and the oil-rich Middle Eastern countries, only the four Asian Tigers successfully became developed economies; and why China has been the fastest growing economy in the world in the past forty years. These are by no means coincidental success stories in economic development.[38]

---

[38] For the past two decades, India and Vietnam have been among the fastest growing populous countries after China. Both countries are known for their cultural focus on education. There are also historical reasons for this. In India's caste system, the Brahmins, the highest caste, were the educated elites who monopolized knowledge of the Vedic texts. Vietnam is another East Asian country historically influenced by Confucian culture. In fact, Vietnam ended the imperial civil examination system later than China.

6 Technological Progress and Innovation

China's rapid economic growth over the past four decades has clearly been driven by investment, as shown in Chapter 4, but critics have pointed out that technological innovation has played a very limited role in this process. Although China is now viewed by many pundits as a threat to Western technological supremacy, just a few years ago the world's second-largest economy seemed notoriously incapable of genuine innovation. The influential *Harvard Business Review* even published an article in 2014 with the title "Why China Can't Innovate."[1]

CAN CHINA INNOVATE?

At the United States Air Force Academy graduation ceremony in 2014, then–Vice President Joe Biden noted that China produces six to eight times more graduates in science and engineering each year than the United States, but he challenged Air Force graduates to name him "one innovative project, one innovative change, one innovative product that has come out of China."[2] Ms. Carly Fiorina, former CEO of Hewlett Packard, echoed Mr. Biden's sentiment. As quoted in the previous chapter, during her unsuccessful presidential campaign in the Republican primary in 2015, she accused China of stealing American technology because of its inability to innovate. Some commentators even claimed that the theft of American technologies is "part of the explanation for China's rapid growth."[3] China's low per capita GDP and technological level compared with the United States and other advanced economies can easily lead many to underestimate

---

[1] See Abrami, Kirby, and McFarlan (2014).   [2] VOA News (2014).
[3] See Lewis (2018).

its ability to innovate, whereas the size and rapid growth of its economy can lead others to overestimate it. Indeed, sentiment in the United States about China's technological capacity seemed to have changed during Trump's presidency as his administration launched sanctions against Chinese tech giants Huawei and Tencent. The United States now appears to be seriously concerned about losing to China in the areas of AI and 5G technologies. However, the very tactics of sanctions betray a belief that China's technological progress can be significantly slowed down if the United States stops selling key technologies to Chinese companies. There seems to be an underlying presumption under the harsh criticism of China's theft of American technology that China's current technological prowess is largely based on American innovations, not its own innovative capacity.[4]

It may be interesting for foreigners to learn that China's own critics of the country's lack of innovation can be even harsher. Type the Chinese words for "lack of innovation" (*chuangxin buzu*) into a search engine, and you will find an overwhelming number of articles and speeches that take China's inability to innovate as an established fact and blame it either on its politico-economic system or on Chinese culture. A prominent economist in China, Professor Zhang Weiying of Peking University, told his school's graduates in 2017 that in the past 500 years, China has contributed almost nothing to the world in terms of technological innovation, and there is no comparison even to Switzerland, let alone the United States or the United Kingdom. Professor Zhang then offered his explanation for this abject Chinese failure: "The problem is obviously due to our system and institutions. Creativity hinges on freedom, the freedom to think and the freedom to act. The basic characteristic of the Chinese system is the restriction of people's freedom, the strangling of people's creativity, and the strangling of entrepreneurial spirit."[5] Many Chinese commentators

---

[4] See White House Office of Trade and Manufacturing Policy (2018).
[5] Translated by the author based on the transcript of Zhang Weiying's Chinese speech "Freedom Is a Duty" (Zhang, 2017).

have been equally critical and worried about China's ability to successfully transition to an innovation-led growth model.

It seems indeed true that almost all manufactured goods we enjoy today were invented in the West and a few non-Western countries like Japan, and although many high-tech products are now manufactured in China, their core technologies still come from developed countries. For example, Apple's iPhones are assembled in China, but China's value added is only a small fraction of the total value of an iPhone.[6] Hundreds of thousands of scientists do research in China, but it was not until 2015 that a Chinese scientist, Ms. Tu Youyou, received a Nobel Prize. In contrast, Switzerland, a small country with only a few million people, has produced more than twenty Nobel laureates in scientific fields.

If the benchmark is the most developed countries, such as the United States, the United Kingdom, or Switzerland, China's capacity for innovation has truly been lacking in the past two centuries. However, the same can be said of all developing countries in the world, including those that, until recently, had higher per capita income than China, such as Brazil, Mexico, and Turkey, not to mention other developing countries that lag further behind. In fact, the problem is not that China did not produce a Nobel laureate in science until 2015, but that almost no Nobel Prize–winning scientific research has been conducted in a developing nation. The relatively low level of innovative capacity compared with most advanced Western countries is not unique to China, but characteristic of all low- and middle-income developing countries. In this sense, the lack of innovation in a developing country is obviously not a simple institutional or cultural problem. After all, there are significant variations in institutions and cultures between developing countries.

Therefore, simply comparing the level of technological innovation of a developing country with that of developed countries does not tell us much about the reasons for the innovation gap other than

---

[6] See Xing and Detert (2010) and Lamy (2011).

the level of economic development. No economically less developed country can be the world leader in science and technology. Those countries with the strongest technological innovation capabilities are also the most developed economically. Asking why China or any other developing country is less innovative than the most developed countries is like asking why China or any other developing country has not yet become the most developed.

For a country far from the technological frontier, the key question is not how big the innovation gap with the most developed countries is, but whether the gap is narrowing and whether it is narrowing quickly enough. By this criterion, as I show in the next section, China has performed extremely well over the past three decades or so, making rapid technological progress, which, as another engine of growth, has contributed significantly to China's rapid economic rise.[7]

MEASURING INNOVATION AROUND THE WORLD USING PATENT DATA

In academic work, economists have often used a method called growth accounting to measure the contribution to growth made by technological progress, which is also called TFP growth, as mentioned in Chapter 4. This method basically treats the growth of GDP per capita that cannot be explained by the contribution of investment and education as resulting from technological progress. In other words, technological progress is not measured directly, but as a residual value. As noted in Chapter 4, some studies have shown that technological progress, that is, TFP growth, contributed around 40 percent of China's economic growth during the first three decades of reform and opening up.

---

[7] Even Ronald Coase, the late Nobel laureate in economics who gave high marks to China's economic transformation, underestimated China's ability to innovate due to what he saw as a lack of "open market for ideas" in China. See Coase and Wang (2012).

It is important to note that technological progress and innovation are not the same thing. If innovation means bringing something new to the world, for a developed country on the technological frontier, innovation is essential to its technological progress. For a developing country that is far from the technological frontier, new-to-the-world innovation is not necessary for technological progress. In fact, a developing country can have faster technological progress than a developed country simply by adopting the latter's current technologies. If the TFP figure cited in Chapter 4 is correct, the speed of China's technological progress during the first thirty years of the reform was around 3.8 percent per year, which is much faster than that of all developed countries.

Over the past forty years, China has certainly relied more on Western technologies than on its own innovation for its technological progress, but that does not mean that China has made no new-to-the-world technological innovation. In what follows, I use several measures of technological innovation to show China's progress in its capacity to innovate. Commonly used indicators of a country's scientific and technological innovation strength include the number of patent applications or grants, the number of scientific publications, the number of R&D researchers, R&D expenditure, and so on, not just the total figures but also the per capita figures. Comparing China with the rest of the world, it becomes clear that whatever the indicators used, the gap between China's capacity for innovation and that of the most developed countries is rapidly narrowing. When compared with all other developing countries, China is leading the pack by far not only in terms of the current level of innovation but, more importantly, in terms of the pace of innovation.

Table 6.1 presents the 2018 patent data for selected countries. All patents mentioned here are limited to inventions and do not include utility models, which are much easier to obtain. Out of approximately 200 economies covered by the WIPO database, 99 economies had more than 100 patent applications in 2018. China had the highest number of patent applications, nearly 1.5 million, more than

Table 6.1 *Patent applications and grants worldwide (2018)*

Country	Total Patent Applications by Country of Origin	Patent Applications per Million People	Total Patent Grants by Country of Origin	Patent Grants per Million People	Total PCT International Patent Applications	PCT International Applications per Million People
China	1,460,244	1,048	377,305	271	53,347	38
United States	515,180	1,575	289,082	884	56,247	172
Japan	460,369	3,638	284,068	2,245	49,710	393
South Korea	232,020	4,493	131,912	2,555	16,922	328
Germany	180,086	2,172	101,556	1,225	19,744	238
United Kingdom	56,216	845	26,442	398	5,630	85
Switzerland	46,659	5,479	26,109	3,066	4,575	537
Italy	32,286	534	22,224	368	3,330	55
Russia	30,696	212	23,627	164	1,035	7
India	30,036	22	8,350	6	2,007	1
Canada	24,483	661	13,542	365	2,424	65
Israel	15,482	1,743	7,482	842	1,898	214
Spain	10,292	220	6,271	134	1,398	30
Turkey	9,360	114	3,703	45	1,403	17
Singapore	7,415	1,315	3,337	592	935	166
Brazil	6,859	33	1,976	9	616	3
Poland	6,757	178	3,973	105	334	9

Table 6.1 (cont.)

Country	Total Patent Applications by Country of Origin	Patent Applications per Million People	Total Patent Grants by Country of Origin	Patent Grants per Million People	Total PCT International Patent Applications	PCT International Applications per Million People
Mexico	2,695	21	1,170	9	273	2
Indonesia	1,451	5	552	2	7	0
Egypt	1,174	12	240	2	44	0
Philippines	736	7	141	1	18	0
Nigeria	153	1	204	1	2	0

Note: All data on patent applications and grants (by country of origin) are from WIPO.

the combined total of the countries ranked 2 to 6 (the United States, Japan, South Korea, Germany, and the United Kingdom). China also ranked first in the number of patents granted, but its advantage over other high-ranking countries was much smaller. However, due to the significant time lag (e.g., three to five years) between the filing of a patent application and its eventual granting, patent application data are a more timely reflection of a country's inventive activities than patent grant data.

Of course, ranking first in the total number of patent applications or grants does not mean that China has become the most innovative country in the world. After all, China is also the most populous country. On a per capita basis, China's patent applications rank below 20. As the second column of Table 6.1 indicates, the number of patent applications per million people in China in 2018 was less than 20 percent of that of Switzerland; less than 30 percent of that of South Korea and Japan; and significantly lower than other major developed countries, such as Germany and the United States. However, it should be noted that even with this measure, China surpassed some major developed countries, such as the United Kingdom, Canada, and Italy, and far exceeded some non-Western countries that had long been more developed than China, including Russia, a former superpower, Poland, and upper middle-income countries, like Turkey, Brazil, and Mexico, let alone other less developed countries.

Some readers may argue that although China has the highest patent applications in terms of quantity, their quality may not be comparable to that of more developed countries. However, according to WIPO regulations, although patent laws may vary from country to country, patents granted in all countries must meet similar standards, that is, they must be novel, nonobvious, and useful. Nevertheless, some researchers have found that the average quality of Chinese patents based on certain measures, such as citation statistics, is lower than that of developed countries.[8] Yet there seems to be no evidence

---

[8] See Zhang and Chen (2012), Thoma (2013), and Song and Li (2004).

that it is also lower than the quality of patents from other developing countries.

To use an internationally more comparable measure, Table 6.1 also presents the numbers of international patent applications filed under the Patent Cooperation Treaty (PCT) administered by WIPO. The PCT system, which currently has 153 contracting states, facilitates patent applications in foreign countries by reducing the requirement to file a separate application in each country. International patent applications filed by China under the PCT are ultimately reviewed by foreign patent agencies; therefore, the number of such applications may provide a better comparison with that of major developed countries. Keep in mind that this measure is biased in favor of small economies like Switzerland and against big economies like China. Indeed, as China has the largest manufacturing sector in the world, many inventors may not find it necessary or worthwhile to apply for patent protection in a foreign country that has little use for their invention.

Table 6.1 shows that the United States surpassed China in the number of PCT international patent applications in 2018, although not by much. But on a per million people basis, China's ranking was much lower, and its thirty-eight PCT applications represented less than a quarter of the US level, less than 10 percent of the Japanese level, and less than most major developed countries. However, even with this more stringent measure, China still outperformed traditionally more developed countries, such as Spain, Russia, Turkey, and Brazil, by a large margin, suggesting that China's innovative capacity is already ahead of its level of development as measured by GDP per capita.

For a developing country that is still some distance from the technological frontier, a more meaningful comparison with developed countries is not the current level of innovation – there is no comparison – but whether the country is growing its capacity for innovation quickly enough. No matter how far behind a country is today, as long as its innovative capacity grows faster than that of more advanced countries, it is only a matter of time before the former catches up with the latter. Let us now examine whether and how quickly the

Table 6.2 *Compound annual growth rate of patent applications*

Country	Growth from 1985 to 1995	Growth from 1995 to 2005	Growth from 2005 to 2015	Growth from 1985 to 2015	Growth from 2015 to 2018
China	9.8%	25.2%	26.3%	20.2%	13.1%
United States	11.2%	7.5%	3.3%	7.3%	−1.0%
Japan	4.0%	2.7%	−1.5%	1.7%	0.2%
South Korea	37.7%	9.4%	3.9%	16.1%	−0.9%
Germany	7.9%	8.2%	1.3%	5.8%	0.9%
United Kingdom	4.2%	4.6%	1.3%	3.4%	1.7%
Switzerland	13.8%	9.3%	4.4%	9.1%	0.5%
Italy	9.5%	12.7%	2.1%	8.0%	14.2%
Russia		3.7%	2.7%		−3.2%
India	5.7%	16.7%	11.6%	11.2%	7.8%
Canada	15.5%	8.5%	2.1%	8.6%	−0.4%
Israel	14.5%	9.8%	6.3%	10.1%	2.2%
Spain	4.9%	8.1%	3.6%	5.5%	−1.8%
Turkey	3.4%	21.0%	19.4%	14.3%	8.7%
Singapore		28.6%	12.5%		6.2%
Brazil	4.7%	4.8%	2.9%	4.1%	1.4%
Poland	−6.1%	−0.6%	10.6%	1.1%	−1.2%
Mexico	0.3%	4.3%	10.4%	4.9%	2.4%
Indonesia	2.4%	15.2%	16.5%	11.2%	7.2%
Egypt	9.3%	1.1%	6.2%	5.5%	12.0%
Philippines	6.4%	5.2%	10.1%	7.2%	0.0%
Nigeria			25.9%	6.2%	36.6%

Note: All figures were calculated based on WIPO data on the total number of patent applications (direct and PCT national phase entries) by country of origin.

innovation gap between China and developed countries has narrowed. Table 6.2 shows the growth rate of patent applications for a selection of countries between 1985 and 2018. I chose 1985 as the starting year because it was the year China implemented its new patent law.

Between 1985 and 2015, China's number of patent applications increased by 20.2 percent per year, faster than all other countries. The growth was particularly rapid between 1995 and 2005 and between 2005 and 2015, more than 25 percent per year. Even with a much larger base, China remained one of the fastest growing countries for patent applications between 2015 and 2018.

Table 6.1 shows that on a per capita basis, there was still a significant innovation gap between China and the most developed countries. However, Table 6.2 shows that the gap has been shrinking rapidly. This is particularly evident in Figure 6.1. Only twenty years ago, in 2000, China had 26,445 patent applications, ranking seventh in the world, which was less than 10 percent of the US level and less than 2 percent of Chinese applications in 2018. In 2012, China overtook the United States to become number one in patent applications. In contrast, the gap between the United States and most other developing countries (e.g., Brazil, Egypt, and Mexico) has not narrowed at all. Figure 6.1 also shows that South Korea and India have performed well in the growth of patent applications. No wonder they

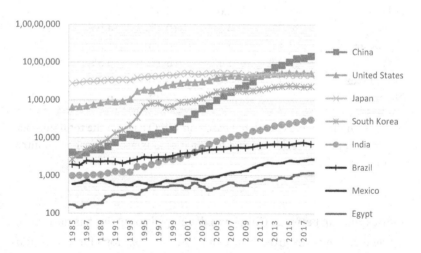

FIGURE 6.1 Growth in patent applications: 1985–2018
Data source: WIPO database

have also been among the fastest growing economies in the past thirty years. A discerning reader may notice that India had around 30,000 patent applications in 2018, just 2 percent of China's level. This is a very low level of innovation for a country of 1.3 billion people. Nevertheless, India's achievements and potential should not be underestimated. They started with a low base of around 1,000 applications in 1985, which implies a thirty-time increase between 1985 and 2018. Less than twenty years ago, in 2001, China was like India today. If India's capacity for innovation grows like that of China over the next twenty years, then in 2040, India will be like China today and will overtake the United States to rank second in patent applications behind China.

SCIENTIFIC RESEARCH: QUANTITY AND QUALITY

Skeptics may point out that the number of patent applications or grants may not be a good indicator of innovation, as not all innovations are patentable or patented, and not all patents are high-quality innovations. Indeed, some researchers have shown that the surge in patent applications in China is to a large extent the result of policy incentives, such as patent subsidy programs, not necessarily because of the increase in real innovation capacities.[9] On the one hand, some inventors may not have bothered to apply for patent rights for their inventions in the absence of subsidies. On the other hand, policy incentives attract many low-quality patent applications. Both cases can lead to a superficial increase in the number of patent applications without a real increase in inventive activities or innovation capabilities. It is certainly true that policy incentives have played a role in the surge in patent applications in China. However, all policy effects are one-off effects and cannot be sustained in the long term. Yet the rapid growth of patent applications and grants in China has been going on for thirty years, as clearly shown in Figure 6.1. More importantly, there is evidence that the quality of Chinese patents has improved

---

[9] See Dang and Motohashi (2015) and Hu, Zhang, and Zhao (2017).

despite its explosive growth in quantity.[10] Therefore, the sustained growth of patent applications in China is more likely to indicate the country's growing capacity for innovation. In summary, China still has some distance to cover before reaching the technological frontier, but it is making great strides and has surpassed all other developing countries with equal or higher per capita income in technological innovation.

Technological innovation may not be sustainable without scientific research. A country's capacity for scientific research may determine the potential and stamina of its technological innovation. So, how is China's scientific research faring? How fast is its progress? The number of scientific articles published is a commonly used indicator to measure a country's scientific research capacity. Based on data from a National Science Foundation report, Figure 6.2 shows that in 2016, China surpassed the United States to produce the largest number of science and engineering (S&E) articles in the world.[11] More importantly, China's S&E publications grew rapidly, at a compound annual growth rate of 13.62% between 2000 and 2018, not only much faster than the United States (1.84%); the European Union (2.99%); and Japan (0.10%), but also faster than the rest of the developing world (e.g., India: 10.7%; South America: 8.39%), as shown in Table 6.3. In 2000, China's share of the world's production of scientific publications was just below 5 percent, but in 2018, that share reached more than 20 percent. Of course, on a per capita basis, China's publication output is still less than a third of the US level. In this sense, China still has work to do to catch up to the United States.[12]

Again, skeptics may argue that although Chinese scientists have published a large number of papers, their quality may not be up

---

[10] See Wei, Xie, and Zhang (2017) and Lin, Wu, and Wu (2019).

[11] See National Science Board, National Science Foundation (2019).

[12] Some authors have argued that the Scopus database used by the NSF underestimates China's contribution to science for two reasons. First, Scopus covers mainly (78 percent) English-language journals and ignores most Chinese-language journals. Second, a significant number of Chinese scholars work for institutions outside of China, and their contributions are credited to other countries in the database. See Xie and Freeman (2019).

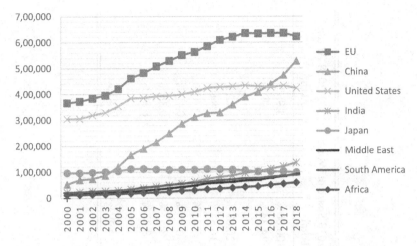

FIGURE 6.2 Published articles in science and engineering: 2000–2018

Note: This figure is based on data obtained from "Publication Output: US Trends and International Comparisons," *Science and Engineering Indicators 2020*, the National Science Board, National Science Foundation, 2019. Available at https://ncses.nsf.gov/pubs/nsb20206. The number of articles in this report comes from a selection of journals in science and engineering from Elsevier's Scopus database, which is the largest abstract and citation database of peer-reviewed literature. Articles are credited on a fractional count basis (i.e., for articles from multiple countries, each receives a fractional credit based on each author's institutional address).

to scratch. How true is this argument? The citation rate is commonly used to measure the quality of scientific publications. It counts the number of publications citing an article. Articles with more citations are supposedly more impactful and of higher quality. A small fraction of scientific publications are classified as highly cited articles (HCA). The National Science Foundation report cited previously compiled an index called the HCA score as an indicator of the quality of a country's scientific output. It represents the percentage share of a country's S&E publications in the top 1 percent most-cited articles in the world each year multiplied by 100. The world's average HCA score is 1 by definition. Figure 6.3 shows the quality index of S&E articles for seven selected countries and regions between 1996 and 2016. The United

Table 6.3 Article counts, growth, and contribution share: 2000–2018

Region or country	S&E Articles in 2000	2000 Share of World Total	S&E Articles in 2018	2018 Share of World Total	2000–2018 Annual Growth
World	1,071,952	100.00%	2,555,959	100.00%	4.95%
European Union	366,366	34.18%	622,125	24.34%	2.99%
China	53,064	4.95%	528,263	20.67%	13.62%
United States	304,782	28.43%	422,808	16.54%	1.84%
India	21,771	2.03%	135,788	5.31%	10.70%
Japan	97,048	9.05%	98,793	3.87%	0.10%
Middle East	15,522	1.45%	91,366	3.57%	10.35%
South America	20,835	1.94%	88,771	3.47%	8.39%
Africa	11,871	1.11%	58,824	2.30%	9.30%

Note: Data source is the same as for Figure 6.2.

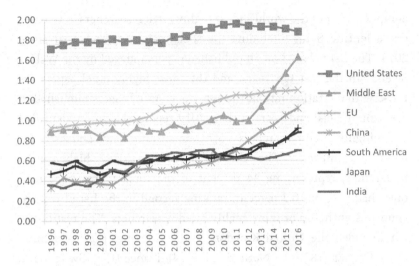

FIGURE 6.3 Quality index of S&E publications: 1996–2016

Note: Both data and the following notes are from the National Science Foundation report "Publication Output: US Trends and International Comparisons" cited earlier. The citation data are based on all citations made to articles in their year of publication and all following years and are normalized by subfield and year of publication to allow comparison between subfields and over time.

States maintained the highest quality in their S&E publications throughout this twenty-year period, but China's quality index improved the fastest among the seven countries or regions. Only twenty-some years ago, in 1996, the quality of China's S&E articles was the lowest at 0.33, one third of the world's average level. However, since 2015, China's HCA score has passed the threshold value of 1, indicating that the quality of China's scientific publications has exceeded the world's average level. It is now better than developed Japan and developing South America and India. The fact that China is still significantly behind the United States, the European Union, and the Middle East (whose HCA score is strongly influenced by Israel and Saudi Arabia, two high-income economies) means that it has room for progress.

Researchers who publish many highly cited articles are the most influential minds in their field. The Web of Science Group has compiled a list of the world's most highly cited researchers in twenty-one scientific fields (including the social sciences) each year since 2014. The list is based on all published papers indexed by the Web of Science in the last ten years, and the most highly cited papers are those with a citation rate in the top 1 percent of papers published in the same field(s) and year. In their 2019 report, the group identified 6,216 highly cited researchers – 3,725 in specific fields and 2,491 for cross-field impact.[13] The United States had 2,737 highly cited researchers, representing 44 percent of the total. China (mainland only) had 636, or 10.2 percent, ranking second in the list of top ten countries with 100 or more highly cited researchers. The rest of the list included the United Kingdom (516); Germany (327); Australia (271); Canada (183); the Netherlands (164); France (156); Switzerland (155); and Spain (116), all developed countries. Japan, with 98, was not in the top ten. In contrast, in 2014, when the Web of Science started compiling its list, China was ranked fourth on the list behind the United Kingdom and Germany and represented less than 5 percent of the highly cited researchers in the world. This is rapid progress for China over a short period of five years.

Most developing countries, including populous countries like Indonesia, Pakistan, and the Philippines, have no highly cited researchers. Among developing countries with a few highly cited researchers, only two countries other than China had more than ten: India with fifteen and Brazil with fourteen. Most impactful and cutting-edge scientific research has almost always been conducted by researchers in high-income developed countries. What is surprising about these results is not why there have not been more world-leading scientific achievements in developing countries, but why China, a middle-income country, could already boast of a considerable number of world-class scholars, which is true even on a per capita basis compared with other middle-income countries.

---

[13] See Web of Science Group (2019).

R&D AROUND THE WORLD: HUMAN RESOURCES
AND FINANCIAL EXPENDITURE

Patents and scientific publications are the output of a country's innovative activities, while R&D personnel and R&D expenditure are the inputs, which are also indicators of a country's innovative capability. Table 6.4 shows the number of researchers in R&D per million people and R&D expenditure as a percentage of GDP for selected countries. Obviously, these two figures are high for developed countries and generally much lower for developing countries. China's proportion of R&D personnel in the total population is less than 16 percent of the level of Denmark, less than 30 percent of the US level, and lower than Turkey, but it is significantly higher than that of most other developing countries. However, China's R&D expenditure ratio is closer to the level of developed countries (but significantly lower than that of South Korea, Japan, Switzerland, and the United States) and much higher than that of all other developing countries.

Again, what is more important for a developing country is not its current level, but the speed of growth of its capacity for innovation, which requires investing in R&D. Figure 6.4 shows the rate of R&D expenditure as a percentage of GDP from 1996 to 2017 for selected countries. It shows that R&D expenditure relative to GDP tends to be higher in developed countries than in developing countries, as expected. The rate of R&D expenditure generally increased over the period in Japan, Germany, and the United States, but barely changed in France and the United Kingdom. Two countries, South Korea and China, saw a dramatic increase. South Korea went from around 2.2% in 1996 to over 4.5% in 2017, the highest in the world (with Israel, not shown here). China started at a rate slightly above 0.5% in 1996, similar to India at the time, and rose to 2.1% in 2017, about the same as France. Given the fact that China also had the fastest GDP growth rate during the period, at 9.1% per year, its R&D expenditure in real terms increased even faster at an annual rate of 16.2% (an increase of

Table 6.4 *R&D researchers and R&D expenditure*

Country	R&D Researchers (per million people) in 2017 (or as noted)	R&D Expenditure (% of GDP) in 2017 (or as noted)
Denmark	7,897	3.10
South Korea	7,514	4.55
Japan	5,305	3.20
Switzerland	5,257	3.37
Germany	5,036	3.04
France	4,441	2.19
United Kingdom	4,377	1.67
United States	4,256	2.80
Canada	4,275	1.59
Turkey	1,386	0.96
China	1,235	2.13
Brazil	881	1.27
Mexico	244	0.49
India	216	0.62
Indonesia	216	0.24
Mali	33	0.29

Note: All data are from the World Development Indicators database. The table is ranked according to the number of researchers per million people, using 2016 data for Canada and the United States, 2015 data for Switzerland and India, 2014 data for Brazil, and 2013 data for Mexico. For R&D expenditure (% of GDP), 2016 data were used for Brazil and Mexico, and 2015 data for Switzerland and India.

twenty-three times in twenty-one years), compared with 7.6% for fast growing South Korea; 3% for the United States; and 1.6% for France.

By now, the answer to the question of whether China can innovate should clearly be a resounding yes given its stage of economic development as an upper middle-income economy. In fact, China's development in science and technology over the past thirty years has been ahead of its income level. Although some Western and Chinese pundits may have underestimated China's ability to

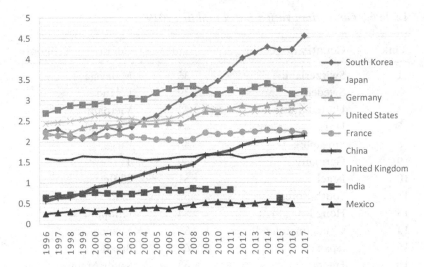

FIGURE 6.4 R&D expenditure as a percentage of GDP (%): 1996–2017
Data source: World Development Indicators

innovate, the Global Innovation Index (GII) ranking, jointly published by WIPO, Cornell University, and INSEAD, has not. The GII uses eighty detailed metrics to measure an economy's innovation performance. In the 2019 GII report, as shown in Table 6.5, China ranked fourteenth in the world. According to the GII criteria, China was the most innovative middle-income country in the world, ahead of all other middle-income countries, such as Turkey, Mexico, and Brazil. However, after examining some important measures of innovation in this chapter, China's fourteenth place on the GII list, ahead of developed countries such as Japan, France, and Canada, seems to have overestimated its true capacity for innovation. On a per capita basis, China still lags behind these developed countries in terms of international patents, high-quality scientific publications, R&D expenditure, and the number of R&D researchers.

In conclusion, China's ability to innovate should neither be underestimated nor overestimated. At the aggregate level, China is already an innovation powerhouse with the largest number of patent applications and grants, R&D researchers, and scientific publications

Table 6.5 *Global innovation index ranking: 2019*

Rank	Country or Economy	Rank	Country or Economy
1	Switzerland	35	Malaysia
2	Sweden	39	Poland
3	United States	42	Vietnam
5	United Kingdom	43	Thailand
8	Singapore	46	Russia
9	Germany	49	Turkey
10	Israel	51	Chile
11	South Korea	52	India
13	Hong Kong SAR	54	Philippines
14	China (mainland)	56	Mexico
15	Japan	66	Brazil
16	France	68	Saudi Arabia
17	Canada	73	Argentina
22	Australia	85	Indonesia
29	Spain	92	Egypt
30	Italy	114	Nigeria

Source: www.globalinnovationindex.org/gii-2019-report (accessed January 30, 2020).

in the world. US sanctions are unlikely to slow down the country's overall rapid technological progress. China is no longer just a copycat, and its position in innovation in the world is comparable to the size of its economy. On a per capita basis, China still has a lot of catching up to do compared with technologically more advanced countries like the United States. Nevertheless, this is not the same as saying that China is just another mid-tier performer in innovation, better than some and worse than others. From the perspective of growth in innovation capacity, China has no competitor. The country has made the fastest progress in science and technology, not just faster than developed countries but also faster than all other developing countries. In this sense, China has already embarked on the path of growth driven by innovation over the past two decades. To give an example at the micro level, in 2018, Chinese tech giant Huawei filed 5,405 PCT international patent applications, the most in the world, nearly 2,600 more applications than second place Mitsubishi. In comparison, in 2005, Huawei filed only 249 applications, ranking thirty-eighth in the world.[14]

For scholars studying technological innovation, the real puzzle is not why China is not as innovative as the United States, Switzerland, or Japan, but why China's innovative capacity has increased more rapidly in the past two to three decades than that of other countries, especially other developing countries.[15] Technological progress and economic growth always go hand in hand, and there is really no sustained growth driven solely by investment. The rapid growth of the Chinese economy has both increased the demand for technological innovation and created better conditions for it. In turn, advances in science and technology have promoted economic growth. Therefore, the puzzle of China's rapidly growing innovation capabilities and the Chinese growth puzzle are two sides of the same coin. As technological innovation requires investment in physical and human capital, Confucian culture that values thrift and education may have very well been a major reason for China's rapid accumulation of physical and human capital, thereby promoting its rapid progress in science and technology.

[14] The figures are taken from WIPO's online database: www3.wipo.int/ipstats/pmhindex.htm?tab=pct (accessed January 30, 2020).

[15] Many studies of China's technological innovations have focused on how economic and policy factors have affected incentives for patenting in China. However, researchers have neglected the question of why China has been able to sustain its extraordinary growth in multiple indicators of innovation for two to three decades, especially compared with other developing countries. See Hu and Jefferson (2009) and Li (2012).

7 Confucian Culture as the Key Differentiating Factor

Let me briefly recap how we came to the conclusion that Confucian culture may have been the key differentiating factor in China's rapid rise over the past four decades. We started by posing the Chinese growth puzzle, which is not why China has grown faster than high-income developed countries, but why it has grown so much faster than other low- or middle-income developing countries. We examined some popular explanations and showed that factors such as cheap labor, demographic dividend, and export orientation in the age of globalization are insufficient to explain the Chinese growth puzzle. We then distinguished between the fundamental causes (i.e., geography, institutions, and culture) and proximate causes (i.e., investment, education, and technological progress) of economic growth. We placed China's rapid economic growth in the context of the East Asian growth miracle and argued that institutional factors, such as market reforms and a strong government, and geographic factors, do not distinguish China (and other East Asian miracle economies) sufficiently from other developing countries. We then suggested that Confucian culture may be the main differentiating factor. We examined the three proximate causes of China's economic growth and argued that Confucian culture's emphasis on hard work, savings, and education seems to have enabled China (and other East Asian economies influenced by Confucian culture) to rapidly accumulate both physical and human capital; as a result, China was able to absorb existing Western technologies and develop indigenous innovation capacity better than other developing countries, leading to its rapid economic rise.

For economists or other skeptical readers, many critical questions come to mind. Isn't the cultural explanation an old and unverifiable theory that has outlived its usefulness? After all, cultural theory was quite popular in the 1980s and early 1990s, at least among noneconomists; but for many critics, it has since been discredited by the bursting of Japan's economic bubble in the early 1990s and the Asian financial crisis in 1998.[1] If Confucian culture is so important, why has China's growth miracle occurred only in the past four decades, but not earlier? How can a cultural explanation do justice to China's rich experience in reform and development? Does it mean that China's experience offers no lesson to other developing countries? If so, isn't that cultural determinism? I address these questions in this chapter.

CULTURAL THEORY AND ITS CRITICS

The first systematic treatise on the idea that culture has a fundamental economic effect can be traced back to the great German sociologist Max Weber. Over 100 years ago, Weber noted that the higher the number of Protestants in a country, the more developed its capitalism. Indeed, in countries with both Protestants and Catholics, the overwhelming majority of capitalists, business leaders, technicians, and skilled workers were Protestants. In his famous 1905 book, *The Protestant Ethic and the Spirit of Capitalism*, Weber attributed these phenomena to the spirit of modern capitalism directly influenced by Protestant doctrines, especially Calvinism, that valued the accumulation of wealth as an end in itself rather than as a means to fund personal consumption. Industry and frugality are the work ethic required by this spirit.

Weber's thesis that the Protestant ethic led to the rise of modern capitalism in northwestern Europe, but not in other parts of the world, is still controversial today. The ethic of industry and frugality is not unique to Protestantism and is often regarded as a hallmark of Confucian culture. Yet in his day, Weber believed that traditional Chinese culture, represented by Confucianism and Taoism, could

---

[1] See, e.g., Krugman (1994), Pye (2000), and Jones (2009).

not inspire a strong enough motivation for people to gain wealth and that the traditional family ideal centered around filial piety was not conducive to the development of rational enterprises. As a result, China failed to give birth to modern capitalism on its own. However, Weber pointed out that China was fully capable of learning, absorbing, and developing capitalism.[2]

Advocates of cultural theory have traditionally discussed the relationship between Confucian culture and the East Asian growth miracle in the Weberian context, trying to show that Confucian culture is also compatible with capitalism.[3] As a result, they have often focused on comparing Eastern and Western cultures. However, to explain the East Asian (including Chinese) growth puzzle, the right comparison is not East versus West, but East versus other non-Western areas. If the world was only made up of East Asia and the West, there would not have been any growth miracle in East Asia, including China, to speak of. After all, East Asian countries have only succeeded in catching up to Western countries, but have not surpassed them in terms of economic development.[4] The central question of the East Asian or Chinese growth puzzle is the following: Why have other developing countries failed to catch up to Western developed countries? Therefore, the cultural analysis in this book is not an East–West comparison, but an exploration of whether Confucian culture is responsible for East Asia's rapid development, including that of China, compared with developing countries in other non-Western geographic regions.

---

[2] See Swedberg (2014).

[3] See, e.g., Yu (1985), Hamilton and Kao (1987), Berger (1988), Redding (1990), and Tu (1996).

[4] As economic historian Eric Jones pointed out, "Asian values" like hard work, thrift, and educational self-improvement were also characteristic of Britain during its industrialization in the nineteenth century (2009, p. 178). However, he used this point to argue against the cultural explanation of the East Asian miracle because he failed to recognize that the right comparison is not East versus West, but East Asia versus other non-Western regions.

While a sociologist may take it for granted that culture plays a key role in economic development, most economists, out of occupational habit, are unwilling to acknowledge it.[5] Economists generally prefer to focus on the roles of capital, technology, policies, and institutions, which are easier to measure, manipulate, and change, than on the effect of culture, which is difficult to define, measure, or influence. For example, Justin Lin, former chief economist of the World Bank, criticized the use of culture to explain the East Asian (and Chinese) growth miracle.[6] He argued that culture is difficult to define precisely, citing a study by two anthropologists who already found 164 definitions of culture in the social science literature in 1952. According to him, this lack of precise definition makes it difficult to validate cultural theories through rigorous quantitative studies. More damning, Lin pointed out that the same Confucian culture was seen as the main obstacle to the modernization of East Asia just a few decades ago.

It may be true that some elements of Confucian culture are not conducive to modernization, but its emphasis on hard work, savings, and education cannot have been an obstacle to modernization. The real question is not whether culture is important, but what specific characteristics of a culture affect the economic development of a country. Lin's criticism may be justified if it is aimed at traditional or amateur culturalists. However, the Achilles heel of traditional culturalists does not lie in their basic ideas, but in the lack of rigorous, quantitative studies supporting these ideas.

Contrary to the beliefs of many critics, cultural values can be measured and their effects quantified. As early as the 1950s, the late Harvard psychologist David C. McClelland attempted to show quantitatively that national culture may play an important role in

---

[5] As an exception to the rule, a World Bank economist, Heng-fu Zou (1994), developed a formal model of the "Spirit of Capitalism" to explain the East Asian miracle, in which people have different cultural preferences for the accumulation of wealth (i.e., savings).

[6] Lin (2014).

explaining cross-country differences in economic performance. Specifically, he tried to prove that a nation's strong motivation for achievement could be the driving force of its economic development.[7] Professor McClelland quantified a country's need for achievement by comparing inspirational stories from children's books across countries. He found that countries with a high need for achievement developed faster. However, his study only covered forty countries, most of which were in the West. His sample only included a handful of developing countries, and China was not included. Since the 1980s, social scientists have used data from values surveys, as mentioned in Chapter 4, to conduct quantitative cultural research.[8] However, many of these early studies tended to consider statistical correlations between cultural characteristics and economic outcomes as proof of causation without taking sufficient account of other factors, such as geography, demography, and institutions.

A CULTURAL AWAKENING IN ECONOMICS

In the past two decades or so, a sign of "cultural awakening" has emerged in economics. An increasing number of mainstream economists have started to use rigorous and quantitative methods to study the impact of cultural values on economic development. There is now a substantial body of research on this topic. In these studies, culture generally refers to beliefs and values that may affect economic outcomes, such as thrift, trust, religiosity, and individualism.[9] Significantly, two recent textbooks on economic growth by leading scholars have devoted entire chapters to the effect of culture on economic development.[10]

---

[7] McClelland (1961).

[8] See, e.g., Hofstede and Bond (1988), Inglehart (1997), and Hofstede (2001).

[9] See, e.g., Knack and Keefer (1997), Guiso, Sapienza, and Zingales (2006), McCleary and Barro (2006), Fernandez (2011), Gorodnichenko and Roland (2011, 2017), and Alesina and Giuliano (2015).

[10] See Aghion and Howitt (2009) and Weil (2013).

Still, most economists, Chinese economists included, seem to be unaware of this recent cultural awakening in economics. Those who are aware of it may not be convinced. Institutionalists are especially hard-nosed. Isn't it obvious, they would ask, that North and South Korea share the same cultural tradition but diverge dramatically in terms of economic performance? What could have caused the striking divergence other than their different institutions? Why has Confucian culture only made its positive mark on China's economic development after 1978, but not before?[11]

The example of the two Koreas is certainly powerful proof that institutions are extremely important in economic development, but it is not proof that culture does not matter. To prove that, one needs to compare countries that have different cultures but are very similar otherwise. No cultural theorist has suggested that culture is the only factor affecting economic performance. Any sensible scholar recognizes the importance of supportive institutions and policies, without which no growth miracle is possible. China's reform and opening-up policy launched in 1978 removed institutional obstacles to the country's economic development. Without it, there would have been no Chinese economic miracle after 1978. However, recognizing the impact of institutions does not mean denying the importance of culture. Few people today believe that central planning is better than a market system, but even with similar economic institutions, whether planned, market-based, or mixed, different countries can still have very different growth performances, for which cultural factors may be responsible. Indeed, some recent economic research using completely different data sources has shown that the effect of culture on long-term economic development at the country, region, or ethnic group level remains very robust even after controlling for the effect of institutions and other factors.[12]

---

[11] See, e.g., Robinson (2006) and Acemoglu and Robinson (2012, p. 57).
[12] See, e.g., Tabellini (2010), Michalopoulos and Papaioannou (2014), and Gorodnichenko and Roland (2017).

Clearly, both institutions and culture are important determinants of economic performance.[13] In fact, growth performance is affected by a plethora of factors, which may be institutional, cultural, demographic, geographic, or related to initial economic conditions. However, we need to distinguish between factors that contribute to the increase (or decrease) in the economic growth of a country and those that make a country grow faster (or slower) relative to a comparison group. The former can be called *contributing factors* and the latter *differentiating factors*. In the case of China, low initial income and labor cost, market reform and opening up, demographic dividend, globalization, and Confucian culture are all contributing factors to its rapid economic growth, but not all of them are factors that differentiate China from other countries. When the comparison group is made up of developed countries, it is China's low initial income and labor cost that is its principal differentiating factor, allowing China to grow faster than this group, thanks to the latecomer advantage (or the advantage of backwardness). When the comparison group is made up of planned economies like North Korea, Cuba, and pre-reform China, the differentiating factor is market reform and opening up. However, when the comparison group is made up of other developing countries, it is Confucian culture's emphasis on hard work, thrift and education that is the principal differentiating factor. As two eminent growth theorists, Philippe Aghion and Peter Howitt, wrote in their popular textbook on economic growth, "under the same initial institutional conditions as China today, other countries with different initial cultures would not grow as fast."[14]

Because I have essentially used what academics call the univariate analysis method (i.e., analyzing one factor at a time) in previous chapters to argue for the cultural view, a doubtful reader may ask whether there could be some factors that I neglected to consider, or some combination or interaction of factors I did consider, that may

---

[13] See, e.g., Greif (1994), Tabellini (2008 and 2010), and Alesina and Giuliano (2015).
[14] Aghion and Howitt (2009), p. 429.

adequately explain the Chinese growth puzzle. This is a legitimate question that a highly cited study published in the prestigious *American Economic Review* in 2004 can help to answer. In that study, Xavier Sala-i-Martin, a leading growth economist, and his coauthors used data from eighty-eight countries or economies (China not included) to analyze the factors determining their average annual growth rates of GDP per capita between 1960 and 1996.[15] They examined sixty-seven possible factors ("explanatory variables"), including geography, colonial history, demographics, policies and institutions, international relations, education, religion, and some initial conditions around 1960, covering almost all factors that could potentially affect a country's economic growth. The conclusion of the study was that the strongest variable correlated with the growth rate of an economy is whether it is located in East Asia. More specifically, if all other factors are the same, the annual growth rate of GDP per capita of an East Asian economy should be 2 percentage points higher than another economy, a very large effect as the average growth rate of these eighty-eight economies was only 1.8 percent during this period. This indicates that at least 2 percentage points of the rapid annual growth in GDP per capita in East Asia cannot be explained by any known factor. From the population figures in their article, the authors included Southeast Asian economies, such as Indonesia and the Philippines, in their defined region of East Asia. As the four Asian Tiger economies grew faster than these Southeast Asian economies during the sampling period, the unexplained portion of economic growth in these four economies was even higher. Indeed, the authors included the fraction of the Confucian population as a variable in their study, which was one of the strongest variables correlated with economic growth. Its effect is very significant: If the fraction of the Confucian population in an economy increases by 20 percentage points, its growth rate of GDP per capita will increase by more than 1 percentage point.

[15] Sala-i-Martin, Doppelhofer, and Miller (2004).

In other words, for a country or economy based on Confucian culture, most of its faster growth compared with that of other countries cannot be explained by any known factor other than its location and culture. China, Japan, and the four Asian Tiger economies of South Korea, Taiwan, Hong Kong, and Singapore are not only all located in East Asia geographically but are also culturally influenced by the Confucian ethic of hard work, frugality, and education. It is this common culture that seems to be the factor that distinguishes them from most other developing economies.

Critics like to say that cultural explanations are just post hoc rationalizations of extraordinary economic outcomes without any predictive power.[16] However, social sciences in general and economics in particular are weak in predictive power and stronger in explanatory power. As with any social science theory, we can make mistakes when using cultural theory to make specific predictions, but that does not mean that the theory itself is necessarily wrong. More importantly, cultural theory has predictive power. As Lawrence Harrison, a staunch advocate of the cultural view of economic development, put it bluntly, "'Confucianism' ... offers 100% predictability with respect to high levels of economic achievement if governments are supportive of economic development."[17] For example, we can use cultural theory to predict that Vietnam, a country historically influenced by Confucian culture, is very likely to experience rapid economic growth over the next thirty years. In fact, nearly fifty years ago, the late Harvard scholar Edwin Reischauer, also a former US ambassador to Japan, already envisioned that China, Vietnam, and North Korea would be able to achieve similar economic success to that achieved by Japan and the four Asian Tigers once "their policies change enough to afford room for the economic drive of which their people are undoubtedly capable." The basis for his prediction was cultural because he believed the peoples of East Asia "share certain key traits, such as group solidarity, an emphasis on the political unit, great

---

[16] See, e.g., Jones (2009).   [17] Harrison (2006).

organizational skills, a strong work ethic, and a tremendous drive for education."[18] Another Harvard scholar, the late economic historian David Landes, even said that "if we learn anything from the history of economic development, it is that culture makes almost all the difference."[19] It may be too strong a claim, but it highlights an important truth that culture matters a lot to economic development.

CONFUCIAN CULTURE AND ITS RELATIONSHIP WITH CHINESE INSTITUTIONS

Ironically, very few Chinese economists have given much thought to the important role of Confucian culture in China's recent economic development. A notable exception is Mr. Mao Yushi, a highly respected institutional economist known for his staunch defense of the free market and the rule of law, who, together with his coauthor Su Dong, argued for a cultural explanation for China's growth miracle in an opinion piece.[20] The two authors argued that China enjoys no institutional advantage over other countries (quite the opposite), therefore its superb economic performance must be explained from the perspective of Chinese culture. They suggested that China has done well economically because Chinese people are eager to get rich and are more hard-working and frugal than others, and that China would have done better with better institutions. Thus, in their view, a growth-friendly culture has more or less successfully substituted for comparatively poor institutions to enable China to develop rapidly.

Culture and institutions are not merely substitutes but also complement each other to affect economic performance. For example, as noted in previous chapters, the Confucian culture of thrift and education has magnified the demographic dividend brought about by China's family planning system (particularly the one-child policy).

---

[18] Reischauer (1974), pp. 347–348. This article was quoted by Wei-ming Tu (2000) as a prophetic statement during the Cold War outlining the trajectory of the rise of Confucian East Asia.

[19] See Landes (2000) and his magnum opus, *The Wealth and Poverty of Nations*.

[20] Mao and Su (2012).

Moreover, there is a two-way causal relationship between culture and institutions. Certain cultural values may lead to the choice of certain institutions, and certain institutions may lead to the survival of certain cultural values.[21] In the case of China, its collectivist Confucian culture may have been more compatible with an authoritarian political system, and the long-lasting historical institution of imperial civil examinations was probably responsible for China's extraordinary cultural emphasis on education.[22]

So far, I have only stressed the culture of hard work, savings, and education in facilitating China's rapid catch-up growth, but other aspects of Confucian culture may have also played important roles. No matter how hard the people of a country try to work, study, and save, if basic law and order are lacking and the necessary infrastructure and public goods are few and far between, economic growth is still difficult to achieve. The free market alone is insufficient. The government must be functional, and there must be some basic level of social trust. Although the Chinese government is not among the most effective or efficient, as shown in Chapter 3, it has still been more effective than that of a majority of developing countries. What has contributed to the relative effectiveness of China's government and public institutions? Again, Confucian culture may have been a differentiating factor.

The Confucian moral system can be summarized by the so-called five constant virtues (*wuchang*), namely, benevolence (*ren*), righteousness (*yi*), propriety (*li*), wisdom (*zhi*), and trustworthiness (*xin*).[23] Historically, Confucian education emphasized the cultivation of these five virtues that every individual was expected to strive for. These virtues were especially demanded of government officials, and benevolent government (*ren zheng*) is one of the most important Confucian teachings. For about 2,000 years, China's government

---

[21] See Alesina and Giuliano (2015).

[22] See Shin (2012) and Elman (2013). In addition, see Sen (1999) for a critique of the view that authoritarianism is implicit in Confucianism.

[23] See Xing (1995) and Zhao (2018).

bureaucracy and Confucian scholarship were almost identical: Government officials were steeped in Confucian scholarship, the main purpose of which was to cultivate the five constant virtues.[24] Political meritocracy as practiced in Imperial China was intimately linked with Confucian ethics. In principle, only virtuous Confucian scholars had the rights and obligations to govern. In reality, self-interest could triumph over Confucian ideals and cronyism and corruption could ensue. However, Confucian teachings were still powerful informal constraints on the selection and behavior of government officials. The CCP, although officially Marxist, has, perhaps unconsciously, more or less inherited the Confucian moral system and its political ideal of benevolent government, that is, to use power to serve the people rather than for personal gain.[25] Former President Liu Shaoqi's famous pamphlet on how to be a good communist reads more like a Confucian sermon than Marxist propaganda.[26] Although Confucianism was publicly denounced during the Cultural Revolution, it experienced a great revival in the reform era.[27] In reality, of course, most CCP cadres may not live up to the ideal of a benevolent servant of the people, but they are at least expected to have the public interest in mind. Like almost all developing countries, China has also suffered from severe corruption, but compared with many African leaders in the post-independence period, Chinese government officials have been much less corrupt.[28] Indeed, according to Transparency International's ranking of countries based on their Corruption Perceptions Index starting in 1995, China ranks below all developed countries, but above the majority of developing countries, as shown in Table 7.1.

As noted in Chapter 3, an influential school of thought has argued for a developmental state view of the East Asian miracle that emphasizes the positive role of active government intervention and judicious industrial policies. If government intervention has indeed

---

[24] See Yao (2000).   [25] See Bell (2015) and Jiang (2018).   [26] Liu (1981).

[27] See, e.g., Billioud and Thoraval (2015) and Ford (2015).

[28] For corruption in post-independence Africa, see, e.g., Meredith (2011).

Table 7.1 *Corruption perceptions index: 1995–2019*

Year	Number of Countries with Sufficient Data to Be Ranked	China's Rank
1995	41	40
1999	99	58
2003	133	66
2007	180	72
2011	183	75
2015	167	83
2019	180	80

Note: The data are from Transparency International (www.transparency .org/en/cpi).

been essential for the success of China and other East Asian economies, why has it been so unsuccessful in the rest of the developing world? To put it another way, what is so unique about China and other East Asian economies that enabled interventionist policies to succeed there, if at all?

Francis Fukuyama, author of the famous *The End of History and the Last Man*, asked this question in his recent book, *Political Order and Political Decay*, and for him the answer lies in the strength of the state. He argued that a strong state is essential for an activist government to successfully pursue industrial policy, and for historical reasons, East Asian countries, like their European counterparts, developed strong state institutions before the age of industrialization, thus laying the institutional foundation for the latter. In fact, he noted that China "invented the modern state at the time of the Qin unification, some eighteen hundred years before its rise in early modern Europe."[29] According to Fukuyama, East Asian countries have used their strong state power (often under authoritarian regimes) to successfully promote economic growth; in contrast, Latin America and

[29] Fukuyama (2014), p. 393.

sub-Saharan Africa had not developed strong states before their encounters with Western colonial powers, and most of the countries in these regions have yet to develop a strong state for various reasons. There is certainly some truth to these arguments, but I suspect that Mr. Fukuyama inferred the strength of East Asian states from their economic success. Would the strength of the state of South Korea or Taiwan have been regarded more highly than that of Argentina in the 1950s? Probably not. In fact, East Asia as a region, and China in particular, has no particular advantage over Latin America in the World Bank's World Governance Indicators, a point that Fukuyama himself acknowledged. After all, what constitutes strong state institutions? If strong state institutions refer mainly to formal rules and organizations, they do not require a long history to be established. If they are mainly informal rules and personnel qualities, then it is not the state apparatus per se, but human capital, and in particular the cultural values embedded in the state apparatus, that really matter. Indeed, Mr. Fukuyama said as much in his fascinating book:

> China and the countries influenced by it were heirs to a Confucian moral and bureaucratic system that oriented rulers, through education and socialization, toward a broader concept of the common good. That, plus the Confucian emphasis on literacy and education, left a critical if unintended benefit for modern economic development. East Asia's rapid rise from the second half of the twentieth century on has been driven by strong technocratic states whose leadership, however authoritarian, remains oriented toward shared goals of economic and social development.[30]

Competent and public-spirited officialdom is needed to produce sensible policies and implement them effectively. If government intervention and industrial policies have indeed made a difference in the economic performance of China and other East Asian miracle economies, much of the credit may be due to Confucian culture,

[30] Fukuyama (2014), p. 394.

shaping the policy orientation and capability of the state. If China's state capacity seems stronger than its income level suggests, it may have little to do with its system of governance and more to do with the culture of the people being governed. It is much easier for a government to pursue an infrastructure-led, investment-driven growth model when its citizens are more inclined to save and invest, and it is much easier to promote export-oriented manufacturing when the labor force is not only cheap but also educated. Moreover, the governing elites themselves belong to the same culture.

In addition to the cultural values of savings and education, economists have found that trust is another important cultural value for economic development and growth.[31] Trust is a cooperative attitude toward people outside the family and plays a vital role in market relationships. As the late Nobel laureate Kenneth Arrow pointed out, "virtually every commercial transaction has within itself an element of trust, certainly any transaction conducted over a period of time. It can be plausibly argued that much of the economic backwardness in the world can be explained by the lack of mutual confidence."[32] Trust is especially important for a developing country where the legal system for contract enforcement is generally weak. In the absence of both trust and formal legal enforcement, marketization alone cannot generate economic growth, as few high-stakes economic exchanges and long-term investments will take place in such an environment. It is thus no coincidence that fast growing China is the most trusting nation among all developing nations according to the WVS. As shown in Table 7.2, just over half of the Chinese respondents answered yes to the WVS question of whether "most people can be trusted," making China the third most trusting society behind Sweden and the Netherlands. After all, trustworthiness is one of the five constant Confucian virtues.

---

[31] For an excellent survey on the topic, see Algan and Cahuc (2014). Also see Knack and Keefer (1997), Zak and Knack (2001), and Algan and Cahuc (2010).
[32] Arrow (1972), quoted in Algan and Cahuc (2014).

Table 7.2 *Social trust around the world*

Country/ Economy	Most People Can Be Trusted (%)	Rank	Country/Economy	Most People Can Be Trusted (%)	Rank
Sweden	60	1	Qatar	21	31
Netherlands	58	2	South Africa	20	32
China	**54**	**3**	Uruguay	20	33
New Zealand	50	4	Argentina	19	34
Australia	45	5	Armenia	19	35
Hong Kong	44	6	Chile	19	36
Iraq	40	7	Nigeria	19	37
Germany	39	8	Azerbaijan	18	38
Japan	38	9	Slovenia	18	39
Kazakhstan	38	10	Morocco	16	40
United States	38	11	Palestine	16	41
Yemen	38	12	Tunisia	16	42
Thailand	37	13	Georgia	15	43
Bahrain	34	14	Romania	15	44
Estonia	32	15	Algeria	14	45
India	32	16	Uzbekistan	14	46
South Korea	30	17	Turkey	12	47
Taiwan	30	18	Colombia	11	48
Kuwait	29	19	Rwanda	11	49
Kyrgyzstan	28	20	Lebanon	10	50
Russia	28	21	Libya	10	51
Singapore	28	22	Zimbabwe	10	52
Belarus	27	23	Cyprus	9	53
Egypt	27	24	Malaysia	9	54
Spain	26	25	Brazil	8	55
Ukraine	26	26	Peru	8	56
Pakistan	25	27	Ecuador	7	57
Jordan	24	28	Ghana	7	58
Poland	22	29	Philippines	6	59
Mexico	21	30	Trinidad and Tobago	4	60

Note: The data are based on each country or economy's average percentage of respondents who agreed with the statement "Most people can be trusted" in the WVS in various waves from 1981 to 2014.

A distinctive feature of China's economic transition in the 1980s and early 1990s was that rural TVEs were the most dynamic driving force of economic growth.[33] A TVE was in principle a firm collectively owned by all residents of a township or village, but was in reality a vaguely defined cooperative with ambiguous property rights.[34] The success of TVEs poses a puzzle to economic theory: How could such enterprises without well-defined property rights perform so well in driving economic growth? In a pioneering article on this important question, economists Martin Weitzman and Chenggang Xu attributed the success of TVEs to China's cooperative culture of trusting others. For them, in a cooperative society characterized by a high level of trust, people may be able to do business with others and make relationship-specific investments even without well-defined formal ownership.[35] Unsurprisingly, their article was much criticized by mainstream institutional economists at the time.

In China, *guanxi*, or personal connections in society, plays an outsized role in business dealings. In a seminal paper, management scholars Katherine Xin and Jone Pearce (1996) argued that *guanxi* acts as a substitute for formal institutional support in a legal environment with weak protection of private property rights. They showed that Chinese private business executives were more dependent on *guanxi* for business than their SOE counterparts and trusted their connections more. Trust is the foundation of *guanxi*, which has enabled China's private sector to prosper after market reforms.

CAN CHINA'S GROWTH EXPERIENCE BE EMULATED?

If China's rapid growth was the result of superior institutions or clever industrial policies, other countries could learn from its experience. Some economists indeed believe that the development experiences of China and other East Asian economies can be distilled into policy recommendations for other developing countries. Most notably,

---

[33] See, e.g., Walder (1995).   [34] See Weitzman and Xu (1994) and Li (1996).
[35] Weitzman and Xu (1994).

Justin Lin and his associates at Peking University have advocated the view that developing countries can learn from China's example and achieve rapid catch-up growth by actively promoting industries compatible with their comparative advantages. According to this view, the main reason most developing countries have not achieved rapid growth is because they have adopted the wrong policies for economic development.[36] In other words, if only they knew the right approach to development, all developing countries would have grown like China. Now, finally, a few Chinese economists have found the magic bullet for development, and any country willing to follow their advice will soon be on the path to prosperity, or so it seems. However, how likely is it that all East Asian economies influenced by Confucian culture have discovered the right approach to economic development, apparently without much guidance from economic theory, whereas other developing countries have to wait for some Chinese economists to teach them a new theory to help them develop their economies? One must have enormous confidence in his or her theory to entertain such a possibility.

In this book, I argue that China's comparative strength in its economic development lies in its Confucian culture that emphasizes hard work, savings, education, trust, and benevolent government. It is this traditional culture that has differentiated China and other East Asian economies from most other developing countries. For this reason, Chinese-style growth cannot be easily emulated.[37] Some Chinese practices such as special economic zones (SEZs) may be replicated, but there is no easy way to raise a country's savings rate, education quality, or trust level. This is not to say that a developing country whose culture does not place as much emphasis on savings and education as Confucian culture cannot achieve catch-up growth. A cultural explanation for extraordinary growth is not cultural

---

[36] See Lin (2014).

[37] From a different angle, economist Barry Naughton (2010) wrote that "the specific character of the Chinese system and the way in which government and business relations have been structured cannot be readily replicated in other countries."

determinism as some critics may believe. It is conceivable that with the right conditions and institutions, any developing country could achieve a sustainable annual growth rate of 3 percent or more of per capita GDP. Given time, it will eventually catch up to developed countries that have a long-term growth rate of 1–2 percent.

Culture is generally sticky and changes very slowly.[38] The late Nobel laureate in economics Oliver Williamson identified four levels of social analysis, and at the top level are culture and other informal institutions, which are taken as fixed by institutional economists because they change very slowly – on the order of centuries or millennia.[39] Therefore, critics may argue that a cultural theory of development has no practical value because there is little we can do with culture. However, cultural values do change and some change faster than others.[40] It is not clear whether the culture of savings and education can be cultivated in a few decades or one to two generations. Some culturalists have indeed attempted to persuade policymakers in developing countries and international development agencies to encourage cultural changes that promote values favorable to economic growth.[41] But their voices have had very little impact in both academia and the real world.

If economic growth is the primary goal of development, and if culture is an obstacle to growth, then promoting cultural change may be a worthwhile endeavor. No matter how difficult it is to change culture, we must first acknowledge the role of culture. Otherwise, changes will not even be attempted. If enough people, especially experts, opinion leaders, and policymakers, recognize the fundamental importance of culture in economic development, then perhaps cultural change will become possible under concerted efforts.

---

[38] Economist Gerard Roland (2004) classified institutions into "slow-moving" and "fast-moving" institutions. His main example of a slow-moving institution is culture, including values, beliefs, and social norms.

[39] Williamson (2000).

[40] See, e.g., Inglehart (1997) and Giavazzi, Petkov, and Schiantarelli (2019).

[41] See Harrison (2000, 2008) and Harrison and Huntington (2000).

However, economic growth is not the only goal of life, and it is not even the only goal of development in Amartya Sen's sense of the removal of unfreedoms.[42] Therefore, a culture conducive to economic development is not necessarily a superior culture. If fast economic growth comes at a high cost to individual well-being or the environment, slower growth may be a good thing. People have long known that economic growth has no necessary bearing on happiness. Economist Richard Easterlin showed many years ago that although high-income people are on average happier than low-income people in a country, increasing the country's income level does not increase overall happiness.[43] In fact, the *World Happiness Report 2020* ranks China 94th out of 153 countries, well below many countries that have both lower incomes and lower growth.[44] Economist Charles Kenny noted that although economic growth has been slow in most developing countries, almost all of them have made significant progress in indicators that reflect people's well-being and quality of life, such as health, life expectancy, and educational opportunities.[45]

---

[42] See Sen (1999).   [43] Easterlin (1974, 1995).

[44] See *World Happiness Report 2020* at https://happiness-report.s3.amazonaws.com/2020/WHR20.pdf.

[45] Kenny (2005).

8   Why Is China Slowing Down?

China's economic growth has fallen sharply in recent years, with its GDP per capita growth rate dropping from 10.1% in 2010 to 5.8% in 2019, the lowest rate since 1990. The average annual growth of GDP per capita over the seven years after 2012 (i.e., 2013–2019) fell to 6.5% compared with the average growth rate of 10.0% during the 2003–2012 period. The long-term average annual growth rate between 1982 and 2012 was 9.1%. Why is China slowing down? Is it caused by cyclical, external factors or by internal structural problems? Is the slowdown inevitable now that the size of the economy is already very large and its per capita income has reached such a level that high growth is becoming difficult, if not impossible? Could it be that China is falling into the so-called middle-income trap?

THE MYTH OF THE MIDDLE-INCOME TRAP

On April 24, 2015, in a speech at the prestigious Tsinghua University, Lou Jiwei, then minister of finance, predicted that China had a 50 percent chance of falling into the middle-income trap in the next five to ten years. It was a very unusual statement for a high-ranking government official and caused quite a stir in the media.[1] Yet even before this controversial speech, the term "middle-income trap" had already gone viral in China. This fatalistic sounding idea had struck a nerve among policymakers, economists, and the general public in the country. As its name suggests, the middle-income trap refers to a situation in which a country is trapped in a middle-income status, unable to become a high-income economy. The term was first used

---

[1] See a news report in Chinese available at www.guancha.cn/economy/2015_04_26_317372.shtml.

casually by two World Bank economists in a bank report published in 2007 without defining it. In a follow-up article almost ten years after its popularization, especially in China, the two authors clarified the meaning of the concept.[2] The idea was based on the observation that many countries in Latin America and the Middle East were stuck in their middle-income status, with lackluster growth for many years. These middle-income countries had lost their competitive advantage in labor costs and could no longer rely on traditional labor-intensive industries to compete with low-income countries. They also lacked sufficient innovative capacity to compete with high-income developed countries. However, the two authors did not believe that the middle-income trap was fate, some economies having managed to get out of it, notably the four Asian Tigers.

Although the creators of the concept did not discuss economic growth in low-income and high-income economies, later proponents have suggested explicitly or implicitly that it is much easier for a country to move from a low-income level to a middle-income level, than from a middle-income level to a high-income level.[3] In other words, low-income countries generally grow faster than middle-income countries. For the concept to make sense, this should be the case. Indeed, if growth is not related to the income level, the concepts of middle-income trap or low-income trap lose their meaning.

The middle-income trap thesis is widely accepted in China and has generated a small but still substantial body of literature in academia.[4] However, I have not seen any studies on the middle-income trap published in top-tier economics journals. This seems to cast doubt on the validity and usefulness of the concept in the study of economic growth and development. Some Chinese economists, including myself, have also questioned the use of the concept, in particular its applicability in the Chinese context.[5] So, is there really

---

[2] Gill and Kharas (2007, 2015).   [3] See, e.g., Agénor, Canuto, and Jelenic (2012).
[4] See, e.g., Cai (2012), Felipe, Kumar, and Galope (2017) and references therein.
[5] See, e.g., Zhu (2015).

Table 8.1 *World Bank's income group thresholds (in US$)*

Year	Low Income	Lower Middle Income	Upper Middle Income	High Income
1987	≤480	481–1,940	1,941–6,000	≥6,001
1992	≤675	676–2,695	2,696–8,355	≥8,356
1997	≤785	786–3,125	3,126–9,655	≥9,656
2002	≤735	736–2,935	2,936–9,075	≥9,076
2007	≤935	936–3,705	3,706–11,455	≥11,456
2012	≤1,035	1,036–4,085	4,086–12,615	≥12,616
2018	≤1,025	1,026–3,995	3,996–12,375	≥12,376

Note: The data comes from the World Bank's website: https://datahelpdesk.worldbank.org/knowledgebase/articles/378833-how-are-the income-group-thresholds-determined.

a middle-income trap? More importantly, is China falling into this trap?

Since 1988, the World Bank has divided all member countries or territories into low-income, middle-income (further divided into lower middle-income and upper middle-income), and high-income economies. As noted in Chapter 1, low- and middle-income countries or economies are collectively referred to as developing countries or economies. It is in this sense that I use the terms "developed" and "developing" in this book. The classification criteria are based on a country's gross national income or GNI per capita in US dollars, similar to GDP per capita. The World Bank adjusts its income criteria over time based on inflation rates in several major developed countries. Table 8.1 presents the World Bank's income group thresholds for selected years.

Under the 2018 criteria, about 36% of the countries or territories in the world (eighty in total) belonged to the high-income group; 27% to the upper middle-income group (sixty in total); 23% to the lower middle-income group (forty-seven in total); and 14% to the low-income group (thirty-one in total). That is, half of the countries or territories were middle-income economies. China's GDP per capita in

2018 was US$9,780 and was therefore an upper middle-income econ-
omy. The minimum standard of US$12,376 for high-income status
was in fact not high, but well below the average income of all
developed economies, and only 20 percent of the US level.

Table 8.1 shows that the initial threshold for high-income
status in 1988 was US$6,001 in 1987 GNI per capita, about 28 percent
of the US level that year. In 2018, it rose to US$12,376, but it was only
20 percent of the US level. This means that the World Bank used
absolute income rather than relative income for its grouping. If the
World Bank continues to use this criterion, as long as a country's
inflation-adjusted real growth rate is greater than 0, it will eventually
become a high-income country; thus, there will be no such thing as a
middle-income trap. There were only forty-one high-income economies in 1988, as defined by the World Bank, while there were eighty
in 2018, indicating that thirty-nine middle-income economies managed to become high-income economies in three decades. Therefore,
based on the World Bank's criteria or any absolute income criteria
used by some researchers, there is obviously no middle-income trap.

For the concept of middle-income trap to make sense, only
relative income criteria should be used to classify high-, middle-,
and low-income economies. Shortly, I use the United States as a
benchmark for a high-income economy and measure a country's relative income by its GDP per capita as a percentage of the US level. If a
developing country wants to catch up to developed countries, its rate
of economic growth must be faster than that of developed countries.
In other words, the relative income of developing countries must
maintain positive growth to reduce the gap with the United States.

In what follows, I propose a relative income criterion to classify
economies into three income levels and show whether there is a
middle-income trap by examining growth performance in the world
over the last fifty years. I classify as low-income economies all countries whose GDP per capita is less than 5% of the US level, which
translates into an income less than US$3,140 in 2018. All countries
with GDP per capita above 30% of the US level, which represents

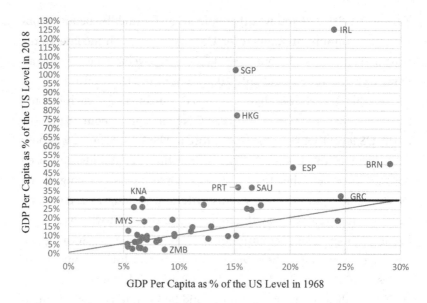

FIGURE 8.1 Change in the relative income of middle-income economies
Data source: World Development Indicators

more than US$18,840 in income in 2018, are classified as high-income
economies. Finally, all countries with GDP per capita between 5%
and 30% of the US level are classified as middle-income economies.
My criterion of middle- and high-income status is higher than that of
the World Bank in 2018, but closer to its level in 1988. This criterion
is of course arbitrary, but I believe that any reasonable relative income
criterion would give us qualitatively similar results.[6]

In the World Bank's World Development Indicators database,
113 economies have data on GDP per capita for the period between
1968 and 2018. There were forty-four middle-income economies in
1968 based on my criterion. How many of them became high-income
economies in 2018? The answer is nine, as shown in Figure 8.1. Each
point represents an economy; the horizontal axis indicates the relative income level in 1968 measured by GDP per capita as a percentage

---

[6] I also used PPP-adjusted GDP per capita figures from the Penn World Table data set
to calculate relative income levels and obtained qualitatively similar results.

of the US level, and the vertical axis is the relative income level in 2018. For example, Singapore's position in the figure indicates that its GDP per capita was around 15 percent of the US level in 1968, but was slightly above the US level in 2018. The figure shows that nine dots are above the thick horizontal line of 30 percent, which means that by my criterion, these nine economies had reached high-income status by 2018. These are the two oil-rich economies of Saudi Arabia and Brunei; the four European economies of Ireland, Spain, Portugal, and Greece; the two East Asian economies of Singapore and Hong Kong; and a small tourist attraction in the Caribbean, St. Kitts and Nevis. Among these economies, Ireland, Spain, Greece, and Brunei already had an income level above 20 percent of the US level in 1968.

Thus, only 20 percent of the middle-income economies have joined the ranks of high-income economies in the past fifty years, and the majority of them have retained their middle-income status. Most of these countries are located in Latin America and the Caribbean. Moreover, twelve of the middle-income economies in 1968, represented by the dots at the bottom right of the diagonal in Figure 8.1, grew more slowly than the United States in the following fifty years. As a result, their relative income level has declined compared with that of the United States. An extreme example is that of Zambia (ZMB in the figure), which started with an income level of more than 8 percent of the US level in 1968, but fell to only 2.5 percent in 2018. In addition to Zambia, four countries, Zimbabwe, Nicaragua, Cote d'Ivoire, and Senegal, started at a middle-income level in 1968 but joined the low-income group in 2018.

These results seem to confirm the existence of a middle-income trap. However, it should be noted that the countries represented by the dots at the top left of the diagonal in Figure 8.1 all grew faster than the United States. There are thirty-two of them, or 73 percent of all economies classified as middle income in 1968. Some of these economies grew much faster than the United States. For example, Malaysia (MYS in the figure) started with a relative income level of about 7 percent of the US level in 1968, but reached almost 20 percent

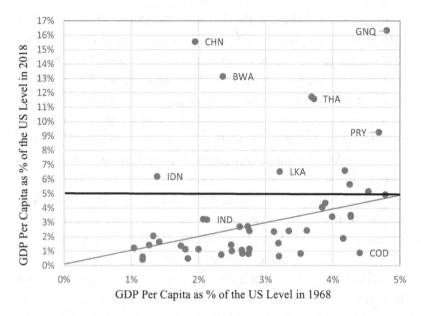

FIGURE 8.2 Change in the relative income of low-income economies
Data source: World Development Indicators

in 2018. Given time, these economies will reach the high-income level in the foreseeable future.

The real question then is whether the stagnation and even decline in relative income growth in many middle-income countries really has anything to do with their middle-income status. What about low-income countries – do they generally grow faster? The answer is a categorical no. The relative income level of most low-income countries did not increase between 1968 and 2018, but actually declined.

Figure 8.2 shows the changing pattern in relative income between 1968 and 2018 for forty-seven economies classified as low income in 1968. Only twelve were above the middle-income threshold of 5 percent of the US level in 2018, including South Korea, China, Thailand, Indonesia, and the two resource-rich economies of Botswana and Equatorial Guinea (GNQ in the figure). South Korea, not shown in the figure, went from a low-income country in 1968 (at 4.2% of the US level) to a high-income country at 50% of the US level in 2018. I omitted South Korea in Figure 8.2 to make the graph more readable. Ten economies, represented by the dots at the top left of the diagonal, below the 5% thick line in Figure 8.2, all grew faster than the United States. For example, India (IND in the figure) started with a relative income level slightly above 2% of the US level in 1968, but it went above 3% in 2018.

However, it may be shocking to some readers that more than half of the low-income economies (twenty-five in total), represented by the dots at the bottom right of the diagonal in Figure 8.2, grew more slowly than the United States, leading to lower relative income compared with that of the United States. For example, the Democratic Republic of the Congo (COD in the figure, formerly Zaire) started with a relative income of 4.4 percent of the US level in 1968, but this fell to less than 1 percent in 2018. Compared with the case of middle-income economies, the majority of which have grown faster than the United States, the probability of a low-income trap is higher than that of a middle-income trap. The term "middle-income trap" often gives people a false impression that it is easier for a country to go from low income to middle income than from middle income to high income. Judging from the two sets of data just displayed, it is the exact opposite!

If the term "trap" is to be used to refer to stagnant economic growth in developing countries, this trap has nothing to do with whether a country has a low- or middle-income level. The fact is that economic growth in most developing countries is not much faster than that of developed countries, resulting in slow or no growth, or even a decline in their relative income levels. In the last sixty years, other than a few resource-rich economies, only a handful of East Asian economies have grown rapidly by more than 6 percent per year for thirty years or more. In addition, with the exception of China, which began the process two decades later and with a lower initial income base, all have successfully transitioned from low income (e.g., South Korea) or middle income (e.g., Singapore) to high-income developed economies (see Table 1.6 in Chapter 1).

Table 8.2 *Episodes of rapid growth: A comparison between East Asia and Latin America*

	Average Annual Growth Rate of GDP Per Capita over Thirty Years of Rapid Growth	Average Annual Growth Rate of GDP Per Capita over Twenty Years of Rapid Growth	Average Annual Growth Rate of GDP Per Capita over Ten Years of Rapid Growth
Chile	3.8% (1982–2012)	4.5% (1983–2003)	6.1% (1987–1997)
Brazil	2.8% (1960–1990)	4.6% (1960–1980)	6.9% (1966–1976)
Singapore	6.9% (1964–1994)	7.7% (1964–1984)	9.4% (1964–1974)
South Korea	6.7% (1965–1995)	6.7% (1975–1995)	7.9% (1981–1991)
China	9.1% (1982–2012)	9.6% (1991–2011)	10% (2001–2011)

Data source: World Development Indicators.

It is instructive to compare East Asia with Latin America in terms of economic growth over the past sixty years. Many Latin American countries are prime examples of economies that supposedly grew rapidly to reach the middle-income level, then stagnated and got stuck in the middle-income trap. Yet, the fact is that no Latin American economy has ever sustained East Asian–style rapid growth for more than twenty years. In terms of average annual growth rate over thirty consecutive years after 1960, the fastest growing Latin American country was Chile, with a GDP per capita growth rate of 3.8% between 1982 and 2012, as shown in Table 8.2, making Chile the Latin American country with the highest per capita income. This growth rate was much lower than that of Singapore at 6.9% (1964–1994); South Korea at 6.7% (1965–1995); and China at 9.1% (1982–2012). For the average growth rate over twenty consecutive years, Table 8.2 shows that Brazil was once the fastest growing country in Latin America, with a GDP per capita growth rate of 4.6% between 1960 and 1980, which was again much lower than that of Singapore at 7.7% (1964–1984); South Korea at 6.7% (1975–1995); and

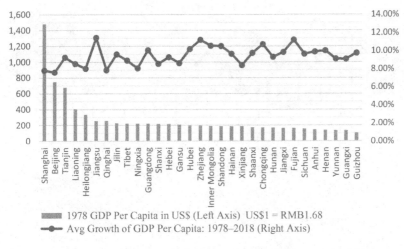

FIGURE 8.3 Economic growth across Chinese provinces: 1978–2018
Note: Based on official NBS data from the CEIC database.

China at 9.6% (1991–2011). For the fastest growth rate over ten consecutive years, East Asian economies also significantly outperformed the two fastest growing countries in Latin America.

The concept of the middle-income trap is particularly inapt when applied to the Chinese economy, with its immense regional disparities in economic development. China is larger in terms of population than the continents of Africa, America, and Europe, and the differences in the level of development between Chinese provinces are no smaller than those between Latin American countries. Figure 8.3 shows the growth performance of the Chinese provinces between 1978 and 2018. All provinces experienced rapid growth during these four decades.

If any Chinese province had been an independent country, it would have been one of the fastest growing countries in the world. In fact, Shanghai and Beijing, the two most developed regional economies in China, have experienced slower per capita GDP growth than the rest of the country in the past forty years. As a result, other provinces have been catching up with Shanghai and Beijing, as can be seen by comparing the bar chart in Figure 8.3 with that in

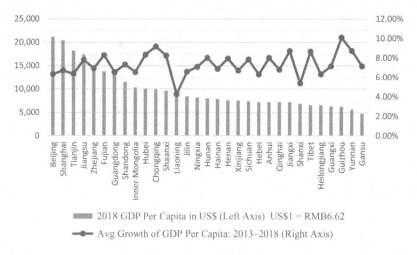

FIGURE 8.4 Income level and growth across Chinese provinces: 2013–2018
Note: Based on official NBS data from the CEIC database.

Figure 8.4. In 1978, the gap between Shanghai's GDP per capita and that of Guizhou, the poorest province at the time, was more than 14 to 1, but in 2018, the gap narrowed to less than 4 to 1. Other than that, economic growth across Chinese provinces during the 1978–2018 period had no correlation with the level of income in 1978.

Based on GDP per capita data for 2018, as Figure 8.4 shows, seven of the thirty-one provincial economies in China already had a high-income level, and some were close to reaching it, as defined by the World Bank. The rest were all at the upper-middle income level. Even between 2013 and 2018, the years of economic slowdown in China, economic growth across Chinese provinces was relatively rapid compared with that of other countries in the world. Again, there was no statistically significant correlation between growth and income level. There were no low-, middle-, or high-income traps in China. It is very likely that in just ten years, two thirds of China's provinces will reach the World Bank's high-income threshold.

The Nobel laureate in economics Amartya Sen said it well: "I don't think there is a middle-income trap. People should identify the causes of the economic slowdown and not use one concept to explain everything."[7] Indeed, the concept of middle-income trap tends to blur the huge differences between middle-income economies, leading people to simplistically link economic growth with income level without looking for the real causes of cross-country differences in economic performance.

EXPLAINING THE SLOWDOWN: EXTERNAL, STRUCTURAL, AND POLICY FACTORS

If the middle-income trap is not the reason, what is causing China's economic slowdown? Is the slowdown cyclical or structural? Or is it something else entirely? Economists, as usual, have not reached consensus.[8]

In Chapter 4, I distinguished between long-term economic growth and short-term economic fluctuations. A country's long-term growth trend is determined by supply-side factors, while short-term fluctuations are mostly determined by demand-side factors. Economic growth is never smooth sailing, and cyclical fluctuations in growth rates are a normal part of economic life. Figure 8.5 shows that although the Chinese economy has grown at an average rate of 8.5 percent over the past forty years, it has experienced four cycles of upturns and downturns. During the same period, the United States and the European Uunion, both with an average growth rate of 1.7 percent per year, experienced a similar number of economic recessions, while the Indian economy experienced more frequent fluctuations. Although economic fluctuations are inevitable, appropriate policies can mitigate them, while bad policies can exacerbate their effects, prolong recessions, and delay recovery.

---

[7] Translated by the author from Chinese based on a quote from Professor Sen in a news report on his speech at Peking University on February 25, 2016. See http://news .hexun.com/2016-02-26/182442302.html.

[8] The English-language journal *Frontiers of Economics in China* covered the topic in its first issue in 2019 (volume 14, issue 1), which included articles by prominent Chinese economists Justin Lin, a proponent of the external factor argument, and Guoqiang Tian, an advocate of the structural argument.

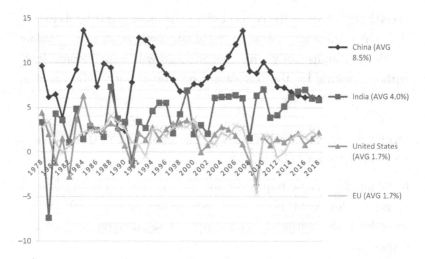

FIGURE 8.5 Economic fluctuations: GDP per capita growth, 1978–2018 (%)
Data source: World Development Indicators

The 2008–2009 global financial crisis plunged developed countries into the worst economic recession since WWII. In 2009, the growth rates of GDP per capita in the United States, Japan, and the European Union were –3.4%, –5.4%, and –4.6%, respectively. In the same year, China adopted a massive 4-trillion-yuan stimulus policy and was able to achieve a per capita growth rate of 8.9%, still well below its peak growth of 13.6% in 2007.[9] Without this stimulus policy, China's economy would certainly have experienced a sharp downturn.[10] The global economy started to recover in 2010, with the Chinese economy following suit. However, the debt crisis in some European countries caused a new recession in the European Union in 2012. As a result, the growth rate of Chinese exports to the European Union fell sharply. China's GDP per capita growth rate also fell from

---

[9] The GDP growth rate initially announced for 2007 was 11.4%, which was revised upward by 2.8 percentage points several years later to 14.2% (i.e., 13.6% growth per capita) after a national economic census found that the value added in the service sector was underestimated in the previous GDP accounting.

[10] See Naughton (2009, 2018).

9.0% in 2011 to 7.3% in 2012, the slowest since 1999. Instead of recovering in 2013 or after, the decline continued, with per capita growth slipping to 5.8% in 2019.

The slowdown in economic growth after the global financial crisis is not unique to China, but rather a general trend worldwide. In terms of growth rates, the world economy has never recovered from the crisis, as Table 8.3 clearly shows; far from it. In the table, I compare global economic growth between two eight-year periods before and after the financial crisis, 2000–2007 and 2011–2018.[11] It is evident that except for India, all other countries and regions in the table experienced a decline in economic growth after the financial crisis. In Japan and the United States, the decline in growth was moderate, but everywhere else, the decline was very significant. Two BRICS countries (Brazil and Russia) and the developing regions of Latin America, the Middle East, and sub-Saharan Africa all experienced a more marked slowdown relative to their long-term growth trend than China.

In a globalized world, the economic slowdown of other countries will negatively affect China's growth via trade links, and vice versa. Indeed, the global financial crisis has significantly slowed the growth of exports and imports around the world, as shown in Table 8.4. Before the crisis, China's exports of goods increased by 23.9 percent per year, but they fell to only 5 percent per year after the crisis, the largest decline among all countries or regions in the table. Naturally, China's exports represent other countries' imports. As a result, import growth fell across the board and sharply in most places.

Therefore, the global economic slowdown since the financial crisis, an important external factor, has clearly contributed to China's slowdown in growth.[12] What about internal factors? Some economists have attributed China's economic slowdown to internal supply-side

[11] To make the comparison more meaningful and symmetric, I eliminated three outlier years: 2008 and 2009, the two years of the crisis, and 2010, the recovery year immediately after the crisis. But the comparison of 2009–2018 and 1999–2008 yields similar results.

[12] See Lin (2019).

Table 8.3 *GDP per capita growth before and after the global financial crisis (%)*

Country or Region	Average Growth (1978–2018)	Pre-crisis Growth (2000–2007 Average)	Post-Crisis Growth (2011–2018 Average)	Change in Growth Rate
Brazil	1.0	2.4	–0.3	–2.6
China	8.5	9.9	6.9	–3.0
India	4.0	4.8	5.6	0.9
Japan	1.9	1.3	1.2	–0.1
South Korea	5.3	4.8	2.4	–2.4
Russia	0.8	7.6	1.2	–6.4
United Kingdom	1.8	2.3	1.2	–1.1
United States	1.7	1.7	1.5	–0.3
European Union	1.7	2.2	1.3	–0.9
Latin America and the Caribbean	1.1	2.1	0.7	–1.5
Middle East and North Africa (excluding high income)	0.5	2.8	0.7	–2.1
Sub-Saharan Africa	0.2	2.7	0.6	–2.1
World	1.5	2.2	1.7	–0.6

Data source: World Development Indicators.

structural causes, such as the disappearance of its demographic dividend, insufficient innovation, and delays or even reversals in market-oriented institutional reforms.[13] It is indeed true that China's economic slowdown coincided with the beginning of negative growth in the working-age population, which, according to official statistics, fell from an average rate of 0.9% during the 2006–2012 period to an

---

[13] See, e.g., Magnus (2018) and Tian (2019).

Table 8.4 *Export and import growth before and after the global financial crisis*

Country or Region	Exports of Goods and Services (Annual Percentage of Real Growth)			Imports of Goods and Services (Annual Percentage of Real Growth)		
	Pre-crisis Growth (2000–2007 Average)	Post-Crisis Growth (2011–2018 Average)	Decline in Growth	Pre-crisis Growth (2000–2007 Average)	Post-Crisis Growth (2011–2018 Average)	Decline in Growth
Brazil	9.3	2.8	-6.5	6.9	0.5	-6.5
China	23.9	5.0	-18.9	18.9	5.8	-13.1
India	16.6	6.1	-10.5	14.9	6.3	-8.6
Japan	8.0	3.1	-4.9	4.4	3.6	-0.8
South Korea	11.9	4.4	-7.5	11.0	4.4	-6.6
Russia	8.6	3.0	-5.5	21.3	2.2	-19.1
United Kingdom	4.6	2.7	-1.9	5.4	3.1	-2.3
United States	4.7	3.2	-1.6	5.7	3.9	-1.8
European Union	6.2	4.2	-2.0	6.2	3.8	-2.4
Latin America and the Caribbean	5.1	2.8	-2.3	6.9	2.6	-4.4
Middle East and North Africa	6.7	3.7	-3.0	9.5	1.7	-7.8
Sub-Saharan Africa (excluding high income)	7.6	3.2	-4.3	12.0	2.9	-9.1
World	6.5	3.9	-2.6	7.1	3.7	-3.4

Note: In the case of China, the growth rates are for imports and exports of goods only without services. China does not report real growth in exports and imports of goods and services. The author calculated China's real growth in imports and exports of goods by subtracting the relevant price indices from nominal growth rates based on data from *China Statistical Yearbook 2019*. The real growth of China's imports and exports of services cannot be calculated because there are no relevant price indices. However, services represent less than 15 percent of China's total imports and exports. All other figures were calculated using data from the World Development Indicators database.

average rate of –0.2% during the 2013–2019 period. This could have reduced the GDP growth rate by 1 percentage point. However, official statistics show that the economically active population (or the labor force) experienced barely any change in growth, dropping from an average rate of 0.5% during the 2006–2012 period to an average rate of 0.4% during the 2013–2019 period.[14] Therefore, if demographic change played a role in the recent economic slowdown, it was a relatively minor one. As for insufficient innovation, Chapter 6 showed that China's ability to innovate has in fact grown rapidly in recent years.

There is a widespread feeling among commentators inside and outside China that market-oriented reforms have stalled or even reversed and that the state has struck back in recent years.[15] However, the Chinese economic system has not become significantly less market-oriented than before. The slow pace of reform is nothing new according to Barry Naughton, who wrote that "after about 2005, the Chinese government's commitment to market-oriented reform was noticeably scaled back."[16] Nevertheless, the Chinese economy grew rapidly between 2005 and 2012 despite the 2008 global financial crisis. However, perhaps it is not the reality of anti-market reform but its perception that matters more. If many economists felt this way, then many business owners and executives would have felt the same, which would affect their investment decisions and therefore economic growth.

In any case, China's recent economic downturn may be attributed partly to the aforementioned supply-side problems, but the sharp drop in growth within a few years should be mainly studied from the demand side. Figure 8.6 shows the growth trajectories of the three demand factors of consumption, investment, and exports between 2011 and 2018. All fell sharply after 2013, but the decline in

[14] These average rates are the author's calculations based on data from the CEIC data set.
[15] See, e.g., Shambaugh (2016), Economy (2018), Lardy (2019), and Tian (2019).
[16] Naughton (2018), p. 31.

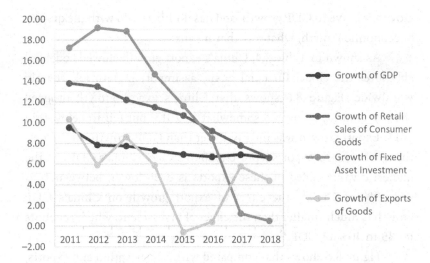

FIGURE 8.6 China's consumption, investment, and export growth: 2011–2018 (%)

Note: (1) For consumption and investment, I chose not to use final consumption expenditure and gross capital formation, the two key components of expenditure-based GDP, but instead used data on the retail sales of consumer goods and fixed asset investment. The reason is that, as explained in Chapter 4 and the Appendix, China's expenditure-based GDP accounting is deeply flawed, underestimating consumption and overestimating investment; (2) All growth rates are real rates after adjustment for the relevant price indices. The growth rates of retail sales of consumer goods and fixed asset investment for most years come from *China Statistical Yearbook 2019*. In the absence of official data, the author calculated real growth rates by subtracting the relevant price indices from nominal growth rates.

consumption growth was smaller than that in GDP growth, and until 2018, consumption growth was significantly faster than GDP growth. This indicates that consumption has not been the force dragging down China's GDP growth, but that slower GDP growth has slowed the country's consumption growth. In fact, consumption as a percentage of GDP has increased as a result. This phenomenon is often cited by the NBS and government officials as evidence that the "quality" of China's growth has improved in recent years. In reality, it is simply a mathematical result of the sharper decline in investment and export growth relative to GDP growth, and has nothing to do with the quality of economic growth, whatever that means.

As shown in Table 8.4, China's export growth slowed considerably after the global financial crisis, as import growth fell sharply worldwide. Figure 8.6 shows that China's export growth dropped sharply in 2012, recovered somewhat in 2013, but fell to below 0 in 2015. Export growth was mostly lower than GDP growth throughout the downturn. As exports represent 20 to 25% of China's GDP and the domestic value added in these exports is even lower, between 15% and 20% of GDP,[17] the effect of export growth on China's GDP growth is much smaller than the effect of investment, which accounts for 35 to 40% of GDP.[18]

Figure 8.6 shows that compared with consumption and exports, China's fixed asset investment growth declined much more dramatically, from 18.8% in 2013 to just 0.5% in 2018. This clearly shows that the most important driver of China's economic slowdown has been a nosedive in fixed asset investment growth. Given the precipitous drop in investment and export growth, the decline of China's official GDP per capita growth rate from 7.2% in 2013 to 6.1% in 2018 appears too small to be credible. According to some economists, China's GDP growth rate in recent years may have been overestimated by as much as 2 percentage points, meaning that the economic downturn may be more severe than the official growth rate suggests.[19]

So, what has caused the free fall in China's investment growth? My own research has suggested two major causes. First, after 2013, when the new leadership came to power, there was a significant shift in policy orientation. China's policy goals became more diversified. Instead of pursuing GDP growth single-mindedly as in the past, the

---

[17] According to OECD data, the ratio of domestic value added in gross exports is around 80 percent for China. See data on the website https://data.oecd.org/trade/domestic-value-added-in-gross-exports.htm.

[18] The official investment rate is between 45 and 50 percent of GDP, but as shown in Chapter 4, China's investment rate may be overestimated by 10 percent of GDP.

[19] See Chen et al. (2019) and Lai and Zhu (2020).

new leadership began to pay more attention to major political and social issues such as corruption and pollution, launching a massive anti-corruption campaign and a sweeping anti-pollution campaign.[20] Many government officials at the central, provincial, and local levels were charged with corruption, and many polluting factories were shut down or scaled back. The resulting cooldown in investment and economic growth was only natural, but it may be a worthy trade-off if a cleaner environment and less corruption can be achieved by sacrificing some economic growth.[21] Shanxi Province is a case in point. On the one hand, Shanxi is a major coal producer and was therefore severely affected by the anti-pollution campaign. On the other hand, Shanxi was also the province with the highest number of provincial officials investigated and charged with corruption during the anti-corruption campaign.[22] National GDP growth between 2014 and 2016 averaged 7.0%, 3.4 percentage points lower than that of the previous decade (2004–2013), while Shanxi Province's growth was only 4.2%, 7.6 percentage points lower than the previous decade. Similarly, growth in the Inner Mongolia Autonomous Region, another major coal producer, fell by 9.2 percentage points in the 2014–2016 period compared with the 2004–2013 period.

The second cause for the slowdown is that China's macroeconomic policies after 2015 became unduly contractionary. We saw in Figure 8.6 that both investment and export growth fell sharply in 2014 and 2015, leading to sluggish economic growth. In 2015, GDP growth fell below 7 percent for the first time since 1990. In this case, the normal course of action would have been to adopt countercyclical – that is, more expansionary fiscal and monetary policies to

---

[20] See, e.g., Economy (2018).

[21] See Bai, Hsieh, and Song (2020) for a theory on why the anti-corruption campaign may have partly led to China's economic slowdown.

[22] According to the website of the Central Commission for Discipline Inspection, between mid-2013 and mid-2015 in the heat of the anti-corruption campaign, around fifty provincial-level officials were investigated nationwide, including eight from Shanxi. In comparison, only three were from the province with the second largest number of officials investigated.

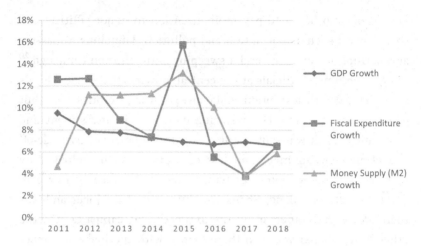

FIGURE 8.7 Fiscal expenditure and money supply growth in China: 2011–2018

Note: All growth rates are adjusted for inflation. The author calculated the real growth rates of fiscal expenditure and money supply by subtracting the GDP deflator from nominal growth rates published in *China Statistical Yearbook 2019*.

stimulate economic growth. However, in 2016, China launched procyclical contractionary macroeconomic control measures, aimed at reducing overcapacity and corporate debt levels as part of supply-side structural reforms.[23] Figure 8.7 shows that in 2016 and 2017, China's fiscal expenditure and money supply (M2) growth plummeted, and in 2017, both were significantly lower than GDP growth. Such contractionary fiscal and monetary policies could only worsen rather than turn around the country's economic slowdown during the 2013–2015 period.

CONFUSED DIAGNOSIS AND PROCYCLICAL POLICIES

Why did China, at a time when its economy was clearly already in a downturn, choose to adopt a procyclical contractionary policy

---

[23] A procyclical policy is one that is expansionary when the economy is in the expansion phase in a business cycle and contractionary when the economy is in the recession phase. This type of policy amplifies the business cycle and makes it worse. A countercyclical policy is one that goes against the business cycle and makes the cycle smoother.

package in 2016? The reason is quite ironic: Policymakers misdiagnosed the real problems faced by the Chinese economy at the time, blaming excess supply, not insufficient demand, for the downturn. They were influenced by economists and pundits inside and outside of China who were critical of its investment-led growth model and believed that the country's monetary policy was too loose and its level of debt too high.

In Chapter 4, I showed that the factors influencing economic fluctuations are different from those determining long-term economic growth. The former are three demand-side factors – investment, consumption, and exports – while the latter are three supply-side factors – investment, education, and technological progress. Only investment is common to both sets of factors, as investment creates short-term demand and long-term supply capacity. Therefore, it is important for both short-term and long-term growth. However, the dominant macroeconomic thinking in China and in the global media on the Chinese economy over the past decade has turned basic macroeconomics on its head: Demand-side factors are applied to explain China's past growth performance, and supply-side factors are applied to explain and deal with the recent downturn.

Specifically, because on the demand side China's investment rate is significantly higher and its consumption rate significantly lower than those of other countries (especially major developed countries), many economists and pundits have suggested that China has relied too much on investment and too little on consumption to drive growth in the past few decades, causing overcapacity in many industries and driving down prices, corporate profits, and economic growth. According to them, high investment rates have led to a very high and unsustainable level of corporate debt in China. When it comes to dealing with the recent downturn, they have suggested that stimulating demand is counterproductive in the long term, as more investment only leads to more debt and diminishing returns. According to this line of thinking, the right course of action for China in 2016 was not to stimulate demand, but to address the problem of oversupply by reducing excess capacity and deleveraging (i.e., reducing debt).[24] These policies, especially when implemented in a top-down fashion through a one-size-fits-all type of rigid administrative measure, naturally led to the collapse of investment growth, and therefore to a further slump in the economy.

China may indeed suffer from excess capacity in certain sectors. However, overcapacity is hardly the reason for the economic slowdown and more likely a result. Chinese policymakers and even some economists have apparently missed the distinction between economic fluctuations and economic growth and have confused the causes of short-term fluctuations with the drivers of long-term growth. They have made the mistake criticized in Chapter 4 and have failed to realize that it is precisely the high rate of savings and investment that is one of China's biggest advantages, enabling it to grow faster than other countries. It has not occurred to them that whether you are dealing with a short-term downturn or long-term growth, investment is always an important part of the solution.

Even economists with a good understanding of the economics of growth have sometimes underestimated the important role of investment. They have argued that long-term growth depends mainly on technological progress or, equivalently, on improving productivity, not investment. This belief is based on the standard neoclassical growth model (the Solow model) and its conclusions in the steady-state equilibrium. However, this model should not be used to analyze catch-up growth (or, to use economic jargon, "transitional" growth between equilibrium states) for developing countries, much less as a tool for analyzing short-term economic fluctuations. Technological progress, treated as a black box in the Solow model, is inseparable from capital investment, and it is difficult to differentiate their separate effects on economic growth. Capital investment is generally not used to purchase more of the same equipment and expand existing

---

[24] See Naughton (2016) for an insightful expert review from outside of China on the debate around the "supply-side structural reforms."

facilities, or to increase production of the same products, but to acquire new technologies, create new facilities, and produce new products. To catch up with developed countries, developing econ- omies will have to rely on capital investment to drive economic growth. There may be excess investment in certain industries or sectors in China for various reasons, but as China's overall capital per worker is still much lower than that of more developed countries, it is unlikely for China to have too much investment at the macro level.

Another related misunderstanding regarding the Chinese econ- omy is the belief that the country's monetary policy has been too loose, leading to an oversupply of money and credit, which in turn results in excess investment and a high level of corporate debt. According to this assessment of the financial state of the economy, China must tighten its money supply and deleverage to avoid a looming financial crisis. Indeed, Table 8.5 shows that China's broad money supply (M2) to GDP ratio reached 2.08 in 2016, among the highest in the world, more than twice that of the United States and three times the global average. In this sense, China's M2/GDP ratio seems too high. However, there is no well-accepted economic theory or evidence that a high M2/GDP ratio is bad for the economy. In fact, researchers studying economic development have often used this ratio as a measure of a country's level of financial development.[25] Table 8.5 shows that low-income sub-Saharan African countries had a very low M2/GDP ratio, while high-income OECD countries had a relatively higher M2/GDP ratio, and in financial centers, such as Hong Kong and Switzerland, the ratio was the highest. In short, the M2/GDP ratio varies enormously across countries and is affected by many factors. However, it is not necessarily correlated with economic growth, inflation, asset price bubbles, or the risk of a financial crisis. Therefore, the M2/GDP ratio is not an indicator that a country must consider when developing its monetary policy. In general, market

[25] See Naughton (2018), p. 694.

economies around the world focus on the rates of GDP growth, unemployment, and inflation when deciding whether to increase or decrease their money supply. Unless inflation exceeds a certain level, it is difficult to say that there is an oversupply of money. In fact, Argentina has had one of the lowest M2/GDP ratios at 0.28, but one of the highest inflation rates in the world in the past decade, and the country has also recently experienced a debt and currency crisis.

Once we understand what M2/GDP really means, it will not be surprising that China has a high M2/GDP ratio. M2, also known as broad money, in China includes all bank deposits plus cash in circulation. As cash only represents 4 percent of M2, the money supply is essentially synonymous with bank deposits. China has one of the highest savings rates in the world, but investment channels in nonbank financial products are relatively underdeveloped, so bank deposits are the predominant form of savings for many people. It is only natural that the country's M2/GDP ratio, which essentially means bank deposits as a percentage of national income, is one of the highest in the world. Therefore, we cannot simply compare China with the United States, a country with a low savings rate and well-developed financial markets, in this regard. In fact, twenty years ago, China's M2/GDP ratio was already very high at 1.34. At the time, some Chinese economists were already worried that it was too high compared with that of the United States. So what? Twenty years of rapid economic growth have passed since then.

Some may agree that a high M2/GDP ratio alone is not alarming, but a rapidly increasing M2/GDP ratio is, as it means that the money supply is growing faster than (nominal) GDP. The excess money supply will presumably lead to asset price bubbles (especially real estate) and high leverage ratios, increasing the chance of a financial crisis. However, is it the increase in the money supply that drives up asset prices, or the increase in asset prices that requires additional money supply to support normal transactions in the real economy? The answer is not straightforward. Asset prices are determined by many factors based on their own demand and supply. The money supply is only one of the factors and does not necessarily play a decisive role. In fact, the M2/GDP ratio of the United States has never been high. In addition, it barely changed during the five years (2001–2005) preceding the 2006 subprime crisis, but a large real estate bubble still emerged in the United States and ultimately led to the 2008 global financial crisis. Argentina is another example with a low M2/GDP, which did not change between 2006 and 2016, but still experienced a severe financial and economic crisis, as mentioned.

Based on the last column of Table 8.5, between 2006 and 2016, when China's M2/GDP ratio reached its peak and the deleveraging campaign started, China's M2/GDP ratio increased by half a point, and the annual percentage change was 2.8 percent. However, the increase in M2/GDP was not unique to China, but a global phenomenon. Indeed, the global average annual percentage change in M2/GDP during this period was 2.7 percent, roughly the same as that of China. The annual growth for the United States was also at 2 percent. Therefore, globally, the money supply has grown faster than nominal GDP since the global financial crisis, while inflation and interest rates have remained low in major economies, including China. This is a new economic phenomenon and an important topic for future research.[26]

For Chinese policymakers and many pundits, the most threatening problem for China was and remains its high level of corporate debt, justifying the policy of deleveraging. Leveraging means increasing debt, while deleveraging means reducing debt. These terms were originally financial jargon used by specialists, but have become familiar terms in China. The so-called macro leverage ratio of a country is the ratio of total debt of the government, household, and nonfinancial corporate sectors to GDP. According to the Bank for International Settlements (BIS), China's macro leverage ratio was 255% in 2018, similar to that of the United States (250%) and the average of all developed countries (265%), but significantly lower than

---

[26] See *The Economist* (October 12–18, 2019 issue) for a special report on this new phenomenon, which the magazine calls "The World Economy's Strange New Rules."

Table 8.5 *Money supply (M2) to GDP ratio around the world*

Country or Region	M2/ GDP (2016)	M2/ GDP (2006)	Ten-Year Change in M2/ GDP	Annual Percentage Change in M2/GDP
Hong Kong	3.77	2.75	1.02	3.2%
Japan	2.42	1.96	0.46	2.1%
China	**2.08**	**1.57**	**0.51**	**2.8%**
Switzerland	1.90	1.34	0.56	3.5%
Vietnam	1.51	0.79	0.72	6.7%
South Korea	1.47	1.19	0.28	2.1%
OECD members	1.18	1.02	0.15	1.4%
Brazil	1.00	0.65	0.36	4.5%
Middle East and North Africa (excluding high income)	0.96	0.64	0.33	4.2%
United States	0.90	0.74	0.16	2.0%
India	0.75	0.70	0.06	0.8%
South Africa	0.73	0.73	−0.01	−0.1%
Global Average	**0.68**	**0.52**	**0.16**	**2.7%**
Latin America and the Caribbean	0.64	0.44	0.21	3.9%
Denmark	0.62	0.53	0.09	1.5%
Russian Federation	0.59	0.38	0.21	4.6%
Indonesia	0.40	0.41	−0.01	−0.3%
Sub-Saharan Africa	0.36	0.36	0.01	0.2%
Argentina	0.28	0.28	0.00	0.1%
Nigeria	0.20	0.12	0.09	5.7%

Note: The table is ranked by M2/GDP in 2016. The global average was calculated by taking the average of the M2/GDP ratios of all economies with data for both 2006 and 2016 (152 economies in total). All data are from the World Development Indicators.

that of Japan (375%).[27] Economists and policymakers were mainly concerned that the macro leverage ratio of nonfinancial corporations in

---

[27] All data are from the Bank for International Settlements, available at https://stats .bis.org/statx/toc/CRE.html.

China was too high, reaching 161% of GDP in 2016 (in the fourth quarter), much higher than that of the United States at 72%, the average of the euro area at 105%, and that of Japan at 100%, as shown in Table 8.6. More seriously, the ratio increased rapidly before 2016, by 63 percentage points compared with 2008, the year of the financial crisis, when it was only 98%. In contrast, the corporate leverage ratio did not increase in major developed economies, such as Japan, the United States, the United Kingdom, and Germany, during the same period.

However, China's relatively high macro leverage ratio in the nonfinancial corporate sector should not be too surprising. It is only the natural result of the country's high savings rate and bank-oriented financial system, and therefore does not constitute in itself a financial risk for the Chinese economy. China's high savings rate means that it has more bank deposits as a percentage of national income, and therefore a higher M2/GDP ratio, as mentioned earlier. More bank deposits mean more bank loans, and more bank loans mean more borrowing (i.e., more debt) by nonfinancial corporations in a country where other sources of financing are underdeveloped, leading to a higher corporate debt to GDP ratio. Thus, in China at least, a high M2/GDP ratio and a high corporate leverage ratio are two sides of the same coin.

What about the rapid increase in the corporate leverage ratio in China? The answer depends on how the debt of nonfinancial corporations is classified. According to research by Zhang Xiaojing and his collaborators from the National Institute for Finance and Development of the Chinese Academy of Social Sciences, the debt of Chinese SOEs accounts for two thirds of the total debt of China's nonfinancial corporate sector, and about half of it is actually borrowed by local government financing vehicles, which are called companies only in name, not in essence. In other words, about one third of China's nominally corporate debt is de facto local government debt.[28] Much of the rapid

---

[28] See reports published on Zhang Xiaojing's official website (www.nifd.cn/Professor/Details/34), all in Chinese, including Zhang Xiaojing (2019) and Zhang, Chang, and Liu (2019a, 2019b).

Table 8.6 *Leverage ratios in the nonfinancial corporate sector (% of GDP): 2008–2018*

Economy	2008–Q4	2010–Q4	2012–Q4	2014–Q4	2016–Q4	2017–Q4	2018–Q4
Hong Kong	130	155	166	206	212	232	219
Netherlands	124	145	162	177	180	174	172
Sweden	150	146	149	152	146	150	156
China	**98**	**122**	**132**	**152**	**161**	**158**	**152**
France	116	119	128	131	139	141	141
Switzerland	90	99	109	103	110	117	118
Euro area	96	101	105	105	108	106	105
Japan	106	103	103	100	99	100	103
United Kingdom	102	95	93	81	83	85	84
United States	73	67	67	68	72	74	74
Greece	62	67	68	68	65	61	58
Germany	58	56	54	53	54	56	57
Argentina	15	14	13	11	12	14	16

Note: The data are from the Bank for International Settlements, available at https://stats.bis.org/statx/toc/CRE.html.

increase in the leverage ratio of China's nonfinancial corporate sector after 2008 was due to the increase in this debt. By reclassifying it in the government debt category, the macro leverage ratio of China's nonfinancial corporate sector would be around 100 percent in 2018, while the leverage ratio of private firms would only be about 50 percent, which is by no means high.

So, if China needed to deleverage, the target should have been the financial arms of local governments and SOEs, rather than private companies. However, during the implementation of the deleveraging policy, private firms bore the brunt of it. According to estimates by Professor Zhang and his collaborators, the proportion of SOE debt to total nonfinancial sector debt increased from 61.4 percent in 2017 to 66.9 percent in 2018, suggesting that private companies were disproportionately affected by the deleveraging policy. In fact, private firms also disproportionately bore the burden of another supply-side policy aimed at reducing capacity. The end result gave the impression that the state sector was advancing while the private sector was retreating (*guojin mintui*). This outcome may not be what Chinese policymakers originally intended, but merely an inevitable consequence of the campaign to reduce capacity and deleverage in an economic system in which SOEs still enjoy certain inherent advantages.

The debt-to-GDP ratio is not the best measure of corporate leverage. Instead, the debt-to-asset ratio, or the micro leverage ratio, is the standard measure of leverage used in the business world. Debt (i.e., liabilities) and assets are two sides of the same coin. High debt is normal when there are also more assets. The overall debt-to-asset ratio of China's private industrial firms has actually declined since 2004 and reached its lowest level in 2016. In contrast, the overall debt-to-asset ratio of SOEs increased after 2007 and peaked in 2013, with much of the 4-trillion-yuan stimulus going to SOEs after the global financial crisis. However, even their debt-to-asset ratio started to drop after 2013.[29]

---

[29] All figures provided in this paragraph were calculated from the official data of *China Statistical Yearbooks* (2019 and other years).

In other words, by a more appropriate measure, China's corporate leverage ratio was already falling (especially for private companies) well before 2016, and therefore further deleveraging in 2016 was really unnecessary.

When evaluating public sector debt, the debt-to-GDP ratio becomes a more reasonable measure, because government debt is less likely to be used for investment, thus there is no corresponding asset. Nevertheless, even with government debt, a simple comparison of the debt-to-GDP ratio between different countries can be misleading. A government's ability to collect taxes and its ownership of income generating assets should also be taken into account. If the debt of local government financing vehicles is included in the calculation of government debt, China's total government debt represents around 90 percent of GDP, which is below the average level of developed countries and is still manageable, as the Chinese government at all levels also holds various forms of assets.[30]

In conclusion, China's economic downturn is neither simply a normal business cycle, nor just the result of lower external demand or some internal structural problems. It is also the result of China's policy choices. In other words, China could have grown faster. Yet, how fast can China still grow? I address this question in the next chapter.

---

[30] According to one authoritative study (Li, Zhang, and Chang 2018), the Chinese government held 27 percent of the country's total net assets in 2016, more than 150 percent of that year's GDP. This contrasts with the United States and the United Kingdom, where the government's net assets are negative.

9 Catching Up to America in a Post–COVID-19 World

On November 12, 1997, the year Deng Xiaoping died at the age of ninety-three, President Jiang Zemin declared the "Two Centennial Goals" for China at the fifteenth Congress of the CCP. These two development goals are set, respectively, for 2021, the centennial of the founding of the CCP, and for 2049, the centennial of the founding of the People's Republic.[1] The first centennial goal is to complete the task set by Deng Xiaoping years ago of building a moderately prosperous society in all aspects by 2021; and the second goal is to make China a strong and fully modernized country by 2049.

China apparently achieved its first centennial goal as the country reached a milestone in per capita GDP in 2019 – over US$10,000 – and basically eliminated absolute poverty in 2020, albeit by a very low income standard. Just when China was about to celebrate the achievement of its first centennial goal and embark on the journey toward the second centennial goal, the Trump administration in the United States launched a trade and tech war with China in 2018, and then in early 2020, the COVID-19 outbreak hit China and soon became a global pandemic, plunging the world economy into the worst recession since the Great Depression.

The start of the trade and tech war with China clearly signaled a shift in US policy from accommodation to confrontation in its approach to the rise of China, which is apparently poised to dethrone the United States as the world's largest economy, a position the country has held for over a century now. The escalation of US–China tensions seems to fulfill a prophecy described by Professor Graham Allison of Harvard University: The two superpowers may

---

[1] Jiang (1997).

fall into the Thucydides Trap, a fateful conflict arising between the emerging new power and the old power.[2]

Can China achieve its second centennial goal in a post–COVID-19 world? Will China catch up to America, and if so, when? Will the superpower conflict derail or at least significantly slow down China's economic growth? What does China's further rise mean for the rest of the world? These are the questions I try to address in this final chapter. I first assess China's potential growth rate over the next thirty years under the assumption that geopolitical challenges, particularly the US–China relations, will not have a significant effect on China's long-term growth trend. I then discuss the impact of the COVID-19 pandemic and geopolitics on China's growth prospects.

PROJECTING CHINA'S ECONOMIC GROWTH OVER THE NEXT THIRTY YEARS

Economists are not known for making accurate forecasts, far from it. After all, how many economists have predicted that China would be by far the fastest growing economy in the past four decades? Understanding this, most academic economists generally refrain from making forecasts. However, if necessary, it is easier to forecast long-term growth (say thirty years) than short-term growth rates, say, 2021 and 2022. I have much more confidence in predicting that the per capita GDP growth of the United States will be around 1.5% per year on average over the next thirty years than in predicting that it will be around 1.5% in 2022. The main reason is that long-term economic growth is quite stable, whereas short-term growth rates fluctuate a lot. For example, the compound annual growth rates of US GDP per capita during four thirty-year periods, that is, 1890–1920, 1920–1950, 1950–1980, and 1980–2010, were 1.66%, 1.97%, 2.24%, and 1.71%, respectively.[3] The long-term growth rates of a large economy at the technological frontier simply do not vary much, which is

---

[2] Allison (2017).   [3] These figures are based on the Maddison Project Database 2018.

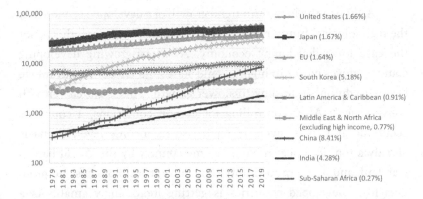

FIGURE 9.1 Long-term GDP per capita growth: 1979–2019
Note: The percentages in brackets after each country or region (continent) are
compound annual growth rates of GDP per capita during the 1979–2019 period.
The data source is the World Development Indicators data set.

amazing given that so much has happened during each of
these periods.

Globally, in the past forty years (1979–2019), developed economies like the United States, Japan, and the European Union essentially had the same GDP per capita growth, at a compound annual rate
of just over 1.6%, as shown in Figure 9.1.[4] In contrast, economies
classified as developing economies in 1979 had very different growth
performances, with South Korea, China, and India rapidly catching up
to developed economies, whereas the developing regions of sub-
Saharan Africa, Latin America, and the Middle East stagnated with
annual growth of less 1%. To paraphrase Leo Tolstoy, developed
countries are all alike, but each developing country develops at its
own pace.[5]

---

[4] During the 1979–2019 period, according to the World Development Indicators, the
compound annual growth rate of GDP per capita of Canada, France, Germany, and
the United Kingdom was 1.44%, 1.29%, 1.54%, and 1.69%, respectively.

[5] Figure 9.1 also corroborates my earlier argument that the middle-income trap does
not really exist: Most developing countries have had low long-term growth, whether
they are low-income (e.g., most sub-Saharan economies); lower middle-income (e.g.,
many economies in the Middle East and North Africa); or upper middle-income

Although the long-term trend growth of a developed economy at the technological frontier may not change much over time, this is not the case for a developing economy. As a fast-growing developing country moves closer to high-income status, its latecomer advantage begins to diminish, leading to slower growth. This is called "growth convergence": After controlling for certain conditions, a country's economic growth is inversely related to its income level. China is already a top tier upper middle-income country by the World Bank's standard, and its room to simply copy current technologies and products from developed countries is getting increasingly small. As a result, the era of double-digit growth is over. Some economists have argued that China's recent slowdown reflects a decline in its rate of potential GDP growth.[6]

Japan and the other four East Asian miracle economies of Hong Kong, South Korea, Taiwan, and Singapore have all gone through the process of growth slowdown. The question is at what income level such a slowdown becomes appreciable and significant. Figure 9.2 may give us an idea of the possible answer to this question. For this scatter chart, I divided the fifty-five years (from 1961 to 2015) covered by the World Development Indicators data set into eleven five-year periods (i.e., 1961–1965, 1966–1970, . . ., 2011–2015) and calculated the average annual growth rate of GDP per capita for every five-year period for Japan and the three tiger economies of South Korea, Hong Kong, and Singapore.[7] I also calculated the relative income level of each economy at the start of each five-year period as a percentage of GDP per capita of the United States, the benchmark economy at the technological frontier.[8] As a result, the chart includes forty-four data points,

countries (e.g., most Latin American economies). But a small number of economies have grown fast, and they are mostly located in Asia.

[6] See Bai and Zhang (2017a). Potential GDP growth refers to growth under the condition of full employment, which does not mean zero unemployment but unemployment at the "natural" rate.

[7] The World Bank database does not include Taiwan.

[8] Here, I used the World Bank's GDP per capita data in current US dollars to calculate relative income levels. Alternatively, one can use PPP-adjusted GDP per capita

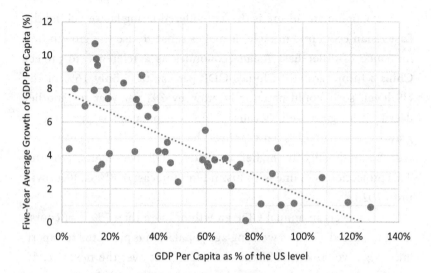

FIGURE 9.2 Growth slowdown and relative development level: The case of the four East Asian economies
Note: The four East Asian economies are Japan, Hong Kong, South Korea, and Singapore. The data are from the World Development Indicators.

each representing the average five-year growth rate (vertical axis) of an East Asian miracle economy at a relative income level in the first year of the corresponding five-year period (horizontal axis).

Figure 9.2 clearly shows that before the 30% relative income mark, the growth rate of the four East Asian miracle economies was mostly above 7%, and it was mostly above 6% between the 30% and 40% relative income marks. However, after the 40% mark, average growth dropped significantly to around 4% or less. In other words, before reaching the high-income threshold defined as 30% of the US level, these East Asian economies had mostly maintained their average growth rate above 7%, so there was no noticeable growth slowdown during the "middle-income" phase.

figures from the World Bank or the Penn World Table data set. The results are very similar. When measured by PPP-adjusted total GDP, China is already the largest economy in the world. However, PPP adjustment is not an exact science and is subject to measurement errors. See Feenstra et al. (2013).

If Confucian culture is the key differentiating factor behind the East Asian economic miracle, it makes sense to use the growth performance of other East Asian economies as a reference to project China's future growth. China's GDP per capita is only 16% of the US level, so it could potentially grow by 7% per year for another decade if all goes well. Because China's population is projected to grow by less than 0.2% per year over the next decade, its GDP growth will be only slightly higher than its GDP per capita growth.[9] This projection is in line with Justin Lin's forecast of 8% GDP growth until 2028.[10]

However, an annual GDP growth of more than 7% is of course not guaranteed. China's working-age population is projected to experience negative growth of about –0.3% per year over the next decade, which, combined with an annual population growth of 0.2%, implies a direct negative impact on GDP per capita growth of about 0.5% per year (i.e., a negative direct demographic dividend). In contrast, the four East Asian economies all had positive direct demographic dividends, ranging from around 0.5% to over 1.5% in the decade after their income level reached 16% of the US level.[11] Thus, on this fact alone, China's GDP per capita growth could be on average 1.5 percentage points lower than that of the four East Asian miracle economies at a similar stage of economic development.[12] In other words, China may be able to achieve an annual GDP per capita growth of 5.5% or slightly higher over the next decade.

---

[9] The projected population growth of China (and later the United States) is taken from the World Bank's "Population Estimates and Projections" data set, available at https://databank.worldbank.org/source/population-estimates-and-projections.

[10] See Lin (2019).

[11] These figures are the author's calculations based on data from the World Development Indicators. See Chapter 2 for the definition of the direct demographic dividend.

[12] Here I assume that the negative direct demographic dividend in China will not lead to a further indirect negative demographic dividend, because China saves more than it invests domestically, so less savings resulting from aging will not lead to a bottleneck for economic growth.

In addition, the US population is projected to grow by 0.5% per year over the next decade. If the GDP per capita of the United States continues to grow at 1.5% per year, its average annual growth rate over the previous thirty years (1989–2019), then its GDP growth rate will be 2% per year. As long as China's GDP can grow by 6% per year (or 5.8% on a per capita basis), a more manageable target, it will catch up to America in total GDP in 2030, that is, China will become the world's largest economy in ten years. However, China's GDP per capita would still be just a quarter of the US level by then.

On the pessimistic side, two Harvard economists, Lant Pritchett and Lawrence Summers, argued in a 2014 article that forecasting China's or any country's growth by simple extrapolation is the wrong approach and believed that reversion to the mean is the rule of economic growth, implying that China's "abnormally" rapid growth may be followed by a more "normal" growth rate or discontinuous declines. They predicted that China's annual growth would fall to 5% during the 2013–2023 period and to 3.3% during the 2023–2033 period.[13] They came to their conclusion because they treated China like any developing country that follows the same general pattern of economic growth, in direct contrast to the theme of this book, that is, that China is not an average developing country.

Now suppose that China can catch up to the United States in total GDP in 2030. How fast can China grow afterward? How big would China's economy be relative to that of the United States in 2050? Can it ever catch up to America in GDP per capita? Some studies have attempted to forecast China's economic growth up to 2050. Three types of methods are generally used to project long-term growth: (1) simple analogies based on growth convergence in comparable economies, as I did to project China's growth over the next decade; (2) predictions based on the growth accounting method, which essentially consists of separately estimating the growth of physical capital, labor and human capital, and productivity (or, more precisely,

---

[13] Pritchett and Summers (2014).

TFP) and then taking a weighted average of these estimates; and (3) a combination of the two methods.[14] Using the second and third method, respectively, Fang Cai of the Chinese Academy of Social Sciences and Chong-en Bai of Tsinghua University, two leading Chinese economists known to be on the more cautious side in their assessment of China's economy, came to similar predictions: China's potential GDP growth rate will drop from 6% now to 2–3% in 2050, with an average annual growth rate of around 4% for the next thirty years.[15] Using a similar approach, Xun Wang of Peking University came up with a slightly more optimistic forecast, giving China an annual growth rate of just over 5% for the next thirty years.[16] All three studies took China's demographic factors into account. Outside of China, an OECD report predicted that China's GDP per capita would grow at an average rate of 6.4% between 2011 and 2030, but only 2.8% between 2030 and 2060. Overall, during the 2011–2060 period, China's GDP per capita is expected to grow by 4.2% per year, while that of the United States is expected to be 1.5% per year.[17]

If the average annual GDP growth rates of China and the United States over the next thirty years are 4% and 2%, respectively, then in 2050, China's total GDP will be 22% higher than that of the United States, and its per capita GDP will be only 34% of the US level (35,600 versus 105,000 in today's US dollars). However, if China's growth rate is 5%, then its total GDP will be 64% higher than that of the United States in 2050, and its per capita GDP will be 45% of the US level (48,000 versus 105,000 in today's US dollars). In either case, China will be a high-income developed economy in 2050 by the usual standard. For comparison, economies with a per capita GDP of around 34%

---

[14] See Wang (2020), and also see Holz (2008) for a growth accounting method that decomposes GDP into four income categories (labor remuneration, depreciation, net taxes on production, and operating surplus).

[15] Bai and Zhang (2017b) and Lu and Cai (2016).

[16] See Wang (2020). For the 2021–2030 period, Wang's projection of China's GDP growth is 6.6%, that of Bai and Zhang is 5.2%, and that of Lu and Cai is 5.3%. For the 2031–2050 period, their projection is 4.3%, 3.4%, and 3.5%, respectively.

[17] Johansson et al. (2012).

of the US level in 2019 include Estonia, Portugal, Saudi Arabia, and the Czech Republic. Economies with a per capita GDP of around 45% of the US level in 2019 include South Korea and Spain.

In these projections, my implicit assumption is that the real exchange rate of RMB to US dollars will remain the same over the next three decades.[18] This is a very conservative assumption because when a developing country grows faster than a developed country, its real exchange rate will normally appreciate.[19] This is called the Balassa–Samuelson effect. The idea behind this effect is that, to take China as an example, as China catches up to the United States, its general price level will also converge to the US level, therefore, either the nominal exchange rate of RMB will appreciate or China's inflation rate will be higher than that of the United States, or both. As a result, China's GDP measured in US dollars will grow faster than that measured in RMB. In the case of the four East Asian economies in Figure 9.2, their real exchange rates during the 1961–1990 period all appreciated against US dollars, and the average annual rates of appreciation ranged from 0.7% for Singapore and 2% for Hong Kong to 2.9% for South Korea and 4.4% for Japan.[20]

Let us suppose, conservatively, that over the next thirty years, China's real exchange rate will appreciate by only 1% per year. Now if its GDP grows by 4% annually as projected by Chong-en Bai, Fang Cai, and their coauthors, then when measured in constant US dollars, it will grow by 5% per year, which implies that China's total GDP will be 64% higher than that of the United States in 2050, and its per capita GDP will be 45% of the US level, assuming that the US GDP growth

---

[18] The real exchange rate of RMB to US dollars is defined as the nominal exchange rate multiplied by the ratio of the price level of China to that of the United States. If the nominal exchange rate does not change and the inflation rates are the same in both countries, then the real exchange rate will remain the same.

[19] See, e.g., Ito, Isard, and Symansky (1999) and Choudhri and Khan (2005).

[20] These numbers were calculated by the author based on data from the World Development Indicators. The rate of appreciation of a country's real exchange rate in a year was calculated as the rate of appreciation of the nominal exchange rate plus the country's inflation rate (measured by the GDP deflator) minus the US inflation rate.

rate remains at 2%. However, if China's GDP grows by 5% per year (in constant RMB) as projected by Xun Wang, then it will grow by 6% in constant US dollars. In this case, China's total GDP will be 120% higher than that of the United States in 2050, and its per capita GDP will reach 60% of the US level. For comparison, Euro area members on average had a per capita GDP of around 60% of the US level in 2019.

In summary, it is quite possible that by the middle of this century, China's per capita GDP will reach about 50% of the US level, and its total GDP will be two thirds larger than or even double that of the United States. To give some perspective, it took Japan thirteen years (1960–1973) for its GDP per capita to go from 16% to 50% of the US level (measured in current US dollars); twenty-four years for Hong Kong (1963–1987); twenty-one years for Singapore (1969–1989); and twenty years for South Korea (1987–2007). If the cultural explanation of the East Asian growth puzzle is correct, there is a good chance that China will achieve the same success in thirty years and accomplish its second centennial goal.

As to whether or when China will ever catch up to America in per capita GDP, I have not seen any projections on that. Even if China succeeded in this feat, it would be very far into the future and need not concern us for now.

SPEED BUMPS ON CHINA'S PATH TO A FULLY DEVELOPED ECONOMY

I made the previous projections without explicitly taking into account the impact of the COVID-19 pandemic and the growing tensions between China and the United States. The pandemic as both a demand- and supply-side shock has certainly had a huge impact on short-term growth, but its impact on long-term growth appears limited, although some pundits have argued that the pandemic could have long-term geopolitical implications.[21] According to the projections of the International Monetary Fund (IMF) in October 2020,

---

[21] See, e.g., Cimmino, Kroenig, and Pavel (2020) and Nye (2020) for discussions about the possible geopolitical implications of the COVID-19 pandemic.

global GDP growth would suffer a 7.2% decline, from 2.8% in 2019 to –4.4% in 2020. In contrast, China was projected to sustain a much smaller 4.2% decline in GDP growth and would be the only major economy to manage a positive growth of 1.9%, thanks to its more effective control of COVID-19. In 2020, China's exports were expected to have positive growth compared with 2019, whereas world merchandise trade would fall by more than 9% and China's share of exports in the world would increase accordingly.[22] The IMF predicts a sharp recovery of the world economy in 2021 with a growth rate of 5.4% (3.9% and 6.0% for developed and developing economies, respectively), while China is projected to grow by 8.2%.

In general, as Table 9.1 shows, the IMF does not predict a deterioration in GDP growth in the post–COVID-19 world. According to its projection, the four-year average growth rate post–COVID-19 during the 2022–2025 period for the world economy will be 3.8%, higher than the pre–COVID-19 four-year average growth of 3.4% during the 2016–2019 period. However, China's growth is projected to decline from a pre–COVID-19 four-year average of 6.6% to a four-year average of 5.7% post–COVID-19. Nevertheless, this projected decline is likely to have little to do with COVID-19 and more to do with a widely perceived downward trend in China's growth in the future.

The pandemic may have led many countries and multinational companies to reevaluate the benefits and risks of relying on current global supply chains. However, so far, the main focus has been on medical supplies and other essential products, the total values of which as a percentage of GDP are negligible. COVID-19's disruption for businesses may have empowered voices in favor of deglobalization. A partial reversal of globalization is certainly a possibility. However, globalization is apparently still very much alive, as evidenced by the recent signing of the Regional Comprehensive Economic Partnership (RCEP) on November 15, 2020 by fifteen Asia-Pacific countries

---

[22] See Huang and Lardy (2020).

Table 9.1 *Impact of COVID-19 on GDP growth and projection to 2025 (%)*

Economies	2016–2019 (Four-Year Average)	2019	2020	2021	2022–2025 (Four-Year Average)
China	6.6	6.1	1.9	8.2	5.7
United States	2.3	2.2	–4.3	3.1	2.2
European Union	2.3	1.7	–7.6	5	2.4
Developed economies	2.1	1.7	–5.8	3.9	2.2
India	6.4	4.2	–10.3	8.8	7.6
Latin America and the Caribbean	0.5	0	–8.1	3.6	2.6
Sub-Saharan Africa	2.8	3.2	–3	3.1	4.3
Developing economies	4.4	3.7	–3.3	6	4.9
World	3.4	2.8	–4.4	5.2	3.8

Note: The data source is the IMF World Economic Outlook (October 2020). Available at www.imf.org/external/datamapper/NGDP_RPCH@WEO/OEMDC/ADVEC/WEOWORLD. The IMF uses the terms "advanced economies" and "emerging market and developing economies" to refer to developed and developing economies, respectively.

(ten member countries of the Association of Southeast Asian Nations and China, Japan, South Korea, Australia, and New Zealand), the largest free trade agreement that represents 30 percent of the world's GDP and population.[23]

Amid the pandemic and the rhetoric of the 2020 US presidential election campaign, China and the United States appeared to be heading on a full-blown collision course. There seems to be a bipartisan consensus in the United States on confronting China, and there is increasing talk of decoupling between the two countries.[24]

---

[23] See Petri and Plummer (2020).
[24] See, e.g., Johnson and Gramer (2020) and Mahbubani (2020).

However, will or to what extent can the United States and China decouple? So far, there seems to have been more rhetoric than action.[25] Even under the Trump administration, the trade war was limited to imposing additional tariffs on Chinese exports, and the aim was not to stop trade with China, but to pressure China to make concessions on IP protection, market opening, and the issues of state subsidies and industrial policy. The tech war has mostly been limited to sanctions on Huawei and a few other Chinese tech companies in the name of national security, to prevent China from dominating sensitive 5G telecommunication technologies. President Trump himself insisted that national security should not be used as an excuse to prevent American companies from selling their products to foreign countries when he rebuked a proposal by his senior officials to block General Electric's jet-engine sales to China in February 2020. The blockage would have dealt a heavy blow to China's ambitious project to develop its own large commercial aircraft.[26]

Despite the fanfare, the overall impact of the trade war on the economic growth of China (and the United States for that matter) has been rather insignificant, an order of magnitude smaller than that of the COVID-19 pandemic. China's slowdown in growth in recent years was not caused by the trade war, but preceded it. China's exports to the United States accounted for less than 4 percent of its GDP before the trade war. Even if the United States imposed a 25 percent tariff on all Chinese exports, it would only represent less than 1 percent of China's GDP, not an unbearable impact, not to mention that much of the cost would be borne by American importers or consumers. Higher US tariffs, if kept in place, could lead to some changes in China's trade structure and a slight realignment of global supply chains. Some low- and middle-end manufacturing facilities may move from China to India, Vietnam, and other countries. However, as long as the United States and China continue to trade, tariffs alone will have minimal effects on China's long-term growth.

---

[25] See Lardy and Huang (2020).   [26] See Donnan (2020).

What about the effect of a tech war? It depends on whether it is limited to a few select technologies, as has been the case so far, or whether it is a full-scale technological decoupling effort. The fact that the United States can impose sanctions that effectively cripple the core businesses of China's technological leaders like Huawei, demonstrates that the United States has a clear technological supremacy over China. If the ultimate goal of the United States is to completely cut China off from American technology, there is no doubt that this will seriously harm China, at least in the short to medium term. However, banning the sales of advanced American technology is a double-edged sword: It hurts sellers as much as it hurts buyers.[27] Advanced technological products inherently have a high upfront fixed cost at the R&D stage but have a relatively low marginal cost at the production stage, the additional cost of producing one more unit of the product, which is virtually zero in the case of software. In other words, a large part of the sales revenue of these hi-tech products is profit, and a 20 percent reduction in sales as a result of the tech war may lead to, say, a 50 percent reduction in profit for US companies. This explains why the news of the sanctions imposed on Huawei sharply lowered the stock prices of American chipmakers and why many hi-tech companies in the United States do not approve of a tech war with China.

In today's highly integrated global economy, it is, for all practical purposes, impossible or very costly to pursue full-scale decoupling between the two largest economies.[28] The world is already "chained to globalization."[29] If full-scale decoupling is not possible, will selective technological decoupling have a significant effect on China's economic growth? The short answer is probably not. A limited tech war will disrupt the activities of affected Chinese companies in the short term, but will have a very limited effect on China's technological progress in the long term. It may instead become a catalyst for China's own technological innovations.

[27] See Bown (2020).   [28] See Lardy (2020).   [29] See Farrell and Newman (2020).

As I showed in Chapter 6, China's capacity for innovation and its role in the country's rapid growth have generally been underestimated. Chinese companies are already trying to move up the value chain, and the inability to acquire blocked American technologies will motivate some of them to develop these technologies for import substitution. So, in the long run, a limited tech war could conceivably harm American interests more than Chinese interests.

Now that effective vaccines for COVID-19 are available and Joe Biden, "an unapologetic globalist" as *The New Yorker* called him, has become the US president, many expect more stable and predictable US–China relations.[30] Joe Biden may not go soft on China, but he does not believe that a tariff war with China is the right approach to address the US–China trade relationship. He believes that the most effective way is to build a united front of allies to meet the Chinese challenge by shaping "the rules of the road" on everything from the environment to labor, trade, technology, and transparency. Biden wants to invest more in R&D to keep the United States ahead in innovation and competitiveness, not to block China's technological progress. He will also seek to cooperate with China on issues of climate change, nonproliferation, and global health security.[31] In short, the China policy of the Biden administration is not to decouple with China, but to try to change China's behavior in trade and competition. There may be more conflict and bickering between China and the United States under the Biden administration over political issues such as human rights, relations across the Taiwan Strait, and territorial disputes in the South China Sea. However, they are unlikely to have a significant impact on the US–China trade relationship or on China's long-term economic growth for that matter.

Many Western leaders and economists seem to agree with Biden's approach. For example, NATO Secretary General Jens Stoltenberg, former prime minister of Norway, believes that China will soon be the largest economy and that its rise presents

---

[30] See Wright (2020) and Hansen (2020).   [31] Biden (2020).

opportunities for Western economies and trade. He argued that it is important to continue to engage with China and not to see it as an adversary of NATO. He called for a strong alliance among NATO members to defend Western values and support human rights in China, but not to slow down China's rise.[32] Glenn Hubbard of Columbia University, former chairman of President George W. Bush's Council of Economic Advisers, pointed out that the US government should not obsess over its bilateral trade deficit with China and that the trade war will not help to resolve the overall US trade deficit. Instead, the solution is to increase domestic savings and reduce the government's fiscal deficit. Professor Hubbard argued that it is better for the United States to work on domestic issues, such as increasing spending on research and education to protect US technological leadership, than to simply protest China's industrial policy or bring back traditional manufacturing.[33]

China's relations with the United States and its Western allies are not the only important challenge for the Chinese economy. Naysayers have also pointed to China's internal factors as the basis for their grim and sometimes alarmist forecasts for the country's economic growth. I addressed several oft-mentioned issues earlier in the book, such as an aging population, overreliance on investment and exports, and high corporate debt. Some pundits have repeatedly predicted the imminent collapse of China's economy based on the perceived inefficiency of its authoritarian and state-dominated development model.[34] None of these predictions have panned out. More cautious commentators, notably the authors of the bestselling

[32] Stoltenberg (2020).

[33] Hubbard (2018). For a similar view, also see Ratner, Rosenberg, and Scharre (2019).

[34] In 2001, Gordon G. Chang, a Chinese-American columnist and author, published a book called *The Coming Collapse of China*. In this book, Chang predicted that the Chinese economy (and the Chinese government) would collapse before 2011 due to its inefficient SOEs and banks. Although his predictions turned out to be completely wrong, the American magazine *Foreign Policy* still decided to publish another article by Chang in 2011, "The Coming Collapse of China: 2012 Edition," predicting that the Chinese economy would collapse in 2012!

book *Why Nations Fail,* have predicted that China's growth under its current political institution could not be sustained after reaching the middle-income level when catch-up growth by importing foreign technology and exporting low-end manufacturing products is no longer viable. Their prediction is based on the premise that "creative destruction" (i.e., innovation) cannot occur under "extractive" (i.e., nondemocratic) political institutions.[35] However, China has already gone well beyond the middle-income stage that these two authors had in mind (i.e., importing foreign technology and exporting low-end manufacturing products) when they wrote their book. I showed in Chapter 6 that China is already an innovation powerhouse. I also showed in Chapter 8 that several provincial economies in China, each with a population of tens of millions, have already reached the status of high-income economies by the World Bank's criterion. Moreover, dozens of cities (or municipalities) in the coastal provinces of Guangdong, Jiangsu, and Zhejiang, each with millions of residents, have reached the level of GDP per capita similar to that of the developed economy of Taiwan or even higher in the case of Shenzhen, Suzhou, and Wuxi. These mainland provincial and municipal economies have the same political institutions as other places in China. Why would the same institutions prevent other provinces and municipalities from becoming high-income economies?

I argued in Chapter 3 that the role of specific forms of political institutions in economic growth and development has been greatly exaggerated by many institutionalists from left to right. In contrast, economic institutions and policies play a much more important role.[36] Comparing China before and after its market reform, it is clear that a more market-oriented economic system is the reason why,

---

[35] Acemoglu and Robinson (2012). According to them, "the Chinese experience is an example of growth under extractive political institutions. Despite the recent emphasis in China on innovation and technology, Chinese growth is based on the adoption of existing technologies and rapid investment, not creative destruction" (p. 439).

[36] See Lin (2001) and Glaeser et al. (2004).

under the same political system, China has grown much faster in the forty years after the reform than the thirty years before the reform. As long as market reforms are not reversed, it is more likely than not that China will be able to grow further to become the world's largest economy in about ten years; and after this milestone, it will still have the potential to grow faster than the United States and other developed countries for another twenty years.

A MULTIPOLAR WORLD

China's further rise is certainly not inevitable, but one would be well advised not to bet against it. The resilience of the Chinese economy has often been underestimated in the past. What does the further rise of China mean for the rest of the world? How should the United States, Europe, and the world in general reckon with it?

For Joschka Fischer, former foreign minister and vice chancellor of Germany, China's rise means the end of Western hegemony, which is why the confrontation between China and the West is escalating now, not two decades ago. However, he doubts the possibility of containing a competitive economy with 1.4 billion people. In a level-headed opinion piece, Mr. Fischer pointed out that it is too late to prevent or delay China's rise, which could not succeed without inflicting serious damage to everyone else. He argued that the West must find a way to live peacefully with China that neither accommodates China without regard for principles, nor coaxes it into becoming a Western-style democracy.[37] Carl Bildt, former prime minister of Sweden, shared this view.[38] They both argued that the West should engage with China on trade and other issues such as climate change, but also protect Western values and interests.

The risk posed by China's rise to Western values and interests may have been greatly exaggerated.[39] If one envisions direct

[37] Fischer (2020).   [38] Bildt (2020).

[39] For a historically informed argument on why the China threat is exaggerated and why engagement instead of decoupling is the right strategy for the United States, see Zakaria (2020).

Table 9.2 *China's relative economic power compared with other countries*

Country	2019 GDP (in PPP US Dollars) as % of World Total	2019 Population as % of World Total
OECD members	47%	18%
China	**17%**	**18%**
European Union	16%	6%
United States	15%	4%
India	7%	18%
Japan	4%	2%
Russia	3%	2%

Data source: World Development Indicators.

competition between the world's centralized autocracies and liberal democracies, China enjoys no advantage either in the size of its economy or in the size of its population. Table 9.2 shows that in terms of current economic power, even measured by the more generous PPP-adjusted GDP, China represented 17% of global GDP in 2019, not much more than the United States (15%) and the EU (16%). The OECD is a thirty-six-member economic alliance made up mainly of Western liberal democracies, and all member countries combined accounted for 47% of global GDP in 2019. The economic power of a possible China-led alliance would be no match to a US-led alliance that includes the European Union, Japan, and India. Even if one day China catches up to the United States and the European Union in terms of GDP per capita, which will take many decades to materialize, if at all, its economic power will be proportional to the size of its population. As China's population will not grow faster than the OECD average in the coming decades, its economic power will be similar to that of the OECD countries combined. By then, India, as the most populous liberal democracy, will also be an economic superpower and a counterweight to China.

Moreover, different political systems do not necessarily imply different fundamental values between two peoples. China is not a Cold War–era Soviet Union, and its official ideology seems to have evolved into something more Confucian than Marxian.[40] Modernization theorists have probably been too optimistic about the effect of economic development on democratization, but time may have been too short to invalidate their theory. Economic development and globalization are likely to affect the political values of new generations, which in turn will shape future political institutions.[41]

We are truly entering the era of a multipolar world, where no country can be the dominant power. Peaceful coexistence between major powers may not be a choice, but a necessity.[42] The rest of the world should focus on how to adapt and benefit from the rise of China, not how to stop it. China, for its part, should make real efforts to ensure that its economic rise is beneficial to and not at the expense of the rest of the world.

China's economic rise appears to have benefited some developing countries. It has helped drive up the prices of many natural resources and has therefore benefited countries that are rich in these resources. One can, of course, point to the negative economic effects of resource dependence, such as excessive price volatility and the crowding out of investments in other sectors. However, the net effect of higher resource prices may still be positive for some developing countries.[43] China's surplus savings can help to finance investment projects in developing countries, although one can also challenge the wisdom of over-indebtedness to China by some of these countries.

More importantly, China's rise will significantly contribute to technological progress in the world. As a percentage of GDP, China already spends more on R&D than the European Union, and Chinese

---

[40] See, e.g., Jacques (2009), Page (2015), Bell (2016), and Mahbubani (2020).
[41] See, e.g., Inglehart and Welzel (2005).   [42] See Rodrik (2019).
[43] See Brunnschweiler and Bulte (2008).

patent applications represent more than 40 percent of the world total. Both are still growing rapidly. Of course, most of the benefits of China's technological innovations accrue to the country itself, but there will be a significant spillover effect on other countries. Moreover, China accounts for nearly 20 percent of the world's scientific publications, which are by nature public goods that can potentially benefit all nations. For the past 200 years, almost all modern technologies were invented by Western countries and a few other developed countries, such as Japan. However, over the next few decades, China will play an increasingly important role in advancing the technological frontier and could potentially contribute up to half of the world's total innovations, which will hopefully accelerate technological progress and therefore economic growth worldwide.

Of course, China's future technological progress may also be seen as a major challenge to the technological supremacy of the United States and the West in general. The further rise of China and Chinese companies will inevitably put strong competitive pressures on many US and other Western companies. It is therefore neither a win-win situation for all nor a pure zero-sum game, but a mixture of the two. However, this is true of any market competition, and it will also be the case when India rises to become another economic superpower.

Instead of trying to decouple or contain China, the US-led alliance should pursue a middle-ground strategy that both addresses Western concerns and aligns with China's long-term interests by pushing for more market-oriented policies and institutional reforms, and better IP protection in China. This is a more legitimate and achievable goal, and it is also what many Chinese economists and reform-minded policymakers have called for.[44] In the face of American (and Western) challenges to its economic system, the Chinese government should redouble its efforts to make the country more market-oriented, more rule-based, and more open to foreign

---

[44] See Wei (2018) and Wu (2018).

competition. If China can do that, there will be less conflict with the United States and the rest of the world.

Economic and political friction between the two superpowers may prove to be the norm over the next few decades, and such friction, like speed bumps on the road, may slow China's rise, but not reverse it. Ultimately, it is the internal growth engines of investment, education, and technological innovation, powered by Confucian culture and institutional reforms, that will determine the speed of China's further rise.

Appendix
A1 China's Underestimated Consumption

China has one of the lowest consumption rates (and therefore one of the highest savings rates) in the world, but it is not really as low as 50 percent of GDP or less. China's household consumption is significantly underestimated in official statistics.[1] First, official statistics cannot account for a great deal of private consumption paid for by company accounts, a very common practice in China, and treated as business costs or, in the case of durable goods like a car, as investment expenditure.[2] However, this part of private consumption paid by companies by its nature is difficult to estimate. Second, Chinese statistics have underestimated housing consumption due to the poor methodology used by the NBS. Third, household consumption statistics are mainly based on household surveys, in which high-income households are significantly underrepresented. Jun Zhang and I attempted to evaluate the extent of the last two sources of underestimation and found consumption rates approximately 10 percentage points higher than the official rates.

Housing consumption includes rent, home maintenance expenses, and utilities. Rent includes actual rent paid by a tenant and "imputed rent" for owner-occupied housing. In theory, the imputed rent of a self-owned home should be equal to the rent that the owner will pay to rent a similar house on the market. In practice, calculating imputed rent is not an easy task. The NBS uses construction costs multiplied by a fixed depreciation rate (2% for urban

---

[1] This section is based on Zhang and Zhu (2015).　[2] See Cai, Fang, and Xu (2001).

Table A1.1 *Housing consumption around the world: 2009*

Country	Housing Consumption to GDP	Rent to GDP (Actual + Imputed)
Australia	11.7%	10.0%
Canada	13.6%	11.4%
France	14.2%	10.4%
Germany	13.7%	9.4%
Japan	14.7%	N/A
South Korea	8.7%	6.2%
Mexico	11.1%	8.2%
Turkey	16.5%	N/A
United Kingdom	14.0%	10.0%
United States	13.6%	11.4%
India	8.6%	6.1%
China	6.2%	N/A

Note: The ratios were calculated by the author based on data from the OECD.Stat website (https://stats.oecd.org) and *China Statistical Yearbook 2012.*

housing and 3% for rural housing) as their estimate. Although this method is easy to apply, it greatly underestimates actual expenses. Construction costs represent only a small fraction of the real market value of a home in urban China. In addition, the depreciation rate of 2% is likely to underestimate the actual rental yield. Take 2009 as an example. China's housing consumption calculated using this method represented only 6% of total GDP that year. However, as shown in Table A1.1, in the same year, housing consumption in the major developed OECD economies (the United States, Japan, the United Kingdom, Germany, France, and Canada) represented about 14% of their respective GDP. Even in developing countries like Mexico and Turkey, housing consumption represented 11.1% and 16.5% of their GDP, respectively. In India, it was 8.6% of GDP. Using the market rent approach for China based on a conservative estimate of the price-to-rent ratio, Jun Zhang and I estimated the imputed rent of owner-occupied urban homes, and showed that China's housing consumption rates were at least underestimated between 2.8% and 4.7% of GDP over the 2004–2011 period.

The most important source of underestimation of household consumption in China is the serious underrepresentation of high-income families in household surveys, on which household consumption expenditure in GDP is estimated. These surveys rely on households supposedly randomly selected to record monthly income and expenditure. These households receive only a small nominal compensation for participating in the survey. The aggregate household consumption expenditure is calculated by multiplying the average per-capita consumption expenditure by the total population. High-income households are known to be underrepresented because they have little incentive to participate in the surveys or to report their income and expenditure accurately.[3] As a result, overall household consumption is significantly underestimated.

Let me illustrate the extent of underrepresentation of high-income families in the household surveys by comparing the figures for family car ownership from two data sources: data from NBS household surveys and data from the Ministry of Transportation based on actual car ownership registrations. Table A1.2 shows that private car ownership based on household survey data is significantly lower than actual ownership based on data from the Ministry of Transportation. With the exception of 2011, household surveys have largely underestimated car ownership in China. As only relatively high-income Chinese households can afford to buy a car, this clearly shows that high-income households were severely underrepresented in the household surveys at least during these years.

Fortunately, aggregate household disposable income in China is also reported in the national income accounts and published in the country's flow of funds (FOF) tables. As the income approach to

---

[3] See Wang (2007).

Table A1.2 *Family car ownership from two data sources*

Year	Car Ownership Estimated from Household Survey Data (in Thousands)	National Car Ownership Based on Data from the Ministry of Transportation (in Thousands)	Household Survey Car Ownership as % of the Ministry of Transportation Car Ownership
2004	4,595.75	10,155.41	45.25%
2005	7,883.12	13,254.39	59.48%
2006	10,293.76	17,561.77	58.61%
2007	15,006.92	22,532.67	66.60%
2008	22,444.85	28,139.61	79.76%
2009	28,575.79	37,396.50	76.41%
2010	37,824.70	49,191.64	76.89%
2011	58,894.38	61,651.33	95.53%

measuring GDP is based on comprehensive information provided by businesses, the government, and other organizations in China, it does not suffer from the same sampling bias as household surveys; thus, its income figures should be more reliable.

Table A1.3 presents the figures for household disposable income obtained from these two sources. It is clear that household disposable income from FOF data is much higher than that from household survey data. This means that household income derived from the NBS household surveys may be underestimated by as much as 30 percent. If household surveys underestimate household income, they also underestimate household consumption. Jun Zhang and I estimated the missing consumption expenditure of high-income households that are underrepresented in household surveys. We basically multiplied the difference in total income between the two sources by an estimated consumption rate for high-income households.

By taking into account the two sources of underestimation of household consumption, we obtained estimates of China's consumption rates between 2004 and 2011. The results are presented in

Table A1.3 *Disposable income from household survey data and flow of funds (FOF) data*

Year	Household Survey Figures (Billion Yuan)	FOF Figures (Billion Yuan)	Ratio of Household Survey Figures to FOF Figures
2004	7,337	9,851	74%
2005	8,325	11,291	74%
2006	9,479	13,143	72%
2007	11,319	15,856	71%
2008	13,199	18,593	71%
2009	14,632	20,730	71%
2010	16,772	24,312	69%
2011	19,647	28,577	69%

Table A1.4. The table ends in 2011 because, for unknown reasons, the NBS stopped publishing statistics on the individual components of consumption expenditure (such as housing, health care, etc.), which were the basis for our reestimation of household consumption. Table A1.4 shows that China's official statistics underestimated consumption by around 10 percentage points. The reestimated final consumption rates for the eight years represented around 60% of GDP, compared with the official rates of around 50%. It is interesting to note that Morgan Stanley's Asia Pacific research team directly estimated China's household consumption expenditure in 2012 using a bottom-up approach at the micro level.[4] They found that China's household consumption rate was 46% in 2012 instead of the 35% officially reported. In other words, China's consumption rate was underestimated by 11 percentage points that year, making the actual consumption rate close to the results we reached using our macro approach.

[4] Garner and Qiao (2013).

Table A1.4 *Reestimated consumption rates in China*

Year	Reestimated Household Consumption Rate	Reestimated Final Consumption Rate	Official Household Consumption Rate	Official Final Consumption Rate
2004	50.38%	63.56%	40.50%	54.40%
2005	49.83%	63.25%	38.90%	53.00%
2006	47.40%	60.53%	37.10%	50.80%
2007	46.70%	59.63%	36.10%	49.60%
2008	45.58%	58.32%	35.30%	48.60%
2009	45.75%	58.42%	35.40%	48.50%
2010	46.06%	58.90%	34.90%	48.20%
2011	46.15%	59.41%	35.40%	49.10%

A2 China's Inflated Investment Statistics[1]

According to official statistics, China's investment rate (i.e., gross capital formation as a share of GDP) between 1982 and 2012 was 40% of GDP and exceeded 45% after the global financial crisis. In comparison, the world's average investment rate was around 24%. At the provincial level, almost half of the Chinese provinces had an official investment rate of more than 60% in 2012 and six provinces (or autonomous regions) exceeded 80%. These numbers are astonishing. Such a high investment rate seems unsustainable. The problem is that these official statistics should not be trusted, as they are greatly overestimated by the official methodology.

GDP on the demand side is made up of final consumption, investment, and net exports. If consumption is underestimated, as shown, then mathematically, investment must be overestimated. But how exactly is investment overestimated in China? To answer this question, we must first understand how GDP is measured in China.

For those who do not know, there are three approaches to measuring a country's GDP: the production approach; the income approach; and the expenditure approach. In theory, these approaches should produce identical results, but in reality, there are always statistical discrepancies. China's annual and quarterly GDP figures published by the NBS are obtained by combining the production approach and the income approach: The former is used to estimate value added in the primary industry (i.e., agriculture, forestry, animal husbandry, and fisheries), and the latter is used for the secondary (i.e.,

---

[1] This appendix is based on Liu, Zhang, and Zhu (2016).

manufacturing, mining, construction, and utilities) and tertiary (i.e., service) industries. In principle, the NBS also uses the expenditure approach to estimate national GDP by adding final consumption expenditure, domestic investment, and net exports.[2]

In GDP accounting, domestic investment expenditure is called gross capital formation (GCF), which is equal to gross fixed capital formation (GFCF) plus changes in inventories. In China, as elsewhere, changes in inventories represent a very small share of GCF, around 4 to 6 percent during 2004–2012. Therefore, investment expenditure is almost entirely captured by GFCF.

A more popular measurement of investment in China is the so-called total investment in fixed assets (TIFA), which is reported monthly and used extensively as an indicator of investment activities in the country. TIFA and GFCF are closely related investment measures, but are conceptually different. TIFA is not a measure of the investment component in expenditure-based GDP. For instance, TIFA includes the costs of purchasing land, old equipment, and old buildings, which are not produced in the current period and therefore do not contribute to GDP. These costs are thus not included in GFCF. Conversely, TIFA does not include investment in fixed assets below a certain threshold value, even if it represents real fixed capital formation and should be included in GFCF. According to the NBS, GFCF is estimated primarily from TIFA, but is adjusted by adding and subtracting a few items.[3]

Before 2004, the two investment figures (TIFA and GFCF) were essentially the same, but after 2004, they started to diverge. The gap has widened significantly over the years, causing much concern. For example, in 2013, TIFA represented 76% of GDP, while GFCF represented only 46% of GDP. In 2015, Fang Liu and Jun Zhang of Fudan University and I tried to find out the reasons for this divergence.

---

[2] At the provincial level, however, expenditure-based GDP is not independently estimated, but is equal to production-cum-income GDP. Provincial statistical bureaus use net exports as a residual term to equalize GDP figures from these two approaches. For provinces with an unusually high investment rate, their net exports as a percentage of GDP are, by design, also unusually high (and negative).

[3] See National Bureau of Statistics (2010).

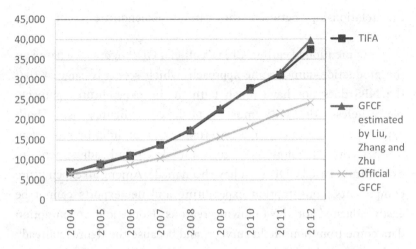

FIGURE A2.1 Two measures of fixed investment (in billion RMB): Gross fixed capital formation (GFCF) versus total investment in fixed assets (TIFA)

We followed the official published method to estimate GFCF between 2004 and 2012.[4] To our surprise, our estimated GFCF using the official formula and data was very close to TIFA but differed significantly from the official GFCF, as shown in Figure A2.1. For 2012, our estimate of GFCF was 64% higher than the official figure, in other words, the official figure was only 61% of our estimated value. If we use our estimated GFCF figure to recalculate expenditure-based GDP for 2012, it would be 31.6% higher than the official production-cum-income GDP figure.

So, why is the official GFCF so different from our result using the official methodology and data sources? The only sensible answer is that the officially published GFCF figures are not estimated as independently as they are purported to be. If so, where do the official GFCF figures come from? It is impossible to know the truth unless the NBS reveals the detailed procedures and data used in its estimation and the adjustment applied to the data, if any, to arrive at the figures they publish. However, we can make some educated guesses based on

[4] See Liu, Zhang, and Zhu (2016).

the relationship between the various expenditure components of GDP.

As mentioned earlier, China's official GDP figures are based on the production-cum-income approach, which seems to suggest that the NBS does not have much faith in the expenditure approach. Nevertheless, the NBS must publish GDP figures using both approaches, and the two figures certainly cannot differ by more than 30 percent. Therefore, a significant downward adjustment to expenditure-based GDP must have been made. Among all expenditure components, consumption expenditure and net exports cannot be easily adjusted for the following reasons. Household consumption data come from household surveys, and because the figure is already underestimated (officially representing only 36 percent of GDP in 2012), there is no room for further downward adjustment. Government consumption data come from the Ministry of Finance and the NBS is not free to modify them. Net export data come from China Customs and the State Administration of Foreign Exchanges and the NBS cannot change them either. Therefore, only GCF is left for the NBS to adjust, and the adjustment can be conveniently implemented as most of the underlying data are under the control of the NBS system. As previously explained, GCF is made up of GFCF and changes in inventories. The latter's share of GCF is too small to have a significant effect on the size of GCF. Thus, GFCF is the only expenditure component that the NBS can adjust to ensure that the GDP figures of both approaches are essentially the same.[5] In other words, the NBS must adjust GFCF to ensure that GCF is more or less equal to the official production-cum-income GDP figure minus final consumption and net exports.

If GFCF is strictly estimated using the official method, it should be very similar to TIFA, as previously stated. Therefore, a downward adjustment to GFCF simply means that the official TIFA must be

---

[5] Because expenditure-based GDP should theoretically be estimated independently, the two GDP figures cannot officially be the same. Of course, the NBS can make sure that the two figures are close but not identical.

"discounted" to a similar extent. Apparently, the NBS believes that GFCF is so much higher when estimated independently because TIFA is significantly inflated at the local level. There are indeed many reports on local governments exaggerating their TIFA figures. Therefore, we believe that the official GFCF figure published by the NBS involves a procedure that significantly "discounts" the TIFA figure in the GFCF estimate.

As TIFA is an inflated measure of real investment, it raises the following question: What discount should the NBS apply to TIFA when estimating GFCF? We do not think that the NBS has any solid basis, much less a well-specified procedure, for choosing a particular discount rate. We believe that the discount for a given year is decided on an ad hoc basis to ensure that the resulting GFCF makes expenditure-based GDP close to production-cum-income GDP. In other words, the official GCF is in effect obtained by subtracting final consumption expenditure and net exports from the official GDP figure. The "desired" GFCF is equal to the aforementioned GCF minus the changes in inventories (a stable 2 to 3 percent of GDP during 2004–2012). Based on the desired GFCF value, the discount rate that must be applied to TIFA when calculating GFCF can be computed by working backward.

It is only our conjecture that the NBS applies a discount rate to TIFA to obtain a desired GFCF value. We do not know exactly how the NBS comes up with the official GFCF figure, but we are almost certain that in practice, neither GFCF nor expenditure-based GDP are independently estimated as they are supposed to be. Instead, we strongly suspect that they are deduced from production-cum-income GDP.

If the official GCF is indeed derived from the official GDP figure minus final consumption and net exports, then its accuracy will depend on the accuracy of the GDP, final consumption, and net export figures. Assuming that GDP and net exports are reliable (at least more reliable than consumption and investment figures), the accuracy of GCF will depend on the accuracy of final consumption. However, as shown in the previous section of the Appendix, China's final consumption is significantly underestimated in official statistics by

Table A2.1 *Reestimated investment rates (GCF/GDP) in China*

Year	Official Final Consumption Rate	Reestimated Final Consumption Rate	Official Investment Rate (Ratio of GCF to GDP)	Reestimated Investment Rate
2004	54.40%	63.56%	42.97%	33.81%
2005	53.00%	63.25%	41.54%	31.29%
2006	50.80%	60.53%	41.74%	32.01%
2007	49.60%	59.63%	41.61%	31.58%
2008	48.60%	58.32%	43.78%	34.06%
2009	48.50%	58.42%	47.15%	37.23%
2010	48.20%	58.90%	48.06%	37.36%
2011	49.10%	59.41%	48.31%	38.00%

around 10 percent of GDP. As a result, as the residual term in expenditure-based GDP, the official GCF figure (i.e., investment) will be overestimated by around 10 percent of GDP.[6]

In Table A2.1, I used the final consumption figures from Table A1.4 to derive a series of "reestimated" investment rates (i.e., GCF-to-GDP ratio) in China for the 2004–2011 period. The reestimated investment rate for 2011 is 38 percent, much lower than the official figure of 48.3 percent. Although this investment rate is still considerably higher than the world average, it is more or less similar to the investment rates reached by the now developed East Asian economies (Japan and the four Asian Tigers) during their own years of rapid growth.

---

[6] Although the official GFCF figure is already significantly lower than that of TIFA, it can still significantly overestimate the true investment level. This implies that TIFA may exaggerate true investment by more than the discount already applied by the NBS.

References

Abrami, Regina M., William C. Kirby, and F. Warren McFarlan. 2014. Why China Can't Innovate. *Harvard Business Review* 92(3): 107–111.

Acemoglu, Daron. 2009. *Introduction to Modern Economic Growth*. Princeton, NJ: Princeton University Press.

Acemoglu, Daron, and James A. Robinson. 2012. *Why Nations Fail: The Origins of Power, Prosperity, and Poverty*, 1st ed., New York: Crown Publishers.

Agénor, Pierre-Richard, Otaviano Canuto, and Michael Jelenic. 2012. "Avoiding Middle-Income Growth Traps." *World Bank-Economic Premise* 98: 1–7.

Aghion, Philippe, and Peter Howitt. 2009. *The Economics of Growth*. Cambridge, MA: MIT Press.

Alesina, Alberto, Arnaud Devleeschauwer, William Easterly, Sergio Kurlat, and Romain Wacziarg. 2003. Fractionalization. *Journal of Economic Growth* 8(2): 155–194.

Alesina, Alberto, and Paola Giuliano. 2015. Culture and Institutions. *Journal of Economics Literature* 53(4): 898–944.

Alfaro, Laura, Sebnem Kalemli-Ozcan, and Vadym Volosovych. 2008. Why Doesn't Capital Flow from Rich to Poor Countries? An Empirical Investigation. *Review of Economics and Statistics* 90(2): 347–368.

Algan, Yann, and Pierre Cahuc. 2010. Inherited Trust and Growth. *American Economic Review* 100(5): 2060–2092.

Algan, Yann, and Pierre Cahuc. 2014. Trust, Growth, and Well-Being: New Evidence and Policy Implications. In *Handbook of Economic Growth*, edited by Philippe Aghion and Steven N. Durlauf, vol. 2, pp. 49–120. Amsterdam: Elsevier.

Allison, Graham. 2017. *Destined for War: Can America and China Escape Thucydides's Trap?* New York: Houghton Mifflin Harcourt.

Anker, Richard. 2011. *Engel's Law around the World 150 Years Later*. University of Massachusetts Political Economy Research Institute Working Paper Series No. 247.

Arrow, Kenneth J. 1972. Gifts and Exchanges. *Philosophy & Public Affairs* 1(4): 343–362.

Bai, Chong-En, Chang-Tai Hsieh, and Yingyi Qian. 2006. The Return to Capital in China. *Brookings Papers on Economic Activity* 37(2): 61–102.

Bai, Chong-En, Chang-Tai Hsieh, and Zheng Michael Song. 2020. Special Deals with Chinese Characteristics. *NBER Macroeconomics Annual* 34(1): 341–379.

Bai, Chong-En, and Qiong Zhang. 2017a. Is the People's Republic of China's Current Slowdown a Cyclical Slowdown or a Long-Term Trend? A Productivity-Based Analysis. *Journal of the Asia Pacific Economy* 22(1): 29–46.

Bai, Chong-En, and Qiong Zhang. 2017b. China's Growth Potential to 2050: A Supply-Side Forecast Based on Cross Country Productivity Convergence and Its Featured Labor Force. [in Chinese] *China Journal of Economics* 4(4): 1–27.

Bandiera, Oriana, Gerard Caprio, Patrick Honohan, and Fabio Schiantarelli. 2000. Does Financial Reform Raise or Reduce Saving? *Review of Economics and Statistics* 82(2): 239–263.

Banerjee, Abhijit V., and Esther Duflo. 2011. *Poor Economics: A Radical Rethinking of the Way to Fight Global Poverty.* New York: Public Affairs.

Barro, Robert J. 1991. Economic Growth in a Cross Section of Countries. *Quarterly Journal of Economics* 106(2): 407–443.

Barro, Robert J. 2001. Human Capital and Growth. *American Economic Review* 91(2): 12–17.

Barro, Robert J., and Xavier Sala-i-Martin. 2003. *Economic Growth*, 2nd ed. Cambridge, MA: MIT Press.

Baumol, William. 1999. Retrospectives: Say's Law. *Journal of Economic Perspectives* 13(1): 195–204.

Baxter, Marianne, and Mario J. Crucini. 1993. Explaining Saving-Investment Correlations. *American Economic Review* 83(3): 416–436.

Bayoumi, Tam, Hui Tong, and Shang-Jin Wei. 2009. *The Chinese Corporate Savings Puzzle: A Little International Comparison Can Go a Long Way.* Unpublished Working Paper, IMF and Columbia University.

Becker, Sascha O., and Ludger Woessmann. 2009. Was Weber Wrong? A Human Capital Theory of Protestant Economic History. *Quarterly Journal of Economics* 124(2): 531–596.

Bell, Daniel A. 2016. *The China Model: Political Meritocracy and the Limits of Democracy.* Princeton, NJ: Princeton University Press.

Benhabib, Jess, and Mark M. Spiegel. 1994. The Role of Human Capital in Economic Development Evidence from Aggregate Cross-Country Data. *Journal of Monetary Economics* 34(2): 143–173.

Berger, Peter L. 1988. An East Asian Development Model. In *In Search of an East Asian Development Model*, edited by P. L. Berger and H. H. M. Hsiao, pp. 3–11. Piscataway, NJ: Transaction Publishers.

Biden, Joseph R. (2020, January 1). Why America Must Lead Again. *Foreign Affairs*, March/April issue. Retrieved December 1, 2020, from www.foreignaffairs.com/articles/united-states/2020-01-23/why-america-must-lead-again.

Bildt, Carl. (2020, June 17). How Europe Can Live with China. *Project Syndicate*. Retrieved December 1, 2020, from www.project-syndicate.org/commentary/europe-changing-approach-to-china-engagement-plus-competition-by-carl-bildt-2020-06.

Billioud, Sébastien, and Joël Thoraval. 2015. *The Sage and the People: The Confucian Revival in China*. New York: Oxford University Press.

Bloom, David, David Canning, and Jaypee Sevilla. 2003. *The Demographic Dividend: A New Perspective on the Economic Consequences of Population Change*. Santa Monica, CA: RAND Corporation.

Bosworth, Barry, and Susan M. Collins. 2008. Accounting for Growth: Comparing China and India. *Journal of Economic Perspectives* 22(1): 45–66.

Botticini, Maristella, and Zvi Eckstein. 2005. Jewish Occupational Selection: Education, Restrictions, or Minorities? *Journal of Economic History* 65(4): 922–948.

Botticini, Maristella, and Zvi Eckstein. 2012. *The Chosen Few: How Education Shaped Jewish History, 70–1492*. Princeton, NJ: Princeton University Press.

Bown, Chad P. 2020. How Trump's Export Curbs on Semiconductors and Equipment Hurt the US Technology Sector. *Peterson Institute for International Economics*. Retrieved December 1, 2020, from www.piie.com/blogs/trade-and-investment-policy-watch/how-trumps-export-curbs-semiconductors-and-equipment-hurt-us.

Brandt, Loren, Thomas G. Rawski, and John Sutton. 2008. China's Industrial Development. In *China's Great Economic Transformation*, edited by L. Brandt and T. G. Rawski, pp. 569–632. Cambridge: Cambridge University Press.

Bremmer, Ian. 2017. How China's Economy Is Poised to Win the Future. *Time* 190 (20). Retrieved December 1, 2020, from https://time.com/5006971/how-chinas-economy-is-poised-to-win-the-future.

Breslin, Shaun. 2011. The "China Model" and the Global Crisis: From Friedrich List to a Chinese Mode of Governance? *International Affairs* 87(6): 1323–1343.

Brunnschweiler, Christa N., and Erwin H. Bulte. 2008. The Resource Curse Revisited and Revised: A Tale of Paradoxes and Red Herrings. *Journal of Environmental Economics and Management* 55(3): 248–264.

Cai, Fang. 2012. Is There a "Middle-Income Trap"? Theories, Experiences and Relevance to China. *China & World Economy* 20(1): 49–61.

Cai, Hongbin, Hanming Fang, and Lixin Colin Xu. 2001. Eat, Drink, Firms, Government: An Investigation of Corruption from the Entertainment and

Travel Costs of Chinese Firms. *The Journal of Law and Economics* 54(1): 55–78.

Carroll, Christopher D., Byung-Kun Rhee, and Changyong Rhee. 1994. Are There Cultural Effects on Saving? Some Cross-Sectional Evidence. *The Quarterly Journal of Economics* 109(3): 685–699.

Carroll, Christopher D., and David N. Weil. 1994. Saving and Growth: A Reinterpretation. *Carnegie-Rochester Conference Series on Public Policy* 40: 133–192.

Carroll, Christopher D., Jody Overland, and David N. Weil. 1994. Saving and Growth With Habit Formation. *American Economic Review* 90(3): 341–355.

Chamon, Marcos D., and Eswar S. Prasad. 2010. Why Are Saving Rates of Urban Households in China Rising? *American Economic Journal: Macroeconomics* 2 (1): 93–130.

Chamon, Marcos, Kai Liu, and Eswar Prasad. 2013. Income Uncertainty and Household Savings in China. *Journal of Development Economics* 105: 164–177.

Chang, Gordon G. 2001. *The Coming Collapse of China*. London: Random House Business.

Chang, Gordon G. (2011, December 29). The Coming Collapse of China: 2012 Edition. *Foreign Policy*. Retrieved December 1, 2020, from https://foreignpolicy.com/2011/12/29/the-coming-collapse-of-china-2012-edition.

Chang, Ha-Joon. 2006. *The East Asian Development Experience: The Miracle, the Crisis and the Future*. London: Zed Books.

Che, Jiahua, Kim-Sau Chung, and Xue Qiao. 2013. The Good, the Bad, and the Civil Society. *Journal of Public Economics* 106: 68–76.

Chen, Wei, Xilu Chen, Chang-Tai Hsieh, and Zheng Song. 2019. A Forensic Examination of China's National Accounts. *Brookings Papers on Economic Activity*, pp. 77–141.

Choudhri, Ehsan U., and Mohsin S. Khan. 2005. Real Exchange Rates in Developing Countries: Are Balassa-Samuelson Effects Present? *IMF Staff Papers* 52(3): 387–409.

Chow, Gregory C., and Kui-Wai Li. 2002. China's Economic Growth: 1952–2010. *Economic Development and Cultural Change* 51(1): 247–256.

Chow, Gregory C. 2012. *China as a Leader of the World Economy*. Singapore: World Scientific.

Cimmino, Jeffrey, Matthew Kroenig, and Barry Pavel. 2020. Taking Stock: Where Are Geopolitics Headed in the COVID-19 Era? *Atlantic Council Strategy Papers*. Retrieved December 1, 2020, from www.atlanticcouncil.org/in-depth-research-reports/issue-brief/taking-stock-where-are-geopolitics-headed-in-the-covid-19-era.

Coase, Ronald, and Ning Wang. 2012. *How China Became Capitalist*. London: Palgrave Macmillan.

Collier, Paul. 2007. *The Bottom Billion: Why the Poorest Countries Are Failing and What Can Be Done About It*. New York: Oxford University Press.

Collins, Susan M., and Barry P. Bosworth. 1996. Economic Growth in East Asia: Accumulation Versus Assimilation. *Brookings Papers on Economic Activity* 1996(2): 135–191.

Commission on Growth and Development. 2008. *The Growth Report: Strategies for Sustained Growth and Inclusive Development*. Washington, DC: World Bank.

Costa-Font, Joan, Paola Giuliano, and Berkay Ozcan. 2018. The Cultural Origin of Saving Behavior. *PloS One* 13(9): e0202290.

Dang, Jianwei, and Kazuyuki Motohashi. 2015. Patent Statistics: A Good Indicator for Innovation in China? Patent Subsidy Program Impacts on Patent Quality. *China Economic Review* 35: 137–155.

Deng, Xiaoping. 1994. *Selected Works of Deng Xiaoping*, vol. 2 [in Chinese]. Beijing: People's Press.

Deng, Xiaoping. 2001. *Selected Works of Deng Xiaoping*, vol. 3 [in Chinese]. Beijing: People's Press.

Diamond, Jared. 1997. *Guns, Germs and Steel: The Fates of Human Societies*. New York: W. W. Norton & Company.

Dollar, David, Yiping Huang, and Yang Yao. 2020. *China 2049: Economic Challenges of a Rising Global Power*. Washington, DC: Brookings Institution Press.

Donnan, Shawn. (2020, February 18). Trump Rebukes His Hardliners, Blocks Curbs on China Sales. *Bloomberg News*. Retrieved December 1, 2020, from www .bloomberg.com/news/articles/2020-02-18/trump-says-china-should-be-allowed-to-buy-u-s-jet-engines.

Doucouliagos, Hristos, and Mehmet Ali Ulubasoglu. 2008. Democracy and Economic Growth: A Meta-Analysis. *American Journal of Political Science* 52 (1): 61–83.

Easterlin, Richard A. 1974. Does Economic Growth Improve the Human Lot? In *Nations and Households in Economic Growth: Essays in Honour of Moses Abramovitz*, edited by Paul A. David and Melvin W. Reder, pp. 89–125. Amsterdam: Elsevier.

Easterlin, Richard A. 1995. Will Raising the Incomes of All Increase the Happiness of All? *Journal of Economic Behavior & Organization* 27(1): 35–47.

Easterly, William. 2001. *The Elusive Quest for Growth: Economists' Adventures and Misadventures in the Tropics*. Cambridge, MA: MIT Press.

Easterly, William, and Ross Levine. 1997. Africa's Growth Tragedy: Policies and Ethnic Divisions. *Quarterly Journal of Economics* 112(4): 1203–1250.

The Economist. (2010, December 9). Keqiang Ker-Ching: How China's Next Prime Minister Keeps Tabs on Its Economy. *The Economist*. Retrieved December 1, 2020, from www.economist.com/asia/2010/12/09/keqiang-ker-ching.

The Economist (2019, October 10). The World Economy's Strange New Rules. Retrieved December 1, 2020, from www.economist.com/leaders/2019/10/10/the-world-economys-strange-new-rules.

Economy, Elizabeth. 2018. *The Third Revolution: Xi Jinping and the New Chinese State*. New York: Oxford University Press.

Edwards, Sebastian. 1996. Why Are Latin America's Savings Rates So Low? An International Comparative Analysis. *Journal of Development Economics* 51(1): 5–44.

Edwards, Sebastian. 2010. *Left Behind: Latin America and the False Promise of Populism*. Chicago: University of Chicago Press.

Elman, Benjamin A. 2013. *Civil Examinations and Meritocracy in Late Imperial China*. Cambridge, MA: Harvard University Press.

Evans, Peter. 1995. *Embedded Autonomy: States and Industrial Transformation*. Princeton, NJ: Princeton University Press.

Farrell, Henry, and Abraham L. Newman. 2020. Chained to Globalization: Why It's Too Late to Decouple. *Foreign Affairs* 99 (1): 70–80.

Feenstra, Robert C., Hong Ma, J. Peter Neary, and D. S. Prasada Rao. 2013. Who Shrunk China? Puzzles in the Measurement of Real GDP. *The Economic Journal* 123(573): 1100–1129.

Fei, Hsiao-tung. 1953. *China's Gentry*. Chicago: University of Chicago Press.

Felipe, Jesus, Utsav Kumar, and Reynold Galope. 2017. Middle-Income Transitions: Trap or Myth? *Journal of the Asia Pacific Economy* 22(3): 429–453.

Fernandez, Raquel. 2011. Does Culture Matter? In *Handbook of Social Economics*, edited by J. Benhabib, M. O. Jackson, and A. Bisin, vol. 1, pp. 481–510. Elsevier.

Fischer, Joschka. (2020, August 24). The End of Western Opportunism. *Project Syndicate*. Retrieved December 1, 2020, from www.project-syndicate.org/commentary/us-china-conflict-values-must-trump-economic-interests-by-joschka-fischer-2020-08.

Flynn, James R. 1987. Massive IQ Gains in 14 Nations: What IQ Tests Really Measure. *Psychological Bulletin* 101(2): 171–191.

Fogel, Robert. (2010, January 4). $123,000,000,000,000. *Foreign Policy*. Retrieved December 1, 2020, from https://foreignpolicy.com/2010/01/04/123000000000000.

Ford, Christopher A. 2015. The Party and the Sage: Communist China's Use of Quasi-Confucian Rationalizations for One-Party Dictatorship and Imperial Ambition. *Journal of Contemporary China* 24(96): 1032–1047.

Frankel, Jeffrey A. 1992. Measuring International Capital Mobility: A Review. *The American Economic Review* 82(2): 197–202.

Frankel, Jeffrey A. 2010. *The Natural Resource Curse: A Survey*. National Bureau of Economic Research Working Paper No. w15836.

Frankel, Jeffrey A., and David Romer. 1999. Does Trade Cause Growth? *American Economic Review* 89(3): 379–399.

Fukuyama, Francis. 2007. Seymour Martin Lipset 1922–2006. *The American Interest*. Retrieved December 1, 2020, from www.the-american-interest.com/2007/01/08/seymour-martin-lipset-1922-2006.

Fukuyama, Francis. 2014. *Political Order and Political Decay: From the Industrial Revolution to the Globalization of Democracy*. New York: Farrar, Straus and Giroux.

Gallup, John Luke, Jeffrey D. Sachs, and Andrew D. Mellinger. 1999. Geography and Economic Development. *International Regional Science Review* 22(2): 179–232.

Garner, Jonathan, and Helen Qiao. 2013. Chinese Household Consumption-Most Likely US$1.6 Trn Larger Than Officially Stated. *Morgan Stanley Research, Asia Insight* 28: 3.

Giavazzi, Francesco, Ivan Petkov, and Fabio Schiantarelli. 2019. Culture: Persistence and Evolution. *Journal of Economic Growth* 24(2): 117–154.

Giles, Herbert. (trans.). 2014. *Three Character Classic*, bilingual ed. Scotts Valley, CA: CreateSpace.

Gill, Indermit, and Homi J. Kharas. 2007. *An East Asian Renaissance: Ideas for Economic Growth*. Washington, DC: World Bank.

Gill, Indermit, and Homi J. Kharas. 2015. *The Middle-Income Trap Turns Ten*. World Bank Policy Research Working Paper No.7403. Retrieved December 1, 2020, from https://doi.org/10.1596/1813-9450-7403.

Glaeser, Edward L., Rafael La Porta, Florencio Lopez-de-Silanes, and Andrei Shleifer. 2004. Do Institutions Cause Growth? *Journal of Economic Growth* 9 (3): 271–303.

Gorodnichenko, Yuriy, and Gerard Roland. 2011. Which Dimensions of Culture Matter for Long-Run Growth? *American Economic Review* 101(3): 492–498.

Gorodnichenko, Yuriy, and Gerard Roland. 2017. Culture, Institutions, and the Wealth of Nations. *Review of Economics and Statistics* 99(3): 402–416.

Greif, Avner. 1994. Cultural Beliefs and the Organization of Society: A Historical and Theoretical Reflection on Collectivist and Individualist Societies. *Journal of Political Economy* 102(5): 912–950.

Guiso, Luigi, Paola Sapienza, and Luigi Zingales. 2006. Does Culture Affect Economic Outcomes? *Journal of Economic Perspectives* 20(2): 23–48.

Hamilton, Gary G., and Cheng-Shu Kao. 1987. Max Weber and the Analysis of East Asian Industrialisation. *International Sociology* 2(3): 289–300.

Hansen, Sarah. (2020, November 8). Biden Will Be More Predictable than Trump on Trade, but Don't Expect Tariff Rollbacks Any Time Soon. *Forbes*. Retrieved December 1, 2020, from www.forbes.com/sites/sarahhansen/2020/11/08/biden-will-be-more-predictable-than-trump-on-trade-but-dont-expect-tariff-rollbacks-any-time-soon.

Hanushek, Eric A., and Dennis D. Kimko. 2000. Schooling, Labor Force Quality, and the Growth of Nations. *American Economic Review* 90(5): 1184–1208.

Hanushek, Eric A., and Ludger Woessmann. 2012. Do Better Schools Lead to More Growth? Cognitive Skills, Economic Outcomes, and Causation. *Journal of Economic Growth* 17(4): 267–321.

Harrison, Lawrence E. 2000. *Underdevelopment Is a State of Mind: The Latin American Case*. Lanham, MD: Madison Books.

Harrison, Lawrence E. (2006, December 15). Response to Clark, Boettke, and Robinson. *Cato Unbound*, Retrieved December 1, 2020, from www.cato-unbound.org/issues/december-2006/how-much-does-culture-matter.

Harrison, Lawrence E. 2008. *The Central Liberal Truth: How Politics Can Change a Culture and Save It from Itself*. New York: Oxford University Press, 2008.

Harrison, Lawrence E. 2012. *Jews, Confucians, and Protestants: Cultural Capital and the End of Multiculturalism*. Lanham, MD: Rowman & Littlefield Publishers.

Harrison, Lawrence E., and Samuel P. Huntington (eds.). 2000. *Culture Matters: How Values Shape Human Progress*. New York: Basic Books.

Higgins, Matthew. 1998. Demography, National Savings, and International Capital Flows. *International Economic Review* 39(2): 343–369.

Hofstede, Geert. 2001. *Culture's Consequences: Comparing Values, Behaviors, Institutions and Organizations across Nations*, 2nd ed. Thousand Oaks, CA: Sage Publications.

Hofstede, Geert, Gert Jan Hofstede, and Michael Minkov. 2010. *Cultures and Organizations: Software of the Mind*, revised and expanded third edition. New York: McGraw Hill.

Hofstede, Geert, and Michael Harris Bond. 1988. The Confucius Connection: From Cultural Roots to Economic Growth. *Organizational Dynamics* 16(4): 5–21.

Hofstede, Geert, and Michael Minkov. 2013. *Value Survey Module 2013 Manual*. Available at https://geerthofstede.com/research-and-vsm/vsm-2013.

Holz, Carsten A. 2008. China's Economic Growth 1978–2025: What We Know Today about China's Economic Growth Tomorrow. *World Development* 36 (10): 1665–1691.

Holz, Carsten A. 2014. The Quality of China's GDP Statistics. *China Economic Review* 30(3): 309–338.

Horioka, Charles Yuji, and Junmin Wan. 2007. The Determinants of Household Saving in China: A Dynamic Panel Analysis of Provincial Data. *Journal of Money, Credit and Banking* 39(8): 2077–2096.

Hsin, Amy, and Yu Xie. 2014. Explaining Asian Americans "Academic Advantage over Whites." *Proceedings of the National Academy of Sciences* 111(23): 8416–8421.

Hu, Albert G. Z., and Gary H. Jefferson. 2009. A Great Wall of Patents: What Is Behind China's Recent Patent Explosion? *Journal of Development Economics* 90(1): 57–68.

Hu, Albert G. Z., Peng Zhang, and Lijing Zhao. 2017. China as Number One? Evidence From China's Most Recent Patenting Surge. *Journal of Development Economics* 124: 107–119.

Huang, Chinchung (trans.). 1997. *The Analects of Confucius (Lun Yu)*. New York: Oxford University Press.

Huang, Tianlei, and Nicholas Lardy. 2020. China Goes from Strength to Strength in Global Trade. *Peterson Institute for International Economics*. Retrieved December 1, 2020, from www.piie.com/blogs/china-economic-watch/china-goes-strength-strength-global-trade.

Huang, Yasheng. 2008. *Capitalism with Chinese Characteristics: Entrepreneurship and the State*. New York: Cambridge University Press.

Huang, Yasheng. 2011. Rethinking the Beijing Consensus. *Asia Policy* (11): 1–26.

Huang, Yiping. 2010. Dissecting the China Puzzle: Asymmetric Liberalization and Cost Distortion. *Asian Economic Policy Review* 5(2): 281–295.

Huang, Yukon. 2017. *Cracking the China Conundrum: Why Conventional Economic Wisdom Is Wrong*. New York: Oxford University Press.

Hubbard, Glenn. (2018, November 2). The US Can Win China Trade War by Getting Its Own House in Order. *Financial Times*, Retrieved December 1, 2020, from www.ft.com/content/e7327d0c-de7f-11e8-b173-ebef6ab1374a.

Huddleston, Tom. (2015, May 26). Carly Fiorina Says the Chinese "Don't Innovate." *Time*. Retrieved December 1, 2020, from http://time.com/3897081/carly-fiorina-china-innovation.

Huntington, Samuel P., and Joan M. Nelson. 1976. *No Easy Choice: Political Participation in Developing Countries*. Cambridge, MA: Harvard University Press.

Inglehart, Ronald. 1997. *Modernization and Postmodernization: Cultural, Economic, and Political Change in 43 Societies.* Princeton, NJ: Princeton University Press.

Inglehart, Ronald, and Christian Welzel. 2005. *Modernization, Cultural Change, and Democracy: The Human Development Sequence.* New York: Cambridge University Press.

Ito, Takatoshi, Peter Isard, and Steven Symansky. 1999. Economic Growth and Real Exchange Rate: An Overview of the Balassa-Samuelson Hypothesis in Asia. In *Changes in Exchange Rates in Rapidly Developing Countries: Theory, Practice, and Policy Issues,* edited by Takatoshi Ito and Anne O. Krueger, pp. 109–132, Chicago: University of Chicago Press.

Jacques, Martin. 2009. *When China Rules the World: The End of the Western World and the Birth of a New Global Order.* New York: Penguin.

Jiang, Yi-Huah. 2018. Confucian Political Theory in Contemporary China. *Annual Review of Political Science* 21: 155–173.

Jiang, Zemin. (1997, September 12). *Speech at the 15th Congress of the Chinese Communist Party.* Retrieved December 1, 2020, from www.gov.cn/test/2007-08/29/content_730614.htm.

Johansson, Åsa et al. 2012. *Looking to 2060: Long-Term Global Growth Prospects.* OECD Economic Policy Paper Series No. 3.

Johnson, Keith, and Robbie Gramer. (2020, May 14). The Great Decoupling. *Foreign Policy.* Retrieved December 1, 2020, from https://foreignpolicy.com/2020/05/14/china-us-pandemic-economy-tensions-trump-coronavirus-covid-new-cold-war-economics-the-great-decoupling.

Jones, Eric L. 2009. *Cultures Merging: A Historical and Economic Critique of Culture.* Princeton, NJ: Princeton University Press.

Kelley, Allen C., and Robert M. Schmidt. 1995. Aggregate Population and Economic Growth Correlations: The Role of the Components of Demographic Change. *Demography* 32(4): 543–555.

Kenny, Charles. 2005. Why Are We Worried about Income? Nearly Everything That Matters Is Converging. *World Development* 33(1): 1–19.

Kim, Jong-Il, and Lawrence J. Lau. 1994. The Sources of Economic Growth of the East Asian Newly Industrialized Countries. *Journal of the Japanese and International Economies* 8(3): 235–271.

King, Ambrose. 1992. *Chinese Society and Culture* [in Chinese]. Hong Kong: Oxford University Press.

Knack, Stephen, and Philip Keefer. 1997. Does Social Capital Have an Economic Payoff? A Cross-Country Investigation. *Quarterly Journal of Economics* 112(4): 1251–1288.

Knight, John, and Sai Ding. 2012. *China's Remarkable Economic Growth*. Oxford: Oxford University Press.

Kohli, Atul. 2004. *State-Directed Development: Political Power and Industrialization in the Global Periphery*. New York: Cambridge University Press.

Koopman, Robert, Zhi Wang, and Shang-Jin Wei. 2014. Tracing Value-Added and Double Counting in Gross Exports. *American Economic Review* 104(2): 459–494.

Kroeber, Arthur R. 2016. *China's Economy: What Everyone Needs to Know*. New York: Oxford University Press.

Krugman, Paul. 1994. The Myth of Asia's Miracle. *Foreign Affairs* 73(2): 62–78.

Kuijs, Louis. 2005. *Investment and Saving in China*. World Bank Policy Research Working Paper No. 3633. Washington, DC: The World Bank.

Kuznets, Simon. 1973. Modern Economic Growth: Findings and Reflections. *American Economic Review* 63(3): 247–258.

Lai, Pingyao, and Tian Zhu. 2020. *Deflating China's Nominal GDP Growth: 2004–2018*. Working Paper of China Europe International Business School.

Lamy, Pascal. (2011, January 24). "Made in China" Tells Us Little about Global Trade. *Financial Times*.

Lamy, Pascal. 2013. *The Geneva Consensus: Making Trade Work for All*. New York: Cambridge University Press.

Landes, David. 1999. *The Wealth and Poverty of Nations: Why Some Are So Rich and Some So Poor*. New York: W. W. Norton & Company.

Landes, David. 2000. Culture Makes Almost All the Difference. In *Culture Matters: How Values Shape Human Progress*, edited by L. E. Harrison and S. P. Huntington, pp. 2–13. New York: Basic Books.

Lardy, Nicholas. 2006. *China: Toward a Consumption-Driven Growth Path*. Peterson Institute for International Economics Working Paper No. PB06-6.

Lardy, Nicholas. 2011. *Sustaining China's Economic Growth after the Global Financial Crisis*. Peterson Institute for International Economics.

Lardy, Nicholas. 2019. *The State Strikes Back: The End of Economic Reform in China?* Peterson Institute for International Economics.

Lardy, Nicholas. (2020, October 20). Memo to the Biden Administration on How to Advance Economic Talks with China. *Peterson Institute for International Economics*. Retrieved December 1, 2020, from www.piie.com/blogs/china-economic-watch/memo-biden-administration-how-advance-economic-talks-china.

Lardy, Nicholas, and Tianlei Huang. (2020, July 2). *Despite the Rhetoric, US–China Financial Decoupling Is Not Happening*. Peterson Institute for International

Economics. Retrieved December 1, 2020, from www.piie.com/blogs/china-eco nomic-watch/despite-rhetoric-us-china-financial-decoupling-not-happening.

Lee, James J. 2010. Review of Intelligence and How to Get It: Why Schools and Cultures Count. *Personality and Individual Differences* 48(2): 247–255.

Levine, Ross, and David Renelt. 1992. A Sensitivity Analysis of Cross-Country Growth Regressions. *American Economic Review* 82(4): 942–963.

Lewis, James Andrew. (2018, March 22). How Much Have the Chinese Actually Taken? *Commentary of the Center for Strategic and International Studies (CSIS)*, Retrieved December 1, 2020, from www.csis.org/analysis/how-much-have-chinese-actually-taken.

Li, David D. 1996. A Theory of Ambiguous Property Rights in Transition Economies: The Case of the Chinese Non-state Sector. *Journal of Comparative Economics* 23(1): 1–19.

Li, Hongbin, and Li-An Zhou. 2005. Political Turnover and Economic Performance: The Incentive Role of Personnel Control in China. *Journal of Public Economics* 89(9-10): 1743–1762.

Li, Wei, and Dennis Tao Yang. 2005. The Great Leap Forward: Anatomy of a Central Planning Disaster. *Journal of Political Economy* 113(4): 840–877.

Li, Xibao. 2012. Behind the Recent Surge of Chinese Patenting: An Institutional View. *Research Policy* 41(1): 236–249.

Li, Yang, Xiaojing Zhang, and Xin Chang. 2018. *The National Statement of Assets and Liabilities of China* [in Chinese]. Beijing: China Social Science Press.

Lin, Jia, Ho-Mou Wu and Howei Wu. 2019. China's Patent Subsidy Policy and Its Impacts on Invention and Patent Quality. Unpublished paper, China Europe International Business School.

Lin, Justin Yifu. 2014. *The Quest for Prosperity: How Developing Economies Can Take Off*. Princeton, NJ: Princeton University Press.

Lin, Justin Yifu. 2019. China's Growth Deceleration: Causes and Future Growth Prospect. *Frontiers of Economics in China* 14(1): 26–52.

Lin, Yi-min. 2001. *Between Politics and Markets: Firms, Competition, and Institutional Change in Post-Mao China*. Cambridge: Cambridge University Press.

Lipset, Seymour Martin. 1959. Some Social Requisites of Democracy: Economic Development and Political Legitimacy. *American Political Science Review* 53 (1): 69–105.

Liu, Fang, Jun Zhang, and Tian Zhu. 2016. How Much Can We Trust China's Investment Statistics? *Journal of Chinese Economic and Business Studies* 14 (3): 215–228.

Liu, Shaoqi. 1981. On a Communist's Self-Cultivation. In *Selected Works of Liu Shaoqi*, vol 1 [in Chinese]. Beijing: People's Press.

Lu, Yang, and Fang Cai. 2016. From Demographic Dividends to Reform Dividends: A Simulation Based on China's Potential Growth Rate [in Chinese]. *Journal of World Economy* 1: 3–23.

Lucas, Robert E. 1990. Why Doesn't Capital Flow from Rich to Poor Countries? *The American Economic Review* 80(2): 92–96.

Lucas, Robert E. 1993. Making a Miracle. *Econometrica* 61(2): 251–272.

Lynn, Richard, and Gerhard Meisenberg. 2010. National IQs Calculated and Validated for 108 Nations. *Intelligence* 38(4): 353–360.

Lynn, Richard, and Tatu Vanhanen. 2002. *IQ and the Wealth of Nations*. Westport, CT: Praeger Publishers.

Maddison, Angus. 2007. *Chinese Economic Performance in the Long Run–Second Edition, Revised and Updated: 960–2030 AD*. Paris: OECD Development Centre Studies.

Maddison, Angus, and Harry X. Wu. 2008. Measuring China's Economic Performance. *World Economics* 9(2): 13–44.

Magnus, George. 2018. *Red Flags: Why Xi's China Is in Jeopardy*. New Haven, CT: Yale University Press.

Mahbubani, Kishore. 2020. *Has China Won? The Chinese Challenge to American Primacy*. New York: PublicAffairs.

Mankiw, N. Gregory. 1995. The Growth of Nations. *Brookings Papers on Economic Activity* 1: 275–310.

Mankiw, N. Gregory, David Romer, and David N. Weil. 1992. A Contribution to the Empirics of Economic Growth. *The Quarterly Journal of Economics* 107(2): 407–437.

Mao, Yushi and Dong Su. (2012, August 23). Hard Work Is at the Root of the Chinese Miracle [in Chinese]. Retrieved December 1, 2020, from www.ftchinese.com/story/001046151?full=y.

Mao, Zedong. 1999. *Collected Works of Mao Zedong* [in Chinese], vol. 7. Beijing: People's Press.

Masson, Paul R., Tamim Bayoumi, and Hossein Samiei. 1998. International Evidence on the Determinants of Private Saving. *The World Bank Economic Review* 12(3): 483–501.

McCleary, Rachel M., and Robert J. Barro. 2006. Religion and Economy. *Journal of Economic Perspectives* 20(2): 49–72.

McClelland, David C. 1961. *The Achieving Society*. Oxford: Van Nostrand.

McGrattan, Ellen R., and James A. Schmitz. 1999. Explaining Cross-Country Income Differences. In *Handbook of Macroeconomics*, edited by J. B. Taylor and

M.Woodford, pp. 669–737. Retrieved from https://doi.org/10.1016/S1574-0048(99)01013-7.

Meng, Xin. 2003. Unemployment, Consumption Smoothing, and Precautionary Saving in Urban China. *Journal of Comparative Economics* 31(3): 465–485.

Meredith, Martin. 2011. *The Fate of Africa: A History of the Continent since Independence*. New York: PublicAffairs.

Michalopoulos, Stelios, and Elias Papaioannou. 2014. National Institutions and Subnational Development in Africa. *Quarterly Journal of Economics* 129(1): 151–213.

Modigliani, Franco, and Shi Larry Cao. 2004. The Chinese Saving Puzzle and the Life-Cycle Hypothesis. *Journal of Economic Literature* 42(1): 145–170.

Mokyr, Joel. 1990. *The Lever of Riches: Technological Creativity and Economic Progress*. New York: Oxford University Press.

National Bureau of Statistics (NBS). 2010. GDP Accounting Methodology in Non-economic-Census Years in China [in Chinese].

National Science Board, National Science Foundation. 2019. Publication Output: U.S. Trends and International Comparisons. In *Science and Engineering Indicators 2020*. Retrieved December 1, 2020 from https://ncses.nsf.gov/pubs/nsb20206.

Naughton, Barry. 2009. China's Emergence from Economic Crisis. *China Leadership Monitor* 29: 1–10.

Naughton, Barry. 2010. China's Distinctive System: Can It Be a Model for Others? *Journal of Contemporary China* 19(65): 437–460.

Naughton, Barry. 2011. China's Economic Policy Today: The New State Activism. *Eurasian Geography and Economics* 52(3): 313–329.

Naughton, Barry. 2016. Supply-Side Structural Reform: Policy-Makers Look for a Way Out. *China Leadership Monitor* 49.

Naughton, Barry. 2018. *The Chinese Economy: Adaptation and Growth*. Cambridge, MA: MIT Press.

Navarro, Peter, and Greg Autry. 2011. *Death by China: Confronting the Dragon–A Global Call to Action*. Upper Saddle River, NJ: Pearson Prentice Hall.

Nelson, Richard R., and Phelps, Edmund S. 1966. Investment in Humans, Technological Diffusion, and Economic Growth. *American Economic Review* 56(2): 69–75.

Nisbett, Richard E. 2009. *Intelligence and How to Get It: Why Schools and Cultures Count*. New York: W. W. Norton & Company.

North, Douglas C. 1990. *Institutions, Institutional Change and Economic Performance*. Cambridge: Cambridge University Press.

North, Douglas C. 2010. *Understanding the Process of Economic Change*. Princeton, NJ: Princeton University Press.

Nye, Joseph S. (2020, October 6). Post-Pandemic Geopolitics. *Project Syndicate.* Retrieved December 1, 2020, from www.project-syndicate.org/commentary/ five-scenarios-for-international-order-in-2030-by-joseph-s-nye-2020-10.

Page, Jeremy. (2015, September 20). Why China Is Turning Back to Confucius. *The Wall Street Journal.*

Pan, Yao. 2016. Understanding the Rural and Urban Household Saving Rise in China. *Regional Science and Urban Economics* 56: 46–59.

Perkins, Dwight H. 2010. China's Pre-reform Economy in World Perspective. In *China's Rise in Historical Perspective,* edited by Brantly Womack, pp. 109–128. Lanham, MD: Rowman & Littlefield Publishers.

Perkins, Dwight H. 2012. Rapid Growth and Changing Economic Structure: The Expenditure Side Story and Its Implications for China. *China Economic Review* 23(3): 501–511.

Perkins, Dwight H., and Thomas Rawski. 2008. Forecasting China's Economic Growth to 2025. In *China's Great Economic Transformation,* edited by L. Brandt and T. G. Rawski. New York: Cambridge University Press.

Petri, Peter A., and Michael Plummer. (2020, November 16). RCEP: A New Trade Agreement That Will Shape Global Economics and Politics. *Brookings Institution.* Retrieved December 1, 2020, from www.brookings.edu/blog/ order-from-chaos/2020/11/16/rcep-a-new-trade-agreement-that-will-shape-global-economics-and-politics.

Pettis, Michael. (2010, August 19). Is China Turing Japanese? *Foreign Policy.*

Pettis, Michael. 2013. *Avoiding the Fall: China's Economic Restructuring.* Washington, DC: Carnegie Endowment for International Peace.

Pomeranz, Kenneth. 2000. *The Great Divergence: China, Europe, and the Making of the Modern World Economy.* Princeton, NJ: Princeton University Press.

Prasad, Eswar, Raghuram Rajan, and Arvind Subramanian. 2007. Foreign Capital and Economic Growth. *Brookings Papers on Economic Activity* 2007(1): 153–230.

Pritchett, Lant. 2001. Where Has All the Education Gone? *World Bank Economic Review* 15(3): 367–391.

Pritchett, Lant, and Lawrence H. Summers. 2014. *Asiaphoria Meets Regression to the Mean.* Working Paper No. w20573. National Bureau of Economic Research.

Przeworski, Adam, Michael E. Alvarez, Jose Antonio Cheibub, and Fernando Limongi. 2000. *Democracy and Development: Political Institutions and Well-Being in the World, 1950–1990,* vol 3. New York: Cambridge University Press.

Pye, Lucian. 2000. Asian Values: From Dynamos to Dominoes. In *Culture Matters: How Values Shape Human Progress,* edited by L. E. Harrison and S. P. Huntington, pp. 244–255. New York: Basic Books.

Qi, Weiping, and Jun Wang. 2002. A Historical Study of the Evolution of Mao Zedong's Thought about "Surpassing Britain and Catching up to America." *Shixue Yuekan* [History Monthly], Issue No 2. Retrieved December 1, 2020, from www.usc.cuhk.edu.hk/PaperCollection/Details.aspx?id=3683.

Qian, Mu. 2001. *New Essays on Chinese History* [in Chinese]. Hong Kong: Joint Publishing.

Qian, Yingyi. 2003. How Reform Worked in China. In *In Search of Prosperity: Analytic Narratives on Economic Growth*, edited by Dani Rodrik. Princeton, pp. 297–333. Princeton, NJ: Princeton University Press.

Qian, Yingyi. 2017. *How Reform Worked in China: The Transition from Plan to Market*. Cambridge, MA: MIT Press.

Ratner, Ely, Elizabeth Rosenberg, and Paul Scharre. (2019, December 12). Beyond the Trade War: A Competitive Approach to Countering China. *Foreign Affairs*. Retrieved December 1, 2020, from www.foreignaffairs.com/articles/united-states/2019-12-12/beyond-trade-war.

Rawski, Thomas G. 2001. What Is Happening to China's GDP Statistics? *China Economic Review* 12(4): 347–354.

Redding, S. Gordon. 1990. *The Spirit of Chinese Capitalism*. New York: Walter De Gruyter.

Reischauer, Edwin O. 1974. The Sinic World in Perspective. *Foreign Affairs* 52(2): 341–348.

Richardson, K. 2004. Review of IQ and the Wealth of Nations. *Heredity* 92: 359–360.

Robinson, James A. (2006, December 13). It's Not Culture. *Cato Unbound*. Retrieved December 1, 2020, from www.cato-unbound.org/issues/december-2006/how-much-does-culture-matter.

Rodrik, Dani. 2006. Goodbye Washington Consensus, Hello Washington Confusion? A Review of the World Bank's Economic Growth in the 1990s: Learning from a Decade of Reform. *Journal of Economic Literature* 44(4): 973–987.

Rodrik, Dani. 2008. *One Economics, Many Recipes: Globalization, Institutions, and Economic Growth*. Princeton, NJ: Princeton University Press.

Rodrik, Dani. (2019, April 20). Peaceful Coexistence 2.0. Retrieved December 1, 2020, from www.project-syndicate.org/commentary/sino-american-peaceful-economic-coexistence-by-dani-rodrik-2019-04?barrier=accesspaylog.

Rodrik, Dani, Arvind Subramanian, and Francesco Trebbi. 2004. Institutions Rule: The Primacy of Institutions Over Geography and Integration in Economic Development. *Journal of Economic Growth* 9(2): 131–165.

Rogers, Henry. 2005. *Writing Systems: A Linguistic Approach*. Hoboken, NJ: Blackwell Publishing.

Roland, Gerard. 2000. *Transition and Economics: Politics, Markets, and Firms.* Cambridge, MA: MIT Press.

Roland, Gerard. 2004. Understanding Institutional Change: Fast-Moving and Slow-Moving Institutions. *Studies in Comparative International Development* 38(4): 109–131.

Romer, David. 2001. *Advanced Macroeconomics.* New York: McGraw-Hill Education.

Ruderman, David B. 1995. *Jewish Thought and Scientific Discovery in Early Modern Europe.* New Haven, CT: Yale University Press.

Sachs, Jeffrey D. 2003. *Institutions Don't Rule: Direct Effects of Geography on Per Capita Income.* National Bureau of Economic Research Working Paper No. w9490.

Sachs, Jeffrey D. (2019, November 7). America's War on Chinese Technology. Retrieved December 1, 2020, from www.project-syndicate.org/commentary/cheney-doctrine-us-war-on-chinese-technology-by-jeffrey-d-sachs-2019-11?barrier=accesspaylog.

Sachs, Jeffrey, and Andrew Warner. 1995. Economic Reform and the Process of Global Integration. *Brookings Papers on Economic Activity* 1: 1–118.

Sachs, Jeffrey, and Andrew Warner. 2001. The Curse of Natural Resources. *European Economic Review* 45(4–6): 827–838

Sala-i-Martin, Xavier, Gernot Doppelhofer, and Ronald I. Miller. 2004. Determinants of Long-Term Growth: A Bayesian Averaging of Classical Estimates (BACE) Approach. *American Economic Review* 94(4): 813–835.

Schaltegger, Christoph, and Benno Torgler. 2009. Work Ethic, Protestantism and Human Capital. *Economics Letters* 107(2): 99–101.

Sen, Amartya. 1999. *Development as Freedom.* New York: Alfred A. Knopf.

Shambaugh, David. 2016. *China's Future.* Cambridge: Polity Press.

Shillony, Ben-Ami. 1992. *Jews and the Japanese: The Successful Outsiders.* Tokyo: Charles E. Tuttle Publishing.

Shin, Doh Chull. 2012. *Confucianism and Democratization in East Asia.* New York: Cambridge University Press.

Shleifer, Andrei. 2009. The Age of Milton Friedman. *Journal of Economic Literature* 47(1): 123–135.

Song, Hefa, and Zhenxing Li. 2004. Patent Quality and the Measuring Indicator System: Comparison among China Provinces and Key Countries. Unpublished Paper, Institute of Policy and Management, Chinese Academy of Sciences.

Stoltenberg, Jens. (2020, June 30). The Geopolitical Implications of COVID-19. Speech at the German Institute for Global and Area Studies. Retrieved December 1, 2020, from www.nato.int/cps/en/natohq/opinions_176983.htm.

Subramanian, Arvind. 2011. *Eclipse: Living in the Shadow of China's Economic Dominance*. Peterson Institute.

Summers, Lawrence H., and Vinod Thomas. 1993. Recent Lessons of Development. *The World Bank Research Observer* 8(2): 241–254.

Swedberg, Richard. 2014. *How to Analyze the Chinese Economy with the Help of Max Weber: A Practical Guide to His Economic Sociology*. CSES Working Paper Series.

Tabellini, Guido. 2008. Institutions and Culture. *Journal of the European Economic Association* 6(2–3): 255–294.

Tabellini, Guido. 2010. Culture and Institutions: Economic Development in the Regions of Europe. *Journal of the European Economic Association* 8 (4): 677–716.

Thoma, Grid. 2013. Quality and Value of Chinese Patenting: An International Perspective. *Seoul Journal of Economics* 26(1): 33–72.

Tian, Guoqiang. 2019. Deceleration of China's Economic Growth: Causes and Countermeasures. *Frontiers of Economics in China* 14(1): 3–25.

Tu, Wei-Ming. 1996. Confucian Traditions in East Asian Modernity. *Bulletin of the American Academy of Arts and Sciences* 50(2): 12–39.

Tu, Wei-Ming. 2000. Implications of the Rise of "Confucian" East Asia. *Daedalus* 129 (1):195–218.

Unz, Ron. (2012, July 17). The East Asian Exception to Socio-economic IQ Influences. Retrieved December 1, 2020, from www.theamericanconservative.com/articles/the-east-asian-exception-to-socio-economic-iq-influences.

Unz, Ron. (2012, July 18). Race, IQ, and Wealth. Retrieved December 1, 2020, from www.theamericanconservative.com/articles/race-iq-and-wealth.

VOA News. (2014, May 29). Biden Slams China over Lack of Innovation. *VOA News*. Retrieved December 1, 2020, from www.voanews.com/usa/biden-slams-china-over-lack-innovation.

Wade, Robert. 1990. *Governing the Market: Economic Theory and the Role of Government in East Asian Industrialization*. Princeton, NJ: Princeton University Press.

Walder, Andrew G. 1995. China's Transitional Economy: Interpreting Its Significance. *The China Quarterly* 144: 963–979.

Wang, Dewen, Fang Cai, and Xuehui Zhang. 2004. The Saving and Growth Effect of Demographic Transition–An Analysis of the Contribution of Demographic Factor to Sustainability of China's Economic Growth [in Chinese]. *Journal of Population Research* 28(5): 2–11.

Wang, Feng, and Andrew Mason. 2008. The Demographic Factor in China's Transition. In *China's Great Economic Transformation*, edited by L. Brandt and T. G. Rawski, pp. 136–166. New York: Cambridge University Press.

Wang, Qing, and Steven Zhang. 2009. *China's Under-Consumption Over-Stated.* A Morgan Stanley Research Report 15.

Wang, Xiaolu. 2007. Grey Income and Household Income Gap [in Chinese]. *China Taxation* 10: 48–49.

Wang, Xun. 2020. Convergence and Prospects. In *China 2049: Economic Challenges of a Rising Global Power*, edited by David Dollar, Yiping Huang, and Yang Yao, chapter 2, pp.29–66. Washington, DC: Brookings Institution Press.

Web of Science Group. 2019. Highly Cited Researchers: Identifying Top Talent in the Sciences and Social Sciences. Retrieved December 1, 2020, from https://recognition.webofsciencegroup.com/awards/highly-cited/2019.

Weber, Max. 2015. *The Protestant Ethic and the Spirit of Capitalism.* Radford, VA: Wilder Publications.

Wei, Shang-jin. (2018, November 1). The Reforms China Needs. *Project Syndicate.* Retrieved December 1, 2020, from www.project-syndicate.org/commentary/trade-war-china-structural-reform-by-shang-jin-wei-2018-11.

Wei, Shang-Jin, and Xiaobo Zhang. 2011. The Competitive Saving Motive: Evidence From Rising Sex Ratios and Savings Rates in China. *Journal of Political Economy* 119(3): 511–564.

Wei, Shang-jin, and Xinding Yu. (2019, December 26). *A Fair Assessment of China's IP Protection.* Retrieved December 1, 2020, from www.project-syndicate.org/onpoint/china-ip-theft-myth-by-shang-jin-wei-and-xinding-yu-2019-12.

Wei, Shang-Jin, Zhuan Xie, and Xiaobo Zhang. 2017. From "Made in China" to "Innovated in China": Necessity, Prospect, and Challenges. *Journal of Economic Perspectives* 31(1): 49–70.

Weil, David N. 2013. *Economic Growth*, 3rd ed. London: Pearson Education.

Weitzman, Martin L., and Chenggang Xu. 1994. Chinese Township-Village Enterprises as Vaguely Defined Cooperatives. *Journal of Comparative Economics* 18(2): 121–145.

Wen, Yi. 2016. *The Making of an Economic Superpower: Unlocking China's Secret of Rapid Industrialization.* Singapore: World Scientific.

White House Office of Trade and Manufacturing Policy. 2018. How China's Economic Aggression Threatens the Technologies and Intellectual Property of the United States and the World. Retrieved December 1, 2020, from www.whitehouse.gov/wp-content/uploads/2018/06/FINAL-China-Technology-Report-6.18.18-PDF.pdf?fbclid=IwAR2vfnzyPLf-zPErnL4UEbSYHIEn8ZjFaF9ws96FD0D1tpMc9MiIwTaamxA.

Williamson, John. 2000. What Should the World Bank Think about the Washington Consensus? *World Bank Research Observer* 15(2): 251–264.

Williamson, Oliver E. 2000. The New Institutional Economics: Taking Stock, Looking Ahead. *Journal of Economic Literature* 38(3): 595–613.

Wolf, Martin. (2006, October 4). Beijing Should Dip into China's Corporate Bank. *Financial Times.* Retrieved December 1, 2020, from www.ft.com/content/09d39538-5302-11db-99c5-0000779e2340.

Wolf, Martin. (2011, June 14). How China Could Yet Fail Like Japan? *Financial Times.* Retrieved December 1, 2020, from www.cnbc.com/id/43403189.

Woo-Cummings, Meredith. 1999. *The Developmental State.* Ithaca, NY: Cornell University Press.

World Bank. 1993. *The East Asian Miracle: Economic Growth and Public Policy.* New York: Oxford University Press. Retrieved December 1, 2020, from http://documents.worldbank.org/curated/en/975081468244550798/Main-report.

World Intellectual Property Organization. 2013. Special Section: The International Mobility of Inventors. In *World Intellectual Property Indicators 2013.* WIPO Publication No. 941E, pp. 21–38. Retrieved December 1, 2020, from www.wipo.int/edocs/pubdocs/en/wipo_pub_941_2013-section1.pdf.

Wright, Robin. (2020, November 11). The Seven Pillars of Biden's Foreign Policy. *The New Yorker.* Retrieved December 1, 2020, from www.newyorker.com/news/our-columnists/the-seven-pillars-of-bidens-foreign-policy.

Wu, Harry X. 2000. China's GDP Level and Growth Performance: Alternative Estimates and the Implications. *Review of Income and Wealth* 46(4): 475–499.

Wu, Harry X. 2002. How Fast Has Chinese Industry Grown?–Measuring the Real Output of Chinese Industry, 1949–97. *Review of Income and Wealth* 48(2): 179–204.

Wu, Jinglian. 2018. *The Process of China's Economic Reform* [in Chinese]. Beijing: China Encyclopedia Press.

Xie, Qingnan, and Richard B. Freeman. 2019. Bigger than You Thought: China's Contribution to Scientific Publications and Its Impact on the Global Economy. *China & World Economy* 27(1): 1–27.

Xin, Katherine K., and Jone L. Pearce. 1996. Guanxi: Connections as Substitutes for Formal Institutional Support. *Academy of Management Journal* 39(6): 1641–1658.

Xing, Fan. 1995. The Chinese Cultural System: Implications for Cross-Cultural Management. *SAM Advanced Management Journal* 60(1): 14–21.

Xing, Yuqing, and Neal C. Detert. 2010. *How the iPhone Widens the United States Trade Deficit with the People's Republic of China.* ADBI Working Paper No. 257. Retrieved December 1, 2020, from SSRN: https://ssrn.com/abstract=1729085 or http://dx.doi.org/10.2139/ssrn.1729085.

Xu, Chenggang. 2011. The Fundamental Institutions of China's Reforms and Development. *Journal of Economic Literature* 49(4): 1076–1151.

Yang, Dennis Tao. 2012. Aggregate Savings and External Imbalances in China. *Journal of Economic Perspectives* 26(4): 125–146.

Yang, Dennis Tao, Junsen Zhang, and Shaojie Zhou. 2012. Why Are Saving Rates So High in China? In *Capitalizing China*, edited by Joseph P. H. Fan and Randall Morck, pp. 249–278. Chicago: University of Chicago Press.

Yao, Xinzhong. 2000. *An Introduction to Confucianism.* New York: Cambridge University Press.

Yao, Yang. 2011. Beijing Consensus or Washington Consensus: What Explains China's Economic Success? *Development Outreach* 13(1): 26–31.

Yao, Yang. 2014. The Chinese Growth Miracle. In *Handbook of Economic Growth*, edited by P. Aghion and S. N. Durlauf, vol. 2, pp. 943–1031. Amsterdam: Elsevier.

Yao, Yang. 2018. The Political Economy Causes of China's Economic Success. In *China's 40 Years of Reform and Development 1978–2018*, edited by Ross Garnaut, Ligang Song, and Cai Fang, pp. 75–92. Acton: The ANU Press.

Young, Alwyn. 1995. The Tyranny of Numbers: Confronting the Statistical Realities of the East Asian Growth Experience. *Quarterly Journal of Economics* 110(3): 641–680.

Young, Alwyn. 2003. Gold into Base Metals: Productivity Growth in the People's Republic of China during the Reform Period. *Journal of Political Economy* 111 (6): 1220–1261.

Yu, Ying-shih. 1985. Confucian Thought and Economic Development: Early Modern Chinese Religious Ethics and the Spirit of the Merchant Class [in Chinese]. *The Chinese Intellectual* 6: 3–46.

Zak, Paul J., and Stephen Knack. 2001. Trust and Growth. *The Economic Journal* 111(470): 295–321.

Zakaria, Fareed. 2003. *The Future of Freedom: Illiberal Democracy at Home and Abroad.* New York: W. W. Norton & Company.

Zakaria, Fareed. 2020, The New China Scare: Why America Shouldn't Panic about Its Latest Challenger. *Foreign Affairs*, January/February: 52–69.

Zhang, Gupeng, and Xiangdong Chen. 2012. The Value of Invention Patents in China: Country Origin and Technology Field Differences. *China Economic Review* 23(2): 357–370.

Zhang, Haifeng, Hongliang Zhang, and Junsen Zhang. 2015. Demographic Age Structure and Economic Development: Evidence from Chinese Provinces. *Journal of Comparative Economics* 43(1):170–185.

Zhang, Jun and Tian Zhu. 2015. Reestimating China's Underestimated Consumption. *Comparative Economic Studies* 57(1): 55–74.

Zhang, Weiwei. 2011. *The China Shock* [in Chinese]. Shanghai, China: Shanghai Renmin Press.

Zhang, Weiying. (2017, July 1). *Freedom Is a Duty* [in Chinese]. Speech at National School of Development, Peking University. Retrieved December 1, 2020, from www.bannedbook.org/bnews/comments/20170705/786792.html.

Zhang, Xiaojing. (2019, May 9). An Anatomy of the Gray Rhino of Chinese Debt [in Chinese]. Retrieved December 1, 2020, from www.nifd.cn/Professor/Details/34.

Zhang, Xiaojing, Xin Chang, and Lei Liu. (2019, January 8). Keep to Structural Deleveraging, and Avoid a "Movement" to Control [in Chinese]. Retrieved December 1, 2020, from www.nifd.cn/Report/Details/1087.

Zhang, Xiaojing, Xin Chang, and Lei Liu. (2019, March 12). Macro Leverage Ratio Falls for the First Time, Deleveraging Goals Partially Realized [in Chinese]. Retrieved December 1, 2020, from www.nifd.cn/ResearchComment/Details/1282.

Zhao, Quansheng. 2018. The Influence of Confucianism on Chinese Politics and Foreign Policy. *Asian Education and Development Studies* 7(4): 321–328.

Zhao, Suisheng. 2010. The China Model: Can It Replace the Western Model of Modernization? *Journal of Contemporary China* 19(65): 419–436.

Zhao, Zhenjiang, and Kexin Chen. (2016, February 25). Amartya Sen at Peking University: The Middle Income Trap Cannot Explain Chinese Economy [in Chinese]. Retrieved December 1, 2020, from www.thepaper.cn/newsDetail_forward_1435842.

Zheng, Jinghai, Arne Bigsten, and Angang Hu. 2009. Can China's Growth Be Sustained? A Productivity Perspective. *World Development* 37(4): 874–888.

Zhu, Tian. (2015, June 5). The "Middle Income Trap" Does Not Exist [in Chinese]. Retrieved December 1, 2020, from www.ftchinese.com/story/001062326.

Zhu, Xiaodong. 2012. Understanding China's Growth: Past, Present, and Future. *Journal of Economic Perspectives* 26(4): 103–124.

Zou, Heng-fu. 1994. "The Spirit of Capitalism" and Long-Run Growth. *European Journal of Political Economy* 10(2): 279–293.

Index